Guidance and Counselling : Research and Applications

Guidance and Counselling
Research and Applications

Dr. Pragya

AMIGA PRESS. INC
Delhi -110051

AMIGA PRESS INC.

AMIGA PRESS INC.
Registered Office:
19 DBS Building, Ansari Road, Darya Ganj, Delhi. 110002, India
Phone: +91-11-23283333 Email: amigapress@gmail.com

This edition is published by Amiga Press.Inc

ISBN : 978-93-84533-02-1

First Published 2018

Reprint 2026

Printed and bound in India by Replika Press Pvt. Ltd.

Preface

Guidance functions whenever choices are made and even when there is no choice, it helps the individual to understand and accept the situation. It is not only needed in crisis situations but throughout the life for personality development. Guidance which comes in just by the way as life goes is informal guidance; the guidance for achievement in our day-to-day life is incidental guidance. The specific form of guidance with a purpose is the formal guidance which helps the individual to find a solution to problem.

Guidance, which is a relatively more comprehensive process includes counselling as its most specialised function. Counselling service forms the central part of the overall assistance given to the individual through guidance programme. Counselling is a process of enabling the individual to know himself and his present and possible future situations in order that he may make substantial contributions to the society and to solve his own problems through a face to face relationship with the counsellor.

The humble effort made in the form of this book will assist in the accomplishment of the understanding of the various concepts, and methods applied in guidance and counselling. Regarding the organisation, the book consists of twenty five chapters. This book is primarily intended to serve as a textbook for graduate and post-graduate students as well as for professionals working in the field of guidance and counselling.

Guidance and counselling, concept that institutions, especially schools, should promote the efficient and happy lives of individuals by helping them adjust to social realities. The disruption of community and family life by industrial civilization convinced many that guidance experts should be trained to handle problems of individual adjustment. Though the need for attention to the whole individual had been recognized by educators since the time of Socrates, it was only during the 20th cent that researchers actually began to study and accumulate information about guidance.

This development, occurring largely in the United States, was the result of two influences: John Dewey and others insisted that the object of education should be to stimulate the fullest possible growth of the individual and that the unique qualities of personality require individual handling for adequate development;

also in the early 20th cent., social and economic conditions stimulated a great increase in school enrolment.

These two forces encouraged a re-examination of the curricula and methods of secondary schools, with special reference to the needs of students who did not plan to enter college. The academic curriculum was revised to embrace these alternative cultural and vocational requirements.

Early guidance programmes dealt with the immediate problem of vocational placement. The complexities of the industrial economy and the unrealistic ambitions of many young people made it essential that machinery for bringing together jobs and workers be set up; vocational guidance became that machinery. At the same time, counselling organizations were established to help people understand their potentialities and liabilities and make intelligent personal and vocational decisions. The first vocational counselling service was the Boston Vocational Bureau, established (1908) by Frank Parsons, a pioneer in the field of guidance. His model was soon copied by many schools, municipalities, states, and private organizations.

The book will provide meaningful insights to all interested in guidance and counselling.

—*Editor*

Contents

1

Introduction

GUIDANCE AND COUNSELLING

In the earlier times, the term 'counselling' was used for guidance. Counselling means to suggest. The relevant reliable informations regarding same special situations and informations related to an individual are co-related and presented to the Individual in such a way that he may suggest himself an the basis of these informations.

In other words, that individual may make decisions on the basis of these informations. In this way, an individual becomes competent to solve his own problems. The organisation of guidance-service involves various services, such as follow-up service, information service, study of an individual etc. Counselling service is also included in the organization of guidance services. Counselling service is very important in order to enable an individual to solve his problems.

According to *Humphrey and Traxler*, all those experiences and activities are included which assist an individual understand himself, making decisions himself and present a development plan effectively. According to these scholars, counselling is a process of delimiting the assistance provided to an individual for developing the existing possibilities to the highest level. Testing and interview are the integral parts of the counselling process.

Hence, guidance is a broader process while counselling is its integral part. The task of guidance cannot be completed without counselling and objective of the guidance cannot be achieved. In the process of counselling, an individual is studied carefully with the help of various methods. The focal point of counselling is a specific person and to know about the obstacles occurring in the way of his development and elimination of these problems. In short, the following differences are observed between guidance and counselling—

Guidance

1. Guidance process is a comprehensive process
2. Guidance can be in individual as well as in groups.
3. Guidance is concerned with educational, vocational and other problems along with personal problems.
4. Any person can provide guidance. Pre-service training is not necessary for guidance.
5. Guidance can be provided through the magazines, books and correspondence.

Counselling

Counselling is an integral part of guidance. Counselling of one individual is possible at a time. Counselling usually helps in solving the problems of mental health and emotions. Pre-service training is must for the counsellor. In counselling, the role of mutual consultation and reasoning is very important.

MEANING OF GUIDANCE

In order to understand the meaning of guidance, it is to be accepted that the focal point of guidance is an individual, not his problem. From this point of view, before starting guidance the potentialities and abilities of the individual are studied. Then that individual is made capable of solving his problems.

This is known as an act of guidance. In this way guidance is a process of all-round development. Hence, we can say that the guidance is that process which makes an individual aware of those methods for knowing his natural powers.

This idea has been expressed in United States Office of Education in this way—

"The process of acquainting the individual with the various ways including special training in which he may discover his natural endowments so that he makes a living to his own best advantage, and that of the society." — United States Office of Education

Jones, Steffire and Stewart have defined guidance as "the help given by one person to another in making choices and adjustments and in solving problems".

In this definition, it is aimed to make the individual self-responsible. Guidance is universal according to them. It cannot be restricted to classes, school or family. Guidance is required in all the phases of life, such as at home, in business, in industries, in government, in social life and in hospitals. Guidance is based on democratic principles. It is involved in all the phases of life. Hence, it is a continuous process. Based on this idea, Emery Stoops and *G.L. Wahlquist* have given the following definition of guidance—

"Guidance is a continuous process of helping the individual to develop to the maximum of his capacity in the direction, most beneficial to himself and to society. Development of insight in an individual is emphasized through guidance so that he can be enabled to solve his own problems. Chisolm has given the definition, of guidance on the same basis are said, "Guidance aims to develop in him insight into the solution of his problems of living as well as a creative initiative whereby he will throughout life be able to meet and solve his own problems adequately."

Jones, in his narrow definition has described guidance merely as "to indicate, to point out, to show the way." Guidance is not a direction. It is also not imposition of one's ideas on others. Guidance is not making decision for others. An individual himself should make decision. To carry over the burden of an individual is also not guidance. In such situations, to what we can call guidance'? Keeping in view these ideas, the definition suggested by *Crow* and *Crow* bears very comprehensive meaning:

"Guidance is assistance made available by competent counsellor to an individual of any age to help him direct his life, develop his own point of view, make his own decisions and carry his own burden." Ruth Strang *has defined guidance in this way, "The purpose of guidance is to promote the maximum development of each child in terms of possibilities available to him."*

In the context of dynamic interpersonal relationships, *Carter V Good* has said in Dictionary of Education (1959), while defining guidance, "Guidance is a process of dynamic interpersonal relationships designed to influence the attitudes and subsequent behaviour of person."

Knapp has given the definition of guidance as "Learning about the individual student helping to understand himself, effect changes in him and his environment which will help him to grow and develop as much as possible."

Hamrin and *Erickson* have defined guidance, considering it assistance in adjustment. They have defined guidance as, "that aspect of educational programme which is concerned especially with helping the pupil to become adjusted to his present situation and to plan his future in line with his interests, abilities and social needs." Like this definition. *Mathewson* has given special importance to educational aspect in his definition of guidance. According to him, "Guidance is the systematic professional process of helping the individual through education and interpretative procedures to gain a better understanding of his own characteristics and potentialities and to relate himself more satisfactorily to social requirements in accordance with Social and moral values."

G.E. Smith, by considering the group of various services for helping an individual has defined guidance as, "the process consists of a group of services to individuals to assist them in securing the knowledge and skills needed in making adequate choices, plans and interpretations essential to satisfactory in varieties of areas.

Lefever, Tussel and *Weitzel* have said, considering guidance as an educational service for the effective use of school training programme, "Guidance is an educational service designed to help students make more effective use of school training programme.

Bernard and *Fullmer* have given a very comprehensive definition in order to make clear the meaning of guidance, "Guidance is all these activities which promote individual self-realization." The meaning of guidance can also be made clear fewer than three headings. *Traxler* has done so. According to him, guidance includes the following activities—

(i) Recognition and understanding of an individual.
(ii) Creating conditions so that the individual can help his capacity fully.
(iii) Enabling the individual to achieve maximum possible self guidance and security both in the economic field and social field.

In the post-independence period, Indian Govt. set up Indian Education Commission (1964-66) who has also defined guidance in its report considering the importance of guidance-

> *"Guidance is a help to the students in making the best possible adjustment to the situations in the educational institutions and in the home and at the same time facilitates the development of all aspects of the personality."*

According to *Skinner*, "Guidance is a process of helping young persons learns to adjust to self, to others and to circumstances."

NATURE OF GUIDANCE

We familiarize ourselves with the following characteristics after analysing the various definitions of guidance. This analysis also throws light on the nature of guidance.

Guidance as an Educational Service

The nature of guidance also includes educational touch. It has been defined as educational service. The meaning of guidance is explained in the context of problems occurring in the field of education and in the context of adjustment in the school environment

Client Centred

Guidance has been accepted as a specialized service. In this form, this process is more client-centred. In other words, it is based upon developmental approach.

Guidance as a Sub-process of Education

Guidance is also considered as a sub-process of education. In education, efforts are made for all-round development of the pupils. Guidance occupies its own place in this process of education. It is being considered as a process like other processes of education.

Wide Scope of Guidance

The scope of guidance is too wide. Any needy person can be guided. This can, include the persons of different age, different interests, various characteristics and persons of different nature. Hence, we cannot draw boundaries around the process of guidance.

Helpful in Adjustment

Guidance helps the person in his adjustment in different situations. This process allows learning to adjust with different types of problems. In this way, the main characteristic of the nature of the guidance is to provide new energy to the demoralized person by adjusting himself in the problematic situation through the process of guidance.

Helpful in Developing the Ability of Self-guidance

The nature of guidance also includes the characteristic of developing self-guidance in a person with the help of guidance process. This enables him in achieving self-dependence by searching out the solution of problems of life.

As a Process

Guidance does not occupy independent place. The chief aim of this process is to assist in the development of an individual keeping in view the social needs.

A Continuous Process

Guidance is a process. Here, it is important to point out that the process of guidance never ceases. It remains dynamic. In this process, an individual understands himself, learns to use maximum his own capacities, interests and other abilities. He continues his struggle for adjustment in different situations. He develops his capacity of decision-making. Hence, we see that it is a non-stop process.

Related with Life

The process of guidance is related to life. This guidance contributes formally or informally to life because life experiences both formal and informal occasions. A person gets informal guidance from his friends and relatives while formal guidance is sought from organised school guidance services and other organised guidance services.

Development of Capacities

During the process of guidance the individual is assisted in such a way that he makes himself enabled to develop his capacities maximum from all angles. Hence, guidance stresses the complete development of possibilities present in an individual.

An individual becomes familiar with his real image. Hence, guidance is helpful in self-realization.

Individual Assistance

Guidance is accepted as individualized help. Through guidance an individual's personal development is provided a direction and not to a group. Hence, it is a process of individualized assistance.

Task of Trained Persons

Providing guidance is not the function of all persons because various techniques and skills are to be used in it. Everybody does not possess the knowledge of the same. For this task, trained persons; psychologists and counsellors are required. Hence, guidance is a skill-involved process.

No Imposition of One's View Point

It is also the main characteristic of guidance not to impose one's view point on others. It depends upon the wish of an individual how he acquires benefit by accepting the decision of the guidance worker.

If he wishes, he may deny to, accept such decisions of the guidance workers. Hence, it is not a process of imposing the decisions.

Helpful in Preparing for Future

The process of guidance is helpful in preparing a person for his future. Hence, a person can succeed in preparing himself for future activities. In this way, guidance is a well-wisher of an individual's future.

Guidance as More than Assistance

Guidance is not merely assistance. It is more than assistance. Limits of this assistance are not fixed or decided. This assistance has a wider scope. It cannot be predicted when and how much help an individual needs. Nothing can be ascertained in advance.

Guidance as an Organized Service: Guidance is an organised service. It is not a single activity of the school. It is a process with broader base and a definite objective. In order to achieve the objective of guidance curriculum is used. Keeping in view this objective changes are also brought about in it. In this way, guidance based education develops.

Guidance is Continuous and Dynamic Process: Guidance is a life-long, flexible and dynamic process and it is concerned with the 'Whole Man'.

Guidance is set apart from Instruction in the Narrowest Sense: Instructions are concerned with acquiring mastery and skills in the subject. Guidance is concerned with the fulfilment of pupil's needs in their growth in the areas other than instructions. Still, guidance helps instructions by providing assistance to the pupils in the various areas of instructions so that they may get adjusted in a better way.

Guidance is both specialized and a Generalized Service: Guidance is both specialized and generalized service in which a teacher, parents and counsellor play important roles. But like other services, guidance service also needs trained staff so that this process may work smoothly. In the guidance programme all have important roles but the main responsibility is of guidance staff because these staff members may solve the problem properly due to their training. Specialized persons include school counsellor, school psychologist, school psychiatrist, curriculum expert, placement worker, co-ordinator of school activities etc.

Guidance is for All: Each and every child needs guidance. It is not so because every person faces problems and he is unable to solve them. He needs guidance because his potentialities are to be developed maximum. A good guidance programme reaches to the entire community without making any demand.

MEANING OF COUNSELLING

The scholars have exhibited variations in their view-points regarding defining the term "counselling". One major cause of these variations is - occurrence of historical changes in the perceptions of the persons. Inspite of this, there was a lot of variation in the philosophy of experts.

In 1945. Good has said, while emphasizing material of knowledge. Immediate decision-making and use of external resources in defining counselling in his educational dictionary, "Counselling is the individualized and personalized assistance with personal, educational, vocational problems in which all pertinent facts are studied and analysed and a solution is sought, often with the assistance of specialists, school and community, resources and personal interviews in which the counselled is taught to make his own decisions." In 1958, English and English gave a new definition in his dictionary. They said. "counselling is a relationship in which one person endeavours to help another to understand and solve his adjustment problems. The area of adjustment is often indicated: Educational counselling, vocational counselling, social counselling etc. They further say that counselling is a two way affair involving both counsellor and counsellee."

Pepinsky and Pepinsky have said while giving more modem definition—

(a) Counselling is a diagnosis and treatment of minor, functional maladjustment.

(b) It is a relationship, primarily individual and face to face between counsellor and client.

According to *Wrenn* (1951), "Counselling is a dynamic and purposeful relationship between the people in which procedures vary with the nature of the students' need, but in which there is always mutual participation by the counsellor and the student with the focus upon self-classification and self-determination by the student." According to *Shostorm* and *Brammer* (1952), "Counselling is' a purposeful reciprocal relationship between two people in which one, a trained person, helps the other to change himself or his environment."

Wolberg (1954) has considered counselling as a form of interview. He has defined it as, "Counselling is a form of interviewing in which the client is helped to understand himself more completely in order to correct an environment or adjustment difficulty."

Gustad (1953) has considered learning too as an important element in order to define the counselling. According to him, "Counselling is a learning oriented process, carried on in a simple, one-to-one social environment, in which a counsellor, professionally competent in relevant psychological skills and knowledge, seeks to assist the client by methods appropriate to the latter's needs and within the contexts of the total personal programme, to learn more about himself, to learn how to put such understanding into effect in relation to more clearly perceived, realistically defined goals to the end that the client may become a happier and more productive member of his society." There is another element in the definition of counselling development of personality On the basis of this element, *Bordin* (1955) has given the definition of counselling as, "The psychological counsellor is a psychological practitioner who aids people with these problems of behaviour in which the critical issues have to do with their emotions and motivations"

Ruth *Strang*, emphasizing mutual relationships of persons, has said, "Counselling is a face-to-face relationship in which growth takes place in the counsellor as well as the counsellee."

Myers has written as, "Counselling means a relationship between two persons in which one person provides special assistance to the other

According to *Harriman,* "Counselling is the psychotherapeutic relationship in which an individual client receives direct help from an advisor or finds an opportunity to release negative feelings and thus clear the way for positive growth in personality."

For *Williamson,* "Counselling is a personalized and individualized process designed to aid the individual to learn school subject-matter, Citizenship tacts and other habits, skills, attitudes and beliefs which go to make up a normally adjusted human being."

The view of *Robinson* is that, "The term counselling covers all types of two-person situations in which one person, the client is helped to adjust more effectively to himself and his environment."

Humphery and *Traxler* think about counselling in this way that "Counselling is the application of the personnel resources of the school or other institution to the solution of the problems that individuals have"

Rogers says about counselling that "Counselling does not mean providing a service by means of which specific problem of an individual may be solved. The process should help the counsellee in gaining clear insight into the problem and in achieving the, self-confidence."

Considering counselling as a problem-solving effort, *Hamrin* and *Erickson* have said that "Counselling is an attempt made by the counsellee to think through and solve the problem that confronts him. It is an experiment in cooperative thinking, who two individuals (the counsellor and the counsellee strike to solve a problem." Considering counselling as a mutual learning process, Willy and Andrew have said. "Counselling is a mutual learning process involving two individuals-one seeking help and the other a professionally trained person helping the first to orient and direct himself towards a goal which leads to his maximum development and growth in his environment"

Arbunckle has mentioned those three points about which various counselling theorists agree-

(a) Counselling is a process between two persons.

(b) The basic aim of counselling is to help the person in solving his problems independently.

(c) Counselling is a professional job of a professionally trained persons.

In the *Webster's* dictionary, counselling means, "consultation, mutual interchange of opinions, deliberating together."

Carl Rogers has said, while defining counselling that the counselling is a definitely structured permissive relationship which allows the client to gain an understanding to himself to a degree which enables him to make positive steps in the light of his new orientation."

CHARACTERISTICS OF COUNSELLING

The following facts become distinct about counselling after studying and analysing the above mentioned definitions-

1. Counselling is a conversation with some one regarding some problem.
2. Normally, not always, one of the two persons possesses facts or experiences or abilities which the other lacks.
3. In the process of counselling, the problem is made clear through discussion. The counsellor explores the problem and its importance through his skilful questioning.
4. Counsellor draws out the facts from the pupils through counselling process.
5. He also informs the pupils certain facts.
6. Counsellor guides the pupils to establish contacts with various factors in the counselling process. He explains the importance of those facts which the pupils consider unimportant.
7. Counselling is a vital part of the entire guidance programme. 2.8. Counselling is only one aspect of guidance.
9. Counselling is a learning oriented process.
10. Counselling helps the pupil in making selections and following those selections.
11. Counselling is an assistance to the persons in their behaviour related problems in which their emotions and motivations are main.
12. Counselling involves interactions in which the counsellor accepts the responsibility of positive contribution in the development of other person's personality.
13. Counselling is a face to face relationship with a person. This relationship is between a counsellor and a client.
14. Counselling is democratic. It lays down the democratic system. The client can behave as he wishes.
15. Counsellor helps the persons in eliminating those defects or disabilities or helps in making modifications in them which obstruct their learning process. These modifications or corrections can be brought about by basic skills, such as reading and social adjustment.
16. Counselling is a professional service.
17. Counselling is problem-oriented.
18. Counselling is based on the appropriateness of counsellor's prediction.
19. Best counselling is in the form of the decision made by the counsellee.

20. Counselling is possible in humorous and cooperative environment only.
21. Counselling is completely based on self-guidance.
22. The term' counselling' cannot be used as a substitute for guidance, teaching, interview and psychotherapy etc.

William Cottle has given the following characteristics of counselling-

(i) A mutual relationship between two persons is necessary.
(ii) There can be various means of consultations between the counsellor and the client or counsellee.
(iii) Every counsellor performs his function with complete knowledge.
(iv) The nature of counselling also changes according to the client's feelings.
(v) Each counselling is interview-based.

COUNSELLING AND OTHER TERMS

Counselling and Advice

No intelligent counsellor gives advice unless and until it is important. In the counselling process, the entire responsibility of decision making is of client. Hence the counsellor is not an advisor. Similarly, the responsibility of quality of the decision also lies with the client. Counselling is also not lecturing and discussion. In counselling, advice-giving is never safe. In the case of advice or suggestion, the counsellor owns responsibility of decision. Hence, the counselling is a process in which the counsellor owns responsibility of those decisions which are taken.

Guidance and Counselling

Guidance and counselling terms are not synonyms. Counselling is only a part of guidance. It is a sort of special or an ordinary part which concerns with behaving with the person at the personal level. All counselling is guidance but all guidance is not counselling. Counselling is a higher order technical job, but guidance can be provided by any person who has sufficient information about that topic for which a person or pupil seeks help. Guidance indicates directive approach i.e., it is like giving an advice. Most of the teachers provide guidance to the pupils in the subjects about which they possess more knowledge. The counsellors are highly trained persons who have some differential personality traits which are different from those of ordinary persons.

It is essential to differentiate counselling and group-guidance. Counselling and group-guidance are not a single process. Group guidance is not counselling. But group guidance and counselling are closely related. After group guidance many counsellees can be benefited through individual guidance, counselling and other methods.

Counselling and Teaching

Counselling and teaching are also not alike. Providing counselling cannot be termed as teaching. Following are the differences between counselling and teaching—

Counselling

1. Counselling is one-to-one relationship. It is individualized.
2. Counselling is concerned with social adjustment and emotional problems.
3. The counsellor applies different techniques, such as diagnostic tools, vocational informations, various tests to understand a person.
4. Counsellor does not know the subject-matter of interview.
5. Interview is the most important technique in the counselling.
6. The informations collected during counselling are concerned with vocations, training etc.
7. Counselling cannot be provided in groups. It is individualized.

Teaching

Teaching is done in groups. When we teach in the class, we don't know the persons.

Teaching is concerned with intellectual and educational problems.

Teacher uses various types of aids so that the teaching may become effective and interesting.

Teacher has the knowledge of subject-matter and its results.

Interview as a technique is never used in teaching.

Information collected by the teacher are concerned with instructional activities.

Teaching is not counselling. It is done in groups.

Counselling and Interview

An interview is a technique which is used in counselling. The term 'counselling' is very comprehensive in itself. According to Jones, it is very difficult to designate the interview as a general method of guidances. Interview is not complete counselling because counselling may occur in informal situations and in the form of short conversation. 'Interview' cannot be used in groups' guidance. In counselling set-up, it is concerned with clinical methods only i.e., when the contact occurs between a counsellor and only one client.

Interview is closely related to the counselling. Interview is a face to face discussion. It is always vital process of counselling. But all this is not an interview. In the other counselling processes, telephonic conversation, a correspondence between two persons is also included. In intelligent counselling, follow-up task is also included which is conducted after counselling interview. In short, there are three main steps of counselling process, which are as follows—

(i) Complete and detailed study of a person,

(ii) Face to face discussion on a problem.

(iii) A systematic follow-up.

The interview is second step in this process i.e., face to face discussion. Hence, we observe that the interview is merely a part of counselling process.

Counselling and Psychotherapy

Psychotherapy is concerned with those persons whose behaviour is like neurotics. These are concerned with repressed individuals. Counselling is related to normal anxieties. Psychotherapy needs medical setting. But in counselling, educational setting is required. The techniques of psychotherapy are-play therapy, psychodrama, social drama etc. In counselling, such techniques can be used in schools.

The scope of counselling is comprehensive while it is deeper in the case of psychotherapy. A counsellor cannot be a psychotherapist but a psychotherapist can become a good counsellor. The counsellor can forward the serious cases to the psychotherapist.

Counselling is a relationship between two persons which includes providing the assistance to an immature person regarding defining his problems, to think about him, and to develop some habits and attitudes for intelligent decision-making. Psychotherapy is defined as a process of adjustment by using psychological methods. In counselling, psychology is not the only basis for appraising an individual, while is, psychotherapy, the basis to study or appraise an individual is only psychology

In counselling, the socioeconomic status of a person is considered as one of the important factors responsible for creating problems, for a person. 'But in the psychotherapy, socioeconomic status plays no role of special importance in solving a person's problems. The aim of the counselling is to help a person in dealing with developmental tasks fit for his age-group. Counselling is related to the situational matters while psychotherapy is concerned with changing the person so that he may face not only present problems but future problems too. Hence, counselling is more peripheral and psychotherapy is central.

Shaw (1957) indicates this too that the counselling should be more concerned with creative help and psychotherapy with mental ailments.

Tyler (1961) has also suggested that the counselling is a process of helping to understand persons identity more clearly, but psychotherapy is an attempt to change the basic developmental structure. According to Tyler, psychotherapy is concerned with the personality changes while counselling is concerned with the use of means. Psychotherapy is concerned with interpersonal conflicts while counselling is related to role conflicts.

According to *Wolberg,* psychotherapy is related to reconstructive goals and counselling to re-educative and supportive goals. Reconstructive goals are related to psychoanalysis. Re-educative attempts are concerned with bringing changes in the behavioural attitudes. Hence, we can say that the counselling focuses on immediate situation while psychotherapy is connected with the complete change in basic character structure.

There are some other differences between counselling and psychotherapy

(i) Counselling is of lesser duration as compared to psychotherapy.

(ii) Lesser number of counselling-sessions occur.

(iii) There is less emphasis on case history in counselling but more emphasis on psychological testing.

(iv) In counselling, suggestions are more and interference is minimum.

(v) A psychotherapist involves his personal guess or diagnosis more while a counsellor uses psychological instruments more frequently.

GUIDANCE VS COUNSELLING

Psychology, the study of behaviour and of mental processes, is a diverse field. It involves the process of understanding the reasons why people behave and think as they do and applies scientific methods in observing and gathering information, in order to come up with an applicable principle of behaviour and motivation. It is subjective and is applied according to the specific requirements of an individual. Among the many branches and applications of psychology are the fields of Guidance and Counselling.

Guidance and Counselling both involve helping an individual in making choices about the different things that might confront and confuse him. They are totally different fields though and to help distinguish between the two, here are some of the things that are used to describe them:

Counselling

Counselling is a psychological specialty that deals with research and applied work in supervision, training, career development, prevention, and health. It focuses on a person's strengths, assets, environmental interactions, educational background, career development and personality. Counselling started as a result of WWII. Since then, it has been used by individuals, institutions, families, rehabilitation agencies and other organizations. It utilizes psychological methods in the collection of case history data through personal interview, testing and aptitude.

It helps clients to choose the best solution to a problem, through the process of listening and questioning. It is important to note that counselling is not a giving of opinion and it is based on a wellness model rather than a medical one. A counsellor's basic concern should go beyond treating dysfunction or pathology. It should deal with a client's self awareness which should help him towards personal growth and wellness.

Guidance

Guidance is defined as the act of guiding, giving leadership, supervision, direction or professional guidance for future actions. It is usually provided to students in preparation for a vocation. Guidance helps a person discover and develop his psychological, vocational and educational potential in order to be happier and more useful in society. Each person is responsible for his decisions and actions, but when he is young he will need someone more mature and experienced to guide him through life and towards making the right decisions for himself.

Like counselling, it assists clients towards a decision or an appropriate course of action. It may be used as therapeutic aid in the treatment of minor emotional disturbances and disorders.

GUIDANCE AND COUNSELLING FOR ADOLESCENTS

Adolescents as we have seen have unique age specific characteristics, needs and problems that need to be rationalized and tackled properly for their adequate adjustment and proper growth and development of their potentialities. Here lies the need of a proper organisation of guidance and counselling. The services as such provided in the form of personal, educational and vocational guidance to them are not enough as the problem being a delicate and gigantic one needs multidimensional efforts well co-ordinate on the part of teachers, parents and school authorities. Let us see what can the teachers, parents and school do for adolescents as a matter of providing guidance and counselling to the adolescent boys and girls. When planned systematically such efforts on their parts may include the things mentioned below.

Adolescence is the bridge between childhood and adulthood. The behaviour of the adolescent and his personality needs a careful study. It is essential to have the knowledge of the adolescents' psychology in order to understand them. What are their specific needs? What types of changes do take place during this period? What are the problems faced by the adolescents?

How should they be treated? All this is essential to be known by the parents, teachers and administrators who have to deal with them.

As we know, the growth stops at the end of adolescence after attaining maturity. Adolescence is the stage where maximum growth takes place. For getting maximum, what one can get with respect to physical and mental growth, suitable environment should be provided by the parents and the teachers at home as well as in schools. Adolescents must be provided with balanced diet. Their eating habits should be properly checked up. They must be given knowledge of health, personal hygiene, cleanliness, various diseases and their prevention etc. to keep them fit for growing. Adequate provision for physical exercise and activities should be made in the school curriculum and necessary facilities should be provided. Sex plays very dominant role at the age of adolescence. The rapid physiological changes, the secretion of sex hormones, the sudden awakening of sex instinct and urges-all necessitate the provision of adequate sex information and education for adolescent. The following things may help in this direction.

(i) They should be helped in making adjustments with regard to their new bodily changes and somatic developments. Girls should know that flow of blood during menstruation is not a disease. It is a natural process which prepares them for becoming mothers. In a similar way, the occasional discharge of semen during sleep among the boys is not in any way harmful to them and should not be in any way a cause of worry. The boys should be told all about this.

(ii) Their curiosity of sex also needs satisfaction. For this purpose the parents and the teachers should provide adequate information regarding the sex hygiene and physiology, the process of the birth of a baby, the hazards of immature and before marriage intercourse etc. in a very frank, scientific, judicious and impersonal manner.

(iii) The sex instinct and urges also need to be cared properly. There should be proper sublimation of sex instinct and canalization of sexual energy. Forceful inhibition, taboos, and restrictions imposed in this direction bring disastrous results. With the provision of wide field of interests, a network of co-curricular activities and social situations, the boys and girls should be given a chance to know and work shoulder to shoulder with each other. This will remove their so many misconceptions about each other and will lead to their healthy adjustments.

Recent researches in the field of Adolescents Psychology have revealed that the adults, the parents, elders and the teachers and their unreasonable ways and points of view are the real problems of adolescence. They are in the habit of criticizing the adolescents and always impose their authority and assert their likings and dislikings. They forget that there is a generation gap between them and adolescents. In dealing with them the parents and the teachers should realize that the demands of their peer group are more important than their own expectation.

Secondly, in the adolescents, there is a craving for recognition and they also try to maintain their self-prestige and status among their peers. They assert that they are now mature individuals. Their opinions should be valued and they should be given a patient hearing. Therefore, it is badly needed on the part of the teachers as well as parents that they should stop treating the adolescents as children and give them due recognition. Their opinions should be invited and they should be given opportunities for free expression. They must refrain from activities damaging to the pupil's self-concept. The adolescents must not feel that they are insulted and their phenomenal self has been attacked unnecessarily. The teachers and parents should stop murmuring and criticizing the attitudes and actions of the adolescents blindly. Youths are more in need of models than critics. The elders must give a deep consideration to adolescents needs and problems. It is futile to punish misbehaviour. The root causes should be removed.

The age of adolescence is marked by too much intensity, force; instability and immaturity of emotions. The adolescent youths are highly inflammable and restless. Their emotions can be aroused with a slight provocation. The political parties and opportunist leaders can easily befool them and use them in destroying national property. Therefore, there is a strong need of emotional education to the adolescents. Their emotions should be properly trained and their emotional energies should be diverted towards the constructive ends.

Moreover, the adolescents suffer from some emotional hungers. They have a strong desire to love and to be loved. They need to be accepted by their age mates and every adolescent aspires that he should be admired and praised. He needs that he should be given freedom to proceed in his own way and adopt his own style of life but on the other hands, needs protection, shelter and affection of the parents, elders and teachers. He becomes disturbed if he is not provided proper security and freedom from anxiety. The parents and the teachers should take care of these needs for the adolescents. They must be given what they need in terms of their emotional requirements.

The adolescence is the age of wide interests and aptitudes. There are wide individual differences among the adolescents with regard to their special interests and aptitudes. A great care should be taken to locate the special interests and aptitudes of the adolescents. According to their interests and aptitudes they should be provided with learning experiences and opportunities for participation in co-curricular activities. The curriculum should provide the open choice for various subjects and activities according to the tastes and temperaments of the adolescents.

Their thirst of curiosity, wandering and adventure should be quenched through excursion, N.C.C., mountaineering, scientific exploration etc. The love for humanity and ideals should be utilized in rendering social services and community services in the neighbourhood and distressed areas. In brief, the adolescents should be provided with useful activities according to their interests so that they can be constantly busy and their mind pre-occupied with healthy and constructive ideas.

One of the causes of increasing restlessness, indiscipline, dishonesty and aimlessness among the youth of India is that there is no proper provision of religious and moral education in our system of education. Ours is a secular state and therefore the doubts are expressed in the provision of religious instruction inside the schools. But it is a false fear standing on erroneous grounds. Actually the roots and the goals of all the religious are one and the same. If we try to do away with the rituals, the essence of all the religions is morality. Therefore, it is education for morality and character formation, which is to be provided by religious education and every school, home and other social agency can work in this direction. The parents, teachers, social workers and administrators should join their hands in creating suitable atmosphere and offering opportunities of practising moral qualities.

There is a strong desire of achieving in-dependence in adolescents. Economic factors obstruct their way. Therefore, they are worried for acquiring self-sufficiency in economic aspect. What occupation should they choose how can they earn their livelihood are some questions, the answers of which they try to seek. Here arises the need of proper vocational guidance and vocational education for them. The youths of today are bewildered and aimless because of the indefiniteness of their vocation. The education imparted to them does not provide jobs and occupations. Therefore, the strong need of today is to provide job oriented and vocation based practical education of the adolescents. The government, society, parents and the teachers should make their efforts in this direction. Lack of guidance creates aimlessness, indefiniteness and restlessness among the adolescents. The adolescents have their problems which need careful attention and proper solution. The adolescents are at the cross-roads of life. A sight mistake can lead them on the wrong path. Therefore, it is the utmost duty of the state, society and school to provide proper guidance services to the students as well as to their parents. Guidance services should be organised in a proper form both inside and the outside the schools. There should be well trained guidance workers and personnel. As far as possible, individual guidance should be provided.

The list of suggestions regarding the solution of the adolescents problems and the satisfaction of their needs cannot be said as complete with above mentioned few points. The task is gigantic and requires strenuous efforts from all directions. Moreover, it is difficult to prescribe some common rule or formula for the direction and guidance of the adolescents with respect to their problems and needs. It is not a mass phenomenon. In actual sense there are no problem adolescents with problems. Therefore, the focus of guidance is always the individual and not the problem. Every adolescent is to be studied carefully as he requires special guidance and help for the solution of his problems and satisfaction of his needs.

BASIC PRINCIPLES OF COUNSELLING PROCESS

According to Mc. Daniel and Shaftal, the counselling process is based on some basic principles—

Principle of Acceptance: According to this principle, each client must be accepted as an individual and dealt with as such. The counsellor should give due regard to the rights of the client

Principle of Respect for the Individual: All the schools of thoughts of counselling advocate for the respect of the individual i.e., respecting an individual's feelings must be an integral part of counselling process.

Principle of Permissiveness: Counselling is such a relationship which develops optimism and the environment shapes according to the person. All the thoughts accept the relative relationship of counselling.

Principle of Thinking with the Individual: Counselling emphasizes thinking with the individual. It is essential to differentiate think for whom'? and 'why to think'? It is the role of the counsellor to think about all the forces around the client to join client's thought process and to work collectively with the client regarding his problem.

Principle of Consistency with Ideals of Democracy: All the principles are associated with ideals of democracy. The ideals of democracy desire to accept a person and want to respect the rights of others. The process of counselling is based upon the ideals of a person's respect. It is a process which accepts individual differences.

Principle of learning: All the assumptions of counselling accept the presence of learning-elements in the counselling process.

BASIC ASSUMPTIONS OF COUNSELLING

Jones has recommended accepting the following four assumptions for the success of counselling—

(a) It is understood that the pupil desires to participate in this process. Unfamiliar process of counselling may create obstruction for a few moments. Unless and until, the pupil does not participate wholeheartedly, counselling cannot be successful.

(b) The counsellor should have proper training, experience and personal attitude for effective functioning. He should have the ability to make contacts. With the pupils very conveniently. He should help the pupil in determining the aims and objectives.

(c) Appropriate environment is must. There should be assurance of confidentiality in such environment.

(d) Counselling should provide such a contact which fulfills immediate and long term needs. The counsellor should be available as and when he is required by the pupil for some special help.

G.W. Aliport has also mentioned the following two basic assumptions—

Behaviour is learned and modifiable: The person should be made sensitive to these changes for their proper adjustment. Counselling owns this responsibility.

Counselling is a learning situation: To help the individual in understanding himself, to help in understanding the environment and to learn new methods of adjustment in life.

Modem approach of counselling concentrates on attitudes, and not on techniques. According to this, the attitude of counsellor should be democratic in addition to authoritarian attitude. Williamson has mentioned the following assumptions concerning-essential conditions for counselling—

(i) The assumption has been expressed that the aims of counselling and the means used for this will help the person for his development or in this direction.

(ii) Uniqueness of individuality has been assumed. But this should not be forgotten that the result of uniqueness of individuality occurs in the context of other persons.

(iii) Counselling is beneficial only when the pupils select it to voluntarily.

(iv) Previously it was thought that the pupils who feel the problem can seek counselling. But this view has been discarded now.

All the pupils can seek counselling to understand themselves in a better way.

(v) Totality of human development should not be assumed. The counsellor should understand this concept.

(vi) Intelligent selection of an occupation by adolescents is a source of motivation. This study has been done by Super, Tyler and Rod.

(vii) It is decided that happily adjusted and matured persons understand their responsibilities properly and they encourage social growth.

(viii) It is assumed that the counsellor should honour the worth and dignity of the counselling-seeking clients.

FIELDS OR FORMS OF COUNSELLING

There are many fields of counselling i.e., it is of various types. Humphreys Traxler and North have described the following four types of fields-

(i) Educational Orientation and Guidance.

(ii) Personal and Social Adjustment.

(iii) Vocational Orientation and Guidance

(iv) Health Adjustment.

Inspite of these types, there are other seven types of forms of counselling—

Vocational Counselling

Vocational counselling is that process in which a person is helped in selecting a proper vocation and preparing for that. The decision regarding a vocation is a very serious affair and hence, it needs special attention. Otherwise, mal-adjustment and unhappiness on be the result.

Educational Counselling

Educational counselling is concerned with helping the pupil in deciding about the curriculum for study. In the context of various aptitudes various capabilities and natural tendencies, pupils can be helped through educational counselling. In nutshell, it helps, a person in problems related to education.

Marriage Counselling

These days, marriage counselling has also started. In this, suggestions are made for the proper selection of life-partners and the person is helped to the maximum. Married clients are helped to solve their married life-problems. There can be various reasons of married life-problems, such as, industrialization, urbanization etc. Families are disintegrating due to these reasons. They need counselling.

Personality Counselling or Psychological Counselling

The solution of personal and emotional problems comes under personality counselling or psychological counselling, e.g., scarcity of friends, isolation, inferiority complexes etc. It is very essential to attend these problems otherwise this affects the school education of the pupils. The lack of such counselling may create disturbed, unhappy and unadjusted mental state. The term 'Psychological Counselling' was used first of all by R.W. White. In psychological counselling, the counsellor is just like a therapist or doctor. The counsellor helps the client in the expression of his suppressed needs, feelings and emotions through this normal talk.

Clinical Counselling

The term clinical counselling was used by H.B. Pepinski According to him, the objectives' of clinical counselling are

(a) Diagnosis and treatment of minor functional mal-adjustments.
(b) A relationship primarily individual and face to face between counsellor and client.

Hence, it is clear that clinical counselling is concerned with the maladjustments related to a person's normal functioning. In this, direct relationship between the counsellor and the client is involved. In clinical counselling process, the problem is analysed and efforts are made to solve the problem.

Clinical psychology is an important branch of psychology. In clinical psychology, a person is helped who develops maladjustment and some problems in self-expression: Clinical counselling and clinical psychology have much similarities.

Psychotherapeutic Counselling

W.V. Snyder has defined psychotherapeutic counselling. According to him. "Psychotherapeutic counselling is the face to face relationship in which a psychologically trained individual is consciously attempting by verbal means to assist another person or persons to modify emotional attitude that are socially maladjusted and in which the subject is relatively aware of the personality reorganization through which he is going."

Regarding the relationship between psychotherapy and counselling. Ruth Strang has said that these both are mutually related. At present, it is agreed that the counselling is remedial in nature. Psychotherapeutic counselling is very useful and important in eliminating social maladjustment.

Placement Counselling

Placement counselling means to help the client in selecting the vocation according to his aptitudes, attitudes and abilities i.e., helping the client in his appointment, in the occupation for which he possesses abilities and from which he gets job-satisfaction.

From these types of counselling we come to know that a person faces problems in these spheres. The type of counselling depends upon the nature of the problem. But the areas of a problem cannot be restricted. The counsellor should be ready to solve or to face all types of problems.

Steps In Counselling Procedure

Williamson and *Darley* have mentioned the following six steps of counselling procedure.

(i) Analysis—It is the procedure in which facts are collected so that the pupil may by study.

(ii) Synthesis—In this step, the collected information is organized.

(iii) Diagnosis—In this step, the reasons responsible for the problem are sorted out.

(iv) Prognosis—The statement regarding the use of diagnosis is known as prognosis.

(v) Counselling—The steps taken by the counsellor and the client for adjustment constitute this step.

(vi) Follow-up—This step includes the evaluation of effectiveness of counselling services or efforts to help the pupil in solving his new problem.

Rogers has also summarized various steps as follows—

(i) A person comes for help and he has taken a tentative step.

(ii) The help-situation is often defined. The client is familiarized with the idea that the counsellor does not possess the answers. The client himself is to search out the answers. Counselling has its own timing if he desires so.

(iii) The counsellors encourage independent expression. This independent expression is in the context of some problem. This prevents anxiety and guilty consciousness. The counsellor does not try to convince the client that he is at fault or he is correct. The counsellors accept the client as he is. He encourages independent expression only.

(iv) The counsellor approves negative feelings, lie identifies them and makes them more distinct. The counsellor should react to the client's feelings.

(v) The tentative positive expression should occur after a person's negative expression.

(vi) The counsellor identifies positive feelings and approves them.

(vii) Self-understanding and insight occur.

(viii) Clarification of possible decisions and possible direction to the tasks.

(ix) Initiation of important positive activities by the person.

(x) Further, more development of insight and proper understanding.

(xi) The developed feeling of independence and increasing need of assistance.

These activities, not necessarily, should occur in this sequence. These steps are client-centred.

TECHNIQUES OF COUNSELLING

The techniques used by the counselling should be according to the pupil's uniqueness and personality. Williamson has described the techniques of counselling under the following five headings—

Cultivating Self-understanding

The pupil or the client should possess the knowledge and understanding of his own abilities and responsibilities very clearly. The client should understand all these before using these abilities and responsibilities.

Therefore, the counsellor should have the experience of test-administration and interpretation of the test scores. The test scores provide a strong base for diagnosis and prognosis in the counselling process.

Advising and Planning a Programme of Action

The counsellor starts with the client's objectives and his attitudes etc. and indicates favourable and unfavourable facts or data. He weighs the evidences and he understands the fact why he is giving special suggestion to the pupil. Williamson believes that the counsellor should state his attitude with definiteness. He should not look like an indecisive.

The counsellor does not fear while giving advice or direct suggestion because the pupil does not understand the utility of scores. Williamson has explained the following methods of advising the pupil after gathering the data—

(i) Direct Advising-In this, the counsellor gives his advice very frankly. This type of method is appropriate for tough-millded people who oppose any activity and who do not fear of failure.

(ii) Persuasive Method - This method is useful when the data indicate clearly some definite alternate. The counsellor analyses only the evidences and observes the alternate actions.

Establishing Rapport

When a client visits the counsellor for the first time, the counsellor should welcome his client. He should make him comfortable and he should be taken into confidence. The main basis of establishing rapport is-the fame of the counsellor's ability, respect for individuality, confidence before the interview and developing relations with the pupil.

Referral to Other Personnel Workers

No counsellor can solve all types of problems of the pupils. He should recognize his limitations and he should be given the knowledge of sources of specialized help. He should suggest the pupils to seek the assistance from other sources.

In addition to above mentioned techniques, there are other counselling techniques which are as follows—

Silence: Sometimes, silent-listening proves more effective in different situations. When a client is describing his problem, the counsellor adopts silence.

This ensures the client about the counsellor's full attention towards the client's narration. It also ensures the client about the counsellor's serious thinking on the client's problem.

Acceptance: The counsellor should grant temporary acceptance to the client's case.

Sometimes, the counsellor utters such words which give the impression that he understands very clearly whatever the client is stating. But the counsellor utters the words in such way that the client's talk remains un-interrupted for example, 'alright' 'very good', 'yes' etc. At many occasions, the counsellor does not utter any word for his acceptance! but he nods expressing his acceptance.

Clarification: At some occasions, the counsellor should clarify what the client says.

It is the duty of the counsellor to make the client familiar with the fact that he understands the client and he accepts him. But sometimes it becomes necessary to clarify the client's explanation. While clarifying, the client should not feel any compulsion.

Restatement: Acceptance and restatement both ensure this client that the counsellor understands and accepts him. Through restatement, the counsellor repeats what the client has stated. But the Counsellor does not apply any correction or clarification during the client's assessment while restating, at his own.

Asking Questions: The counsellor should ask some questions to inspire the client to express more ideas. These questions should be asked just after the client's statement is over.

Approval: The client, expresses his different views regarding his problems. The counsellor approves some of them and disapproves others. The ideas which are approved affect the client very much. The client is also influenced by the knowledge possessed by the counsellor and his personality. If the counsellor 'grants approval to the client's ideas intermittently, then the approval becomes ineffective. Attention should be paid towards this.

Humour: Use of humour just to remove the client's tension and to make the conversation interesting has become the necessity of the day.

Summary Classification: Some part of the client's statement may not be useful Hence, the problem looks vague in itself In such situation, it becomes necessary for the counsellor to shorten the client's statement and to organize it properly so that the client may understand the problem more distinctly. The counsellor should always try not to add his own ideas.

Analysis: The counsellor can take initiative by presenting some solution to the client's problem. But the counsellor cannot force the client to act upon that solution. He leaves it upto the client whether to accept or reject that solution or to apply some modification. The client cannot be put under pressure in this regard.

Interpretations: The counsellor should have the right to interpret the client's statement or explanation only. He should not add from his own side. He concludes the result out of client's statement. The client alone is unable to derive results. It is important to note here that the results concluded by the counsellor and results derived" from the tests may agree or may not agree.

Regression: Sometimes it is erroneous whatever the client thinks or speaks. Such faulty ideas should be given up. The counsellor should act very carefully In order to give up such ideas so that the client may not turn agitated and the client may not think otherwise in negative sense.

Assurance: The technique of providing assurance to the client develops optimism in the client regarding the solution of his problem. Through assurance the counsellor approves the statements of the client and also provides support along with approval.

Effects of assurance are equally observed. Assurance is considered more comprehensive than the approval. Hence, the approval is included in the assurance.

Explanatory Method

Explanatory method is the most desirable method in the counselling. In this, the counsellor gradually understands very carefully the diagnostic data and indicates those situations in which the pupil's potentialities can be used. In this, the, use of data are explained in detail and carefully. Then after knowing the decision or interest of the client, the counsellor helps directly in order to execute the decision. This help includes the remedial work, educational or teaching plans etc.

DIFFERENCE BETWEEN COUNSELLING AND GUIDANCE

Guidance and counselling, concept that institutions, especially schools, should promote the efficient and happy lives of individuals by helping them adjust to social realities. The disruption of community and family life by industrial civilization convinced many that guidance experts should be trained to handle problems of individual adjustment. Though the need for attention to the whole individual had been recognized by educators since the time of Socrates, it was only during the 20th cent that researchers actually began to study and accumulate information about guidance.

This development, occurring largely in the United States, was the result of two influences: John Dewey and others insisted that the object of education should be to stimulate the fullest possible growth of the individual and that the unique qualities of personality require individual handling for adequate development; also in the early 20th cent., social and economic conditions stimulated a great increase in school enrolment.

These two forces encouraged a re-examination of the curricula and methods of secondary schools, with special reference to the needs of students who did not plan to enter college. The academic curriculum was revised to embrace these alternative cultural and vocational requirements.

Early guidance programmes dealt with the immediate problem of vocational placement.

The complexities of the industrial economy and the unrealistic ambitions of many young people made it essential that machinery for bringing together jobs and workers be set up; vocational guidance became that machinery. At the same time, counselling organizations were established to help people understand their potentialities and liabilities and make intelligent personal and vocational decisions. The first vocational counselling service was the Boston Vocational Bureau, established (1908) by Frank Parsons, a pioneer in the field of guidance. His model was soon copied by many schools, municipalities, states, and private organizations.

With the development of aptitude and interest tests, such as the Stanford-Binet Intelligence Test and the Strong Vocational Interest Blank, commercial organizations were formed to analyse people's abilities and furnish career advice. Schools organized testing and placement services, many of them in cooperation with federal and state agencies.

Under the provisions of the National Defence Education Act (1958), the federal government provided assistance for guidance and counselling programmes in the public secondary schools and established a testing procedure to identify students with outstanding abilities.

The U.S. Dept. of Labor has been an active force in establishing standards and methods of vocational guidance, helping states to form their own vocational guidance and counselling services. The personnel departments of many large corporations have also instituted systems of guidance to promote better utilization of their employees.

Modern high school guidance programmes also include academic counselling for those students planning to attend college.

In recent years, school guidance counselors have also been recognized as the primary source for psychological counselling for high school students; this sometimes includes counselling in such areas as drug abuse and teenage pregnancy and referrals to other professionals (e.g., psychologists, social workers, and learning-disability specialists).

Virtually all teachers colleges offer major courses in guidance, and graduate schools of education grant advanced degrees in the field.

2

Guidance: Needs and Principles

A person deserves guidance in order to develop all the areas of his life. Guidance is more essential when he is acquiring education and he is being trained so that he may play some productive role in the society. A person can acquire this during his schooling only.

At this level, a person's energies, abilities, capacities and skills are identified and developed. During this period a person's habits and attitudes are developed along with his social and emotional development. During this period of growth and development various problems arise. If these problems are left as such, various adverse effects start appearing which encourage maladjustment. A research was conducted regarding the need of guidance. This study was conducted by all India Association of Guidance and Counselling, in this study, 1508. Questionnaires were received. Each questionnaire contained 40 questions. These were circulated in the various universities of the country. In these questionnaires it was asked about the assistance being provided to the pupils and the assistance which they require.

In their responses, the pupils made it clear that most of the assistance they get from their parents and guardians. They got very limited guidance from the persons concerned in their colleges. From this, it can be concluded that either colleges don't have organised guidance services or they are failing in achieving their objectives. We can feel the necessity of guidance from different view-point. There can be various cause of need of guidance. The need of guidance may by discussed from the following points of views—

1. from Individual Point of View.
2. from Social Point of View,
3. from Educational Point of View.
4. from Psychological Point of View.
5. from Urban Areas Point of View.
6. from Political Changes Point of View.

From Individual Point of View

Baqer Mehdi, in his article "Guidance in Schools" (A NCERT Booklet), has divided the need of guidance from individual point of view in the following three steps—

(i) Academic Growth

(ii) Vocational Maturity

(iii) Personal-Social Development.

Academic Growth

It is essential to remove the problems related to the subject matter and to develop the abilities and skills according to the changing capacities of the pupils for the academic growth of the pupils. It is desirable for the teacher to understand the pupil first for this purpose. Only then he can teach a subject effectively. Classroom teaching cannot be done properly unless and until the classroom needs and interests of the pupils are not adjusted according to their abilities.

An effort to adjust the teaching according to the needs, abilities and interests of the child means to implement the guidance view point in education. The pupils select those subjects which they know better. With this, their academic growth and adjustment occur better. By removing their problems related to the subject-matter they can avoid their backwardness.

Vocational Maturity

It is essential to develop proper attitudes towards work and polytechnical skills. The need of guidance is made felt by creating proper attitude towards school assignments and philosophy of the work produced according to the pupil's expectations. As a result of this need proper vocational selection is possible. In the selection of a vocation, not only abilities and aptitudes are related with the vocation, but also the development of interests, attitudes and skills is included. Interests, attitudes and skills are not inborn. These can be developed. Hence, if we don't do like this, the guidance programme in the schools will become ineffective.

Personal-Social Development

For the individual and social development of a person, self-understanding, adjustment with self and society is necessary. *Baqer Mehdi* has classified the problems into three categories—

(a) Orientational

(b) Adjective

(c) Developmental.

In order to solve these problems, self-appraisal and self-understanding are necessary. Generally guidance is related to orientational and adjustive problems because these problems can be easily identified.

Mathewson (1955) has considered the third type of problems very important. From this point of view, guidance programme cannot be restricted only to educational and vocational orientation but it can be extended to life-orientation and life-philosophy so that a person's thinking process may become an integral part of his life. For this objective, guidance programme should be continuous and dynamic.

OBJECTIVES OF GUIDANCE

Guidance process is purposeful process. Without determining the objectives, this process connot be completed or concluded. Due to the variations in the scope, guidance has a variety of objectives. If we start guidance process without any objective it cannot be concluded because various sub-processes involved in the guidance cannot be given any direction and these activities remain meaningless.

Objectives of guidance change at each level of education. Every stage of education enjoys different objectives of guidance. For example, the functions and objectives of guidance at primary level will be different from those of middle stage. Similarly, objectives of guidance at high school or higher secondary stage will be different from those of middle stage.

Objectives of Guidance at Primary Stage

Every activity at primary stage includes guidance. At primary stage, there is need to pay special attention towards the health of the children. At this stage there is great need to co-ordinate the functions of a teacher, guidance worker, school, staff members of medical service and school social service workers. All these person help in learning properly essential skills for primary education, for acquiring basic knowledge, for adapting according to the social traditions and for developing proper attitude towards school activities. These too are the objectives of guidance at this stage. In addition to these helping children in their physical development, emotional stability and adjustment in the school are other objectives of guidance at this stage. When a child leaves home and enters into the school environment, he has to make many co-ordinations. School environment is very comprehensive for a child. In school, the child comes in contact with various types of persons, children and teachers. Also he lacks security in the school and he becomes very fearful, hesitating and remains suppressed in the school. Those children are more in difficulty who are fully dependent on their parents. In this situation it is also included in the objectives of guidance that the person imparting guidance should search out such children and their adjustment problems should be controlled. A person providing guidance at the primary stage aims at making the child self-dependent. Hence, it is the objective of guidance too to make the pupils self-dependent. Also a guide organizes his activities to create a feeling of co-operation among children.

Primary stage ranges upto fifth class. During this period, children make their place in the school. Gradually they get themselves established in the school and they consider themselves an honourable member of the school. When these children cross over from primary stage to higher stage, they feel suffocated. Behaviours of primary stage sometimes look like a joke. The traditions of new school, rules, administration, curriculum etc. are all new. In such situations, the guidance worker plans the guidance programme in order to prepare the children of primary stage for next higher school stage, such as arranging the visits of primary stage children to high schools, inviting high school teachers to primary schools explaining the procedure for getting admission to high schools after leaving the primary schools, making them familiar with the curriculum of high schools etc.

Similarly, guidance programme also includes the supply of booklets and other materials to the children and their parents which explain the activities of high schools.

In nutshell we can say that the following are the objectives of guidance at the primary school stage—

1. To co-ordinate all the activities of all the workers such as a teacher, medical service staff members, school social workers and the activities of a person providing guidance etc.
2. To assist children adapting according to the school traditions and rules-regulations of the School.
3. To assist developing higher attitude towards school activities.
4. To assist children in developing their physical and emotional stability.
5. Objective of finding out problems regarding adjustment in the school and to control them
6. Objective of making children self-dependent.
7. Objective of creating the feeling of co-operation in the children.
8. Objective of making children ready for crossing over from primary school to next higher stage.
9. Objective of supplying various informations to children regarding higher stage such as curricula of next higher classes and distribution of booklets regarding various school functions among the children and their parents.

Objectives of Guidance at Secondary Stage

The child leaves primary stage and enters secondary stage. At this stage the scope of guidance becomes more comprehensive as compared to the scope of guidance at primary stage. At this stage, guidance becomes more important as a result of multiple reasons. At this stage teachers too teach according to the subjects. Therefore, all the children cannot contact all the teachers. At high and higher secondary schools, only subject specialists teach. At these stages, personal, social and vocational problems of the children come into light and solution of these problems is necessary. In order to achieve this objective, a comprehensive and organized guidance service is continuously required. In this way, we see the following are the objectives of guidance at secondary and higher secondary stages. A child is not familiar with the life of new school when he leaves the primary school and enters to a new higher school. He has to face a number of problems regarding admission. Also it may become difficult for him to co-ordinate with new classmates and new friends. Hence, the objective of guidance service existing in the school should be to eliminate such problems of the pupils. After reaching at this higher level, the selection of subject becomes necessary. In this task, the pupil may face difficulty. He is unable to understand in which subject he is competent and which subject he should not opt. The selection of subjects has become very difficult task due to the variety of subjects. Hence, the objective of guidance should be to understand this type of problem and the same should be solved.

The objective of guidance service existing in the school is to take care of needs related to the health of the children and to inform timely the relevant persons regarding those health deficiencies so that the necessary action can be taken.

Co-curricular activities are being considered very important for the physical development of the children, such as debates, sports, cultural activities, programmes of social service etc. Hence, the important objective of guidance services is to guide the children for such activities so that their physical development may be given proper direction.

In schools it is important to maintain the records regarding the development of the pupils, education, psychological development, cultural activities, because the entire guidance programme is to be conducted on the basis of these records. Hence, the objective of guidance programme workers should be to maintain such record so that the counsellor may feel convenience during counselling. In solving the problems of the children co-operation plays an important role. This co-operation is desirable in guidance at all levels. The objective of guidance services should be to create a feeling of co-operation among all the workers involved in this service. This cooperation acts as a substantial base for guidance at the next higher level. When an individual enters adolescence, an individual experiences emotional and personal needs. Therefore the objective of guidance services should be to solve the problems related to such needs.

According to Crow and Crow, the creation of academic environment in accordance with the adolescent stage is very essential so that the pupils may be motivated in order to acquire higher education and they may be helped in selecting the subject according to abilities.

Baqer Mehdi, in his booklet 'Guidance in Schools' published by NCERT has pointed out the functions of guidance at this stage which are the other form of objective of guidance. These functions are as follows—

(a) Aiding pupils to orient themselves to the new purposes of education.
(b) Aiding pupils to orient themselves to the need for good planning.
(c) Aiding pupils to adjust themselves to their education by making wise choices of the subjects of study.
(d) Aiding pupils to make progress in their education by removal of subject difficulties and development of good study skills.
(e) Aiding pupils to build proper motivation for study.

OBJECTIVES AT COLLEGE AND UNIVERSITY STAGE

When a child enters the college, he becomes a complete young man and his personality acquires his own pattern. Some of them have clear objectives. Some start feeling their responsibilities. They are also very serious in their studies because they know the meaning of success and failure. But there are some persons who failed to understand what the college education means. They come to college without knowing what they can do. After securing admission to the college they face multiple difficulties. They consider their studies meaningless. That is why they go to college without any objective.

In such situations, the objective of college guidance programme is that the needs of such students should be looked into immediately who are unable to make progress in the college affairs and who can use their talent in their activities on providing proper educational facilities. In college, the objective of guidance service should also be to help the pupils in selecting the subject so that they may acquire specialization because such specialisations help the pupils in their future vocational plans.

Similarly other objectives of guidance service include organized programmes of tutorials and providing help to the pupils for making progress by studying the books existing in the library. It would be very meaningful if the students are made aware of objectives, nature and scope of college educations before its commencement in the college. According to other objectives of guidance service, the pupils should be informed regarding the various facilities existing in the college such as library facilities. If such were not informed, it would lead towards the wastage of pupil's time. In this way, we see that there is no much difference between the functions and guidance objectives of high, higher secondary and college stage. Hence, the guidance objectives at college and University stage can also be presented in the following manner

(i) To make available informations regarding admissions to college and university.
(ii) To provide informations regarding co-curricular activities in the college and university.
(iii) To help pupils selecting subjects so that they may achieve their future programme and objectives.
(iv) To help the children eliminating their financial difficulties.
(v) To make aware the pupils regarding the existing hostel facilities so that the problems of their boarding and lodging may be removed.
(vi) To provide vocational informations to the pupils so that they may take decision regarding their future.
(vii) To arrange for testing the pupils.

The objectives of guidance can also be expressed as follows—

(a) Objectives from pupils' point of view.
(b) From institution's point of view.

Objectives from Pupils' Point of View

From this point of view the objectives of guidance are as follows—

(i) To help the individuals in their proper placement in all the fields of their personal life and helping them in their development to their full capacity.
(ii) To help the individual in his balanced physical, mental, emotional and social progress.
(iii) To be helpful in solving the personal problems of an individual so that there proper adjustment may take place.

From Institution's Point of View

The objectives of guidance from institution's point of view are as follows—

(i) To help to understand pupils and teachers through guidance programme.
(ii) To provide organized training to in-service teachers.
(iii) To provide guidance services by the teachers to the needy students.
(iv) Guidance programme acts as a bridge between school and the society.

The persons involved in the guidance programme may announce the school programmes in the society.

(v) To conduct research work by institutions regarding teaching and guidance so that reforms may be brought about.

In this way, we see that the objectives of guidance are broad based. In order to bring reforms and to analyse the results of these objectives, this programme must be dynamic. For this, we shall have to insist upon research work so that this programme may be implemented more effectively.

TYPES OF GUIDANCE, NEEDS AND PRINCIPLES

Man is a social animal. He has to face various problems while living in the society. Social problems are related to the various aspects of the society. If the problems related to various aspects are not dealt with properly, many difficulties may arise and the person cannot adjust himself with reference to that aspect of the society. It is very difficult to study these problems and the solution of these problems is more difficult. In order to solve these problems we need various types of guidance services. Hence, if the guidance services are classified to solve the problems related to the various aspects of the society, these guidance services can be used more effectively. Hence, for the solution of the problems it is important to classify guidance. On the basis of this classification, we can manage for various elements of guidance services.

Hence, the classification of guidance services is based upon the fact that in this modern age, revolutionary changes have occurred in the industrial, social and cultural areas as a result of scientific progress. Civilization and culture have also adopted modernism and thrown away the old. Also, new principles have been adopted. Due to the changes in various areas, different types of guidance are available. This classification of guidance has broaden its scope too. Hence, to study the scope of guidance, study of its classification is also equally important.

CLASSIFICATION OF GUIDANCE

Different scholars have given various types of guidance. Its description is given below—

Proctor's Classification

In his book, entitled 'Educational and Vocational Guidance' William Martin Proctor (1930) has mentioned the following six types of guidance—

(i) Vocational Guidance.

(ii) Educational Guidance

(iii) Guidance for Social and Civic Activities.

(iv) Guidance in Character Building Activities.
(v) Guidance related to the Health and Physical Activities.
(vi) Guidance for the use of Leisure Time.

In this above mentioned classification only two types, i.e., educational and vocational guidance are more familiar. Rest four types of guidance can be placed under the category of guidance from social point of view instead of placing them independently a four different types.

Brewer's Classification

John M. Brewer, in his book "Education is Guidance", has described the following ten types, of guidance—

(i) Educational Guidance.
(ii) Vocational Guidance.
(iii) Religious Guidance
(iv) Guidance for Home Relationships.
(v) Guidance for Citizenship.
(vi) Guidance for Leisure and Recreation.
(viii) Guidance in Personal wellbeing.
(viii) Guidance in Right Doing.
(ix) Guidance in Co-operation and Thoughtfulness.
(x) Guidance related to the Cultural Activities.

By analysing the above classification, we shall come to know that only educational and vocational guidance is more familiar. Rest of the types of guidance can be associated with personal and social life. Guidance related 'to the religious and home relationships have individual as well as social aspects. Guidance regarding citizenship, utilization of leisure time, personal well being, guidance in right doing, guidance in co-operation and thoughtfulness, cultural activities etc. can be placed under individual and social guidance. Hence, types of guidance suggested by Brewer can be placed under four headings, i.e., educational, vocational, personal and social.

Koof and Kefauver's Classification

Koof and Kefauver have given the following five types of guidance—

(i) Educational Guidance
(ii) Vocational Guidance
(iii) Recreational Guidance
(iv) Health Guidance
(v) Civic-Socio-Moral Guidance.

It is very clear from the classification given by Koof and Kefauver educational and vocational guidance are common to all classifications. In the next pages of this book educational, vocational, and personal guidance have been described in detail.

Paterson's Classification

Paterson has suggested five types of guidance. He has included personal guidance too. Paterson's classification is as follows-

(i) Educational Guidance
(ii) Vocational Guidance
(iii) Personal Guidance
(iv) Economic Guidance
(v) Health Guidance.

In the above-mentioned classification, much importance is given to the personal guidance, because this class includes social, psychoemotional and leisure time guidance. Hence, after knowing the various types of guidance, it is essential to know what the different types of guidance mean and what their different aspects are. Hence, the description of main types of guidance is given below.

VARIOUS TYPES OF GUIDANCE

Educational Guidance

The most important type of the various types of guidance is educational guidance. Educational guidance is directly concerned with the pupil. In the student life educational guidance is very important. The chief aim of educational guidance is to develop the ability of co-ordinating with the school environment in the pupils and to create necessary awareness and sensitivity so that they may select themselves proper learning objectives, devices and situations. If we study and analyse Indian conditions, we shall find the educational guidance is more needed in Indian conditions. Therefore guidance is considered an integral part of education because educational guidance is viewed in the context of child's growth.

According to *Jones*, educational guidance is concerned with that assistance to be provided to the pupils, which is expected for their adjustments in the schools selection of curricula and school-life.

Four Main Functions of Educational Guidance

(i) To plan education according to the capacity, interest and resources of the pupil.
(ii) To collect information regarding the future possibilities of the pupils.
(iii) To be helpful for necessary progress in educational programme.
(iv) To fulfil the needs of the pupils.

Myers has also described educational guidance as a process of creating favourable conditions for the pupil's development or education. From this point of view, educational guidance is required at each level during the pupil's education. For example, educational guidance at primary level, secondary level, at higher secondary level and at college level. Psychological research has also proved that the educational guidance must be given to the pupils at each level. In order to study educational guidance, we shall have to go through its various aspects. Various aspects of educational guidance have been described in detail in the next units.

Personal Guidance

Personal guidance includes personal-psychological or emotional relationships which a person develops himself *Paterson* has included social, emotional and leisure time guidance in personal guidance. In fact, the problems regarding health, emotional adjustment, social adjustment and leisure and recreational problems are included in personal guidance for solution. Under social adjustment, an individual's economic problems are included. The aspect of the life's character and spiritual fields can also be included in the personal guidance In other words, the problems, which cannot be included in educational and vocational guidance, can include them in personal guidance.

In this way, the main aim of personal guidance is to establish balance between the individual's mental, social and physical aspects, because it is often seen that a person sometimes is surrounded by abnormal behaviours and social demerits even though they possess educational competencies and satisfactory progress in the professional areas. Such persons lead neglected life among their families, neighbourers and members of the community. Due to lack of balanced personalities in the families and neighbourhood and due to vague identification of mental and emotional deficiencies, the resultant conditions do not allow the person to imagine a peaceful and progressive life. In such conditions, personal guidance can prove helpful in solving such problems.

Hence, the solution of the following types of problems is possible in personal guidance—

(i) Problems related to the health and physical development.
(ii) Problems related to emotional behaviour.
(iii) Problems related to home and family relationships.
(iv) Problems related to sex, courtship and marriage.
(v) Problems related to religion, morals, ideals and values.
(vi) Economic problems.
(vii) Problems related to social relationships.

Vocational Guidance

Vocational guidance is not a mere technical process by which a person can be fitted in some vocation. Also he is not born for some vocation. The persons having normal intelligence can be adjusted in various vocations. In vocational guidance, a person is evaluated with regard to his capacities, capabilities and the changed conditions in the vocational areas and needs. In the vocational guidance the help is included in order to solve various problems related to the selection of a vocation, which is provided keeping in view the expected capabilities. According to Super too, the main aim of vocational guidance is to enable a person for co-ordination with his vocation, he can use his energies properly and can develop the society financially by the existing facilities.

Crow and Crow have also given the objectives of vocational guidance. The process of vocational guidance is organised by keeping in view these objectives. In the process of vocational guidance, vocational charts, vocational information booklets and talks can provide information to the pupils relating to the vocations.

In nutshell, we can say that vocational guidance helps the persons to adjust in the various vocations. The function of guidance is not only to help in selecting the proper vocation, but also to help in placement and progress. If all the persons possess same powers and abilities, then no guidance is required for various guidance processes. Hence, in all the vocations, same abilities are not required. Every vocation has its own needs. Persons are selected who are fit for those vocations. Hence, vocational guidance is needed. Therefore vocational guidance is—

(i) a process.
(ii) must for selection of a vocation or adjustment in a vocation.
(iii) to know the necessary features of various vocations and abilities.
(iv) a process of introduction with various vocations.

A detailed description of vocational guidance has been given in other unit.

BASIC ASSUMPTIONS OF GUIDANCE

The whole guidance is based upon some basic assumptions. In order to understand the meaning and nature of guidance it is essential to understand those assumptions. These assumptions are as follows—

Each Individual is Different from Others

The influences of psychology on modem educational system can not be denied. It has become very clear as a result of psychological researches that all individuals are different from each other and they cannot be alike. Such individual differences are clear through various media, such as body size, intelligence interests, aptitudes etc. The causes of these differences or variations are not in the hands of a person. These variations or differences Occur as a result of hereditary and environmental effects. By knowing these variations we can predict the limit to which an individual can achieve success in the future life because his behaviour is controlled by these variations. In other words, we can also say that these variations of an individual provide a shape to his individual and social behaviour.

A guidance programme can be conducted only by measuring these variations or differences. These can be measured with the help of a variety of psychological tests. The concept of individual differences forces us to think that the effect of these variations acts on the capacity of functioning the individual and on accomplishment of the task. The role of an individual should be determined with reference to all these variations.

Prediction of Development is Possible

Modern psychology has proved that the prediction regarding a person's achievements is possible now. For this purpose, the tests developed by psychology are used. These tests are highly objective. These tests include intelligence tests, personality and its assessment, interest and aptitude tests etc. All these tests play' an important role in the development of a person and collect Informations regarding the various aspects, of a person's personality. With the help of these tests, the superiority demonstration of a person can be known. It can also be known on the basis of the demonstration of superiority what type of achievements a person can have. These types of informations are very essential because this collection of informations helps the guidance process in providing a proper direction to a person.

Social Development through Adjustment

It is very essential to develop favourable conditions in order to make adjustment of an individual. In other words, a person should enable to face the difficult situations instead of running away from that situation. In this way, we see that by developing adjustment ability and efficiency in an individual, the development of a person and the society is possible. Guidance service tries to develop both the aspects. As a result of these efforts, the entire nation's progress becomes certain. Hence, on the basis of adjustment ability, personal and social development of an individual can be made.

Every Human Being needs Adjustment

It is the assumption of guidance that for desirable development of an individual, his adjustment capacity should be developed and this development should be made in time. Due to lack of development of such ability, both the aspects, i.e., a person and the society are adversely, affected. As a result of this, neither a person nor society will develop. From psychological point of view, the adjustment ability develops only when the individual is provided with the various opportunities according to his abilities and also the capacity to solve and to understand the difficult situations are developed. If we see from psychological point of view, we shall feel that if a person is not provided with such opportunities, the development of inferiority complex cannot be avoided. Such persons lose their mental and emotional balance in such circumstances which give rise to pessimisticism and create tension in the society. Such persons cannot adjust in these situations.

Sometimes, some persons are well educated and they are professionally well satisfied but they are surrounded by other problems such as family problems, neighbourhood problems and social problems. There are some other persons who are the victims of bad habits inspite of satisfactory achievements. These bad habits hurt the social environment. Similarly, some persons who rise from lower economic status develop many problems and get themselves involved in anti-social activities. Hence, in such circumstances every person requires guidance otherwise it would be difficult for the person to get rid off such difficult situations.

Selection of Appropriate Opportunities

In order to do a task and to succeed in it, availability of proper opportunities is essential. These opportunities are influenced by the ideologies, presumptions and changes occurring in a nation. It is often observed that the conditions of every nation differ from one or the other point of view. Due to these variations, various opportunities are offered.

A selection or proper opportunity is very essential out of these varieties of opportunities. It is the presumption of guidance programme that the selection of proper opportunity gives proper direction to the development of a person. The problem of an opportunity is different in itself In order to solve it, a person needs guidance at each step.

A.J. Jones has also mentioned the following presumptions in addition to the above-mentioned presumptions

(i) Inborn capacities, abilities and interests of a person are important for guidance programme.

(ii) The successful solution of an individual's problems is impossible in the absence of any assistance.

(iii) The main aim of guidance is not to give orders but to develop the capacity of self-guidance.

(iv) The in born abilities of a person are generally not specific.

(v) School plays a very vital role in running the guidance programme. Hence, the presumptions by Jones are helpful in formulating the guidance principles.

The following are the assumptions stated by *Asha Bhatnagar* in her article compiled in a book 'Readings for Careers Teachers, 1985' edited by Swadesh. Mohan and published by NCERT.

(i) Guidance is a pupil personnel service, which is executed in order to meet the personal needs of the pupils. Guidance is different from instruction but it helps the pupil in proper adjustment in instruction and teaching learning. In this way, it is an integral part of education and it is the objective of guidance to achieve educational objectives.

(ii) It is well known to all that the professional assistance is needed to acquire the self-information in this complex society. In addition to this information, other existing educational and vocational informations in the society are also required.

(iii) Guidance is a co-operative effort in which the teacher, parents, administrator and community have to extend their co-operation. In the absence of full time counsellor, the, school teacher has to take over guidance work.

(iv) Guidance is provided to the individual to make him more self dependent. Guidance should develop person's potentialities.

(v) Every person-possesses the innate urges of growth and development and to make him something. Guidance helps him in this regard.

(vi) Guidance identifies the dignity and worth of a person and gives importance to these.

(vii) Guidance is a continuous and dynamic process of providing assistance to a person. A person is the focal point for all the guidance activities.

(viii) In addition to the personal needs, guidance programme also gives rise to the social norms and social needs.

MEANING OF EDUCATIONAL GUIDANCE

Before going through the meaning of educational guidance, it is more important to know what education means. It is, because by interpreting the term 'education' and by differentiating it from the term 'guidance' and relating it with the 'guidance', the meaning of 'educational guidance' can be best explained. The term 'Education' is very comprehensive in itself. Its comprehensive interpretation is very difficult. But in its narrow interpretation, education means to impart knowledge to the pupils in the classroom by the teachers. As it is well known that human life has two aspects—

It is the bodily aspect of human being. Its development is also essential and it is possible through the rich diet only. Due to scarcity of nutritious food the biological aspect will remain, undeveloped or under developed.

The development of sociological aspect of an individual is also important like the development of his biological aspect. Without the development of sociological aspect of a person, he is like an animal. Hence, education is must for a person's sociological development. Sociological development is just equivalent to zero without education. The basis of this sociological development of a person is his intelligence. Intelligence separates the human beings from the category of lower animals.

While defining education, T. *Raymont* has described it as a developmental process. According to him, "Education is defined as a process of development which consists the passage of human being from infancy to maturity, the process by which he adapts himself gradually in various ways to his physical, social and spiritual environment."

Considering education as a process of development, *John Dewey* has also defined education as - "Education is the development of all these capacities in the individual which enable him to control his environment."

In the above both definitions education has been considered as the process of developing a person's capacities so that he may be able to develop co-ordination with the environment.

AIMS OF EDUCATIONAL GUIDANCE

For every type of guidance programme, there are specific aims or objectives or functions. Educational guidance too has its own aims or objectives or functions. Jones has described the following objectives or goals of educational guidance

In Indian circumstances, pupils face the problem of getting admission in the school after passing fifth, eighth and senior secondary classes. Where they should get admission? This problem seems to be very simple problem visually and in hearing, but it is very serious and important problem. Because a child commits a mistake in selecting a school, this will adversely affect his future life and further education. Hence, in this condition, a goal of providing educational guidance to the pupils should be fixed. There are various types of schools due to various types of curricula. Every type of school has its own functions and goals, for example, multipurpose schools, medical schools, vocational schools and agriculture schools etc. The pupils can be admitted to these schools according to their mental abilities, interests etc. The aim and function of educational guidance should be to provide the knowledge of functions and objectives of these schools to the pupils.

As it has already been told that in various types of schools, different curricula are taught. For example, in some schools only arts curricula are taught while in some other schools only science curricula are taught. Similarly, some schools concentrate on the subjects related to agriculture only. Hence, due to the multiplicity and variety of subjects, the objective of educational guidance should be to help the students selecting the subjects out of this variety of subjects in accordance with their ability. Providing the informations regarding these subjects and curricula can help the students. The various types of schools have their own administrative pattern and their rules are well-defined. In some schools, some specific subjects are compulsory. Some schools conduct the examination or interview of the student or both. These schools have prescribed the minimum desirable educational qualification. Hence, making aware of these rules etc. should be the goal of educational guidance in these schools so that no pupil may face any difficulty while seeking admission in any school.

With the change of a school, the pupil enters a new environment. He gets new social life in this new environment. In this new environment, the adjustment of the pupil is very essential. In this new environment, the pupil may feel the following needs—

(i) New formation of study habits.

(ii) Help in subject selection.

After school education, there are so many jobs or vocations in which people desire placement. For a few vacancies there are so many applicants. In such situation, the best way is competitive examinations, for example, Public Service Commission, Staff Selection Board and Entrance Tests in various curricula. Complete information is necessary about these tests because pupils are not aware of functions of these institutions, their objectives and procedures. Hence, the main objective and function of educational guidance should be to help in the dissemination of complete information to the pupils about such competitive examinations.

After the completion of education, a person wants placement in some vocation. Multiplicity of vocations may affect a person's selection. Sometimes after completing education, a person fails to understand or he is unable to take decision that what vocation he should adopt? Various types of informations associated with every vocation are not known to the person, such as, what qualifications for a vocation are required, which vocation is in accordance with his abilities'? In order to get a vocation what a person should do? From where he will get the informations related to the vocation'? And, what is the future of that vocation in the country etc.'? The objective of educational guidance should be the passing on all such types of informations to the pupils.

Imparting all above mentioned informations is advantageous only in case we make the pupils aware of his likings, interests and aptitudes because all persons are not alike. Some have low capacity while others have higher capacity. Some are more intelligent while others are less. Hence, making a person aware of individual differences means to tell him for what vocation he is fit or which vocation is in accordance with the personality, behaviour and competency of that person. Hence, this objective of educational guidance acts as the basis of entire process of educational guidance.

In spite of above mentioned objectives of educational guidance as described by Jones there can be some more objectives which are as follows—

One main objective of educational guidance should be to improve the study or learning methods, because the pupils don't have so much intellect that they may select the proper study or learning methods according to their capacities. These study methods too possess the variations, such as—

(a) Method of memorizing.
(b) Whole and part method.
(c) Recitation method.
(d) Spaced and Unspaced method.
(e) Mode of taking notes.
(f) Reading method.
(g) Rote or Cramming method.
(h) Method of summarization.

The objective of educational guidance should be to select proper method according to the competencies of the pupils out of the above-mentioned learning methods. The scope of guidance is not restricted to help the normal persons only but the objective of educational guidance should also be to guide those normal persons who become backward in the field of education. It is because of various reasons responsible for the backwardness of the pupils or persons, which can be controlled, with the help of educational guidance. These causes of backwardness include indiscipline, physical defects such as hard of hearing weak eve-sight low I.Q., left-handedness, defective pronunciation, domestic reasons, economic conditions, broken families, divorce of parents, step parents, bad company, incompetent or untrained teachers, monotonous environment, defective teaching methods, absence from the school etc. The objective of educational guidance to eliminate a person's backwardness and steps for remedy should be suggested, such as provision of special schools, special curriculum and special teaching methods etc.

The educational guidance should not be aimed at helping the backward children only, but it should also aim at guiding the gifted children so that they may well utilize their talent. The objective of educational guidance should be fixed by providing facilities of library, enriching co-curricular activities and helping them in providing education according to their talent.

The objective of educational guidance should be to induce self-realization in pupils so that they may determine their aspiration level on the basis of realities after knowing their capacities." competencies, interests and drawbacks. If the aspiration levels are not determined on the basis of realities, and those aspirations are not fulfilled, then the pupils may face problems.

After analysing the above objectives of educational guidance, we reach at the conclusion that the chief aim of educational guidance is to create sensitivity and awareness in the pupils regarding educational problems and educational activities so that they may make full use of their capacities and abilities.

NEED OF EDUCATIONAL GUIDANCE

Human being has two forms: biological and social. In order to develop his second form *i.e.*, social form, the process of socialization is needed. In order to start this process attention must be paid to the various aspects of the social development of an individual, Hence, for the social development of human being, education and educational guidance is required at each step. Continuous changes in the various social aspects are occurring, such as social ideology, aims of education, methods of achieving these objectives, social needs, social values and traditions etc.

In addition to these changes in social aspects, there are influences of psychological researches on education, an individual and the society. And, as a result of these researches, revolutionary social and educational changes are being observed, such as, at present, education according to the pupil's aptitude, ability and interest, is being insisted. But, practically, providing such education faces many difficulties. In such conditions, the need of educational guidance can be realized. Hence, there is no single factor but variety of factors is responsible which create the need of educational guidance. The description of these factors is given below:

In India, the problem of wastage and stagnation has taken a very serious turn. Most of the wastage occurs at the primary stage of education. It is found that many children get admission in primary education.

They go to school for some period, but due to one or the other reasons they fail to complete their primary education and their parents withdraw them from the school due to their financial problems. Hence, wastage in education has grown too much. In addition to primary level, educational wastage is also found at other levels too. Pupils fail to complete the courses and leave them prematurely.

Similarly, the problem of stagnation has become equally serious. Pupils stick to one educational level for more than desired duration. Its reason may be any such as illiteracy of parents, narrow attitude of parents, unsatisfactory economic condition of parents, shortage of sufficient schools, lack of favourable environment in schools etc. The problems of wastage and stagnation are more frequent in rural areas as compared to urban areas. In Indian Constitution, there is a provision of compulsory school education for the children of 6 to 14 age group, but this objective could not be achieved due to one or the other reason. The pupils their guardians and the teachers wish to control these problems by knowing the causes of wastage and stagnation, by analysing them and by applying remedy to them. In order to achieve this objective, educational guidance services can play appreciable role.

At present, the comprehensiveness of the curriculum and multiplicity of subjects are an indication of expansion and enrichment of the knowledge. From psychological viewpoint, if we observe an individual or a pupil we see that all individuals or pupils are not alike with regard to intelligence levels, interest and aptitude. If the selection of subjects and curriculum does not occur according to their intellectual level their interests and aptitudes, the pupils fail to gain that much success in that subject or curriculum which they should have.

Sometimes high expectations of the pupils or their parents encourage them for the wrong selection of the curriculum or subjects, such as many pupils achieve very unsatisfactorily in science subjects, but their achievement level increases appreciably in arts subjects. Sometimes its reverse too happens. Also low expectations of the pupils or their parents make the wrong selections of subjects while they are capable of studying difficult subjects.

In many circumstances, pupils are not aware which subjects they should select in order to enter some specific vocation. In solving these subject-selection related problems, the educational guidance service acts as light in the darkness and saves many creative lives from destruction. Hence, at the time of selecting curriculum and subjects, the need of educational guidance service is very significant.

The entering behaviours of pupils must be studied in order to enter any level of education. If these behaviours are identified properly, only then the pupils can be guided properly for their future education. The parents and the pupils wish that they should be guided properly in order to enter from one level to the other level of education so that the pupils may prepare themselves for selecting their higher education and entering those courses. Such a situation comes usually after high school or + 2 stage. Guidance given at this stage changes the entire life of a pupil. The pupil always remains in a fix, regarding the knowledge of higher education arid on what basis he should take decisions regarding their future education. The pupil is unable to decide whether he should expand his academic achievement. Should he prepare for some? Competition in order to enter some vocation or should he learn some skill'? Sometimes pupils restrict their future education by making a wrong decision. For this, they face the music throughout life. Also, they have to face the problem of mal-adjustment. Hence, in order to provide the knowledge of future education, educational guidance is needed.

As a result of preparing various plans for various training and for education in the country, opportunities of knowing various educational curricula are sought. For example, in our country, many five-year plans were prepared after independence. Eighth five year plan in our country started with effect from first April 1992. Opportunities for various trainings and many courses were increased appreciably in these plans. If these opportunities are not extended upto pupils, then how the pupils can benefit? Hence, in order to provide the knowledge of such opportunities, the existence of educational guidance services is very essential. But our country lacks such services. Its adverse effect is that the pupils are gaining one type of education. They don't know the scope of that education. This has created the problem of unemployment in the country and now this problem has become so much uncontrolled that the other plans of the country have become unbalanced. If some knowledge regarding the future scope of certain subjects is given to the pupils in the schools through educational guidance, the problem of unemployment can be curbed to some extent. It is necessary to note here that the number of vocations has also got multiplied. Every vocation is related to some specific curriculum and subjects. Knowledge of such vocations and subjects must be provided to the pupils. Hence, in nutshell it can be concluded that for providing such knowledge, a well-organised programme is needed. Such a programme is needed in the form of educational guidance service.

It is essential to keep the pupil busy in learning process so that the achievement level of the pupil may be maintained. If the pupil is not kept busy in the learning process, the sequence of the learning process will break up. That pupil will lag behind the other pupils. In order to keep the pupil busy, the motivation of the pupil plays a very important role. By motivating the pupils for learning their achievement level also increases. In spite of this, their memory and capacity also keeps them busy in learning. Hence, in order to keep the pupils busy in the learning process, factors like motivation of the pupils, memory and capacity, should be encouraged. For doing so selection of various methods is needed. In order to select these methods, the use of educational guidance procedure is essential. In other words, in order to keep the children busy in the learning process, educational guidance is needed in the selection of proper methods. The problem of adjustment is very deep. No one can make desirable progress in any field without proper adjustment. However, maladjustment may lead to damages.

Whenever any pupil enters a new school he has to face adjustment problem first of all. For example, if a pupil moves from Hindi medium school to English medium school, then it becomes difficult for him to adjust in that environment because of much difference in language as well as teaching methods. The pupil cannot adapt these changes very quickly. He feels the need of some help from outside.

Similarly, if a child shifts from rural school to the urban school, he is unaware of those rules and regulations of that schools which are being followed. The pupil also feels difficulty in adjustment when he shifts from one level to the other level of education. In spite of these problems, the pupil faces other personal, emotional and social problems, which are barrier in his adjustment. For example, if a handicapped child enters a normal school, he can face many emotional and social problems. The other 'Pupils of the school or class may make joke of his defects. They may avoid his inclusion in their group or handicapped child may develop many inferiority complexes and he is unable to adjust himself in that school environment. Similarly, a visually and hearing impaired child hated his school because handicapped children were asked to sit on the floor while the same child usually sees his friends sitting in beautiful, attractive and comfortable chairs. Lack of furniture always pinched him. For this reason he could not adjust himself in that school environment hence he became a truant.

Many pupils with such various problems will come across in schools. If these adjustment problems of the pupils are not checked immediately they will start running away from the schools. Hence, the need of educational guidance cannot be denied in order to know their problems, analysing them and to suggest them some remedy. On one side, knowledge expanded in the field of education, while on the other side important changes have taken place in school organisation, administration and teaching methods. In educational administration, narrow mindedness has been replaced by broad mindedness these days. Formerly education was merely a process of intellectual development but these days knowledge is being considered as a means of solving individual and social problems. Similarly, traditional teaching methods too were not well developed. But today a change has occurred in the teaching methods too. These days, child-centred teaching methods are more popular. Hence, after accepting the principle of individual variations, school administration and teaching methods are selected. In this selection too educational guidance is needed.

When a person deviates from the social norms, he is termed as a delinquent. This type of anti-social behaviour is termed as a friction between individual and society. The society gives birth to these delinquents. It is the society, which is responsible for providing the opportunities to a person. Hence, providing these opportunities is only possible when there are means of proper guidance in the educational system.

RELATIONSHIP BETWEEN EDUCATION AND GUIDANCE

In order to establish relationship between education and guidance, the following nature of education should be considered—

Without education, a human being is merely a human being. Guiding a person's moral, emotional, physical and intellectual development is must. It is one of the social responsibilities. Guidance is required for these aspects of development. From this point of view, there is deep relationship between education and guidance. Education and guidance cannot be separated.

Education is a comprehensive process. Considering the needs of the society to start this process. On the other side, society also has its goals or ends. A teacher must have the knowledge of these goals or ends. He should be aware of various methods in order to achieve these ideals and goals. With the help of these methods, one can achieve the goals of the society. But it is possible only if a teacher himself is active. In this process, the pupil remains passive. On the basis of facts received as a result of psychological development, these days an ideology has developed that helping a child in learning is teaching, and the child is the focal point during the teaching activity. In other words, child-centred education is being emphasized. In order to determine these objectives or goals a teacher expects help. This 'help' can be termed as guidance. There are various methods in order to achieve these goals or objectives. If a teacher selects some method to achieve these goals, it is termed as teaching. If a teacher helps the pupil in selecting such methods, it is known as guidance.

After birth, the person is a helpless organism. He is more dependent upon others. After birth, he cannot adjust with environment. For adjustment bringing a change in the person is must. But the process of bringing change in the person is very tough job. In order to adjust a person in the environment, some special assistance is needed. Education is the only process, which can bring necessary changes in a person for adjustment. From this point of view, education has been considered as an 'individual activity'. Guidance too is needed to bring about a change through education. From the above description, it is very clear that education is goal-oriented. The main goal of today's education is an all-round development of the child. Guidance service proves useful in achieving this goal.

After explaining the relationship between education and guidance, in the term 'educational guidance', it is now very essential to explain the meaning of educational-guidance. The different scholars have sought, the help of various definitions in order to explain the meaning of educational guidance.

Ruth Strang has defined educational guidance as assistance. According to him, "Educational guidance is intended to aid the individual in choosing an appropriate programme and in making progress in it."

Myers, while defining educational guidance, has described it as a process of establishing a relationship between a person and his characteristics in order to develop him. According to him, "Educational guidance is a process concerned with bringing about between an individual pupil with his distinctive characteristics on the one hand and differing groups of opportunities and requirements on the other, a favourable setting for the individual development or education."

Jones has also described educational guidance as an assistance to be provided to the pupils so that they may adjust in the schools, with curricula and school life. According to *Arthur J. Jones,* "Educational guidance is concerned with assistance given to pupils in their choices and adjustments with relation to schools, curriculum, courses and school."

Brewer has tried to make bar by considering educational guidance as an effort in consciousness to develop intelligence that educational guidance and learning process go side by side. According to Brewer, the definition of educational guidance is as follows - "Educational guidance may be defined as a conscious effort to assist in the intellectual growth of an individual."

Traxler has also presented educational guidance as a comprehensive process. According to *Traxler,* "Educational guidance is vitally related to every aspect of the school, the curriculum, the methods of instruction, the supervision of instruction, disciplinary procedures, attendance, problems of scheduling, the extra-curricular, the health and physical fitness programme and home and community relations."

Hopkins has also interpreted the term "Educational guidance" in a definition which realizes the compre-hensiveness of the meaning of guidance in the field of education.

According to Hopkins, "The emerging school theory recognize that guidance is an aspect of all proper learning and must therefore be centred in the intelligent management of the learning situation."

This definition of *Hopkins* has explained the comprehensiveness of the term educational guidance by relating it with the creation of learning conditions. In the similar way. *Hamrin* and *Erickson* have also stated while giving a generalized definition of educational guidance, "It offers methods diagnosing the abilities, interest, background and needs of individual students." In the above definition given by *Hamrin* and *Erickson,* a generalized meaning of guidance has been presented. This interpretation can be used in every field of guidance. This definition also suits for educational guidance.

Carter Good has also given the definition of educational guidance According to him. "Educational guidance is concerned principally, with matters relating to schools, courses, curricula and school life, rather than vocational, social or personal matters."

The following facts regarding the nature of educational guidance have come to light after analysing all the above mentioned definitions -

(i) Educational guidance is a comprehensive process.

(ii) Various types of educational problems can be discussed in educational guidance, such as, how to study'? adjustment of school life with other activities, regular attendance in the school, to complete the given task, interview, conversation, sitting in examination, use of libraries, use of common devices regarding learning capacity of making decisions in life etc.

(iii) Educational guidance is a process of providing assistance to the pupils by analysing the elements inhibiting the progress.

(iv) Educational guidance is a process of removing the adjustment problems facing while entering new institutions after crossing the various stages of education.

(v) Educational guidance is a process of providing assistance to the pupils in case they don't show the desired progress in the educational achievements.

(vi) Educational guidance is a process of providing assistance for eliminating the difficulties while selecting the subjects and curricula at all levels of education.

EDUCATIONAL GUIDANCE AT VARIOUS STAGES

There are various stages of education too. At these stages pupils face different problems. Different methods have to be applied to solve the problem of every stage because pupil is surrounded by problems at each stage.

Hence, educational guidance is needed at each stage. It is the reason that we talk about the importance of educational guidance and consider it as an integral part of entire educational process. The following description shows the importance of educational guidance at each stage of education

Educational Guidance at Secondary and Higher Secondary Stages

The child enters middle stage as he leaves the primary stage. Then he has somewhat noval relationships with education. At this stage, the friendships and links start increasing. The way of thinking of the child too changes and the relationships get established with the new fields. At this stage, the most important situation arises when he finds himself in a fix whether he should go to school or not, whether he should sit in the class or not, whether he should be present in the class of a particular teacher or not, etc.

At this stage, attitudes towards the school and teachers are made or about to be formed. Some interests get matured. Some likes and dislikes are also developed. Intelligence and competencies acquire complete development at this stage.

Those children who fail to get opportunities of development at this stage, their development is not possible after this stage. The personality traits related to the successful actions also get stabilized. As a result of all such developments, the child establishes a unique relationship with the environment. This relationship affects the intellectual behaviour of the child.

If we don't provide educational guidance at the primary stage, the task of educational guidance becomes too much difficult and complicated. At this stage the child can be helped in understanding educational and vocational environment by collecting all the means. In other words, the aims of education are 'good' and 'efficient' life. The child is to be made fit so that he may adjust himself according to his education. He can do this by selecting the curriculum intelligently and by removing the difficulties of subject-matter. The child should be provided with the Opportunities for the development of new interests and new skills so that every child may contribute effectively in the society.

For doing so, a well-organised guidance programme is essential. At this stage educational guidance can be provided through the following activities.

It is essential to guide the children at this stage regarding the type of education which can be helpful to them in spending a happy life and the type of education which can make them prosperous personally and socially. Educational guidance helps the children at secondary and higher secondary stage regarding the areas into which they are to enter according to their capacities and resources. After this stage the pupils advance towards professional training and curricula Hence, at this stage it has become very essential to make the pupils aware of the objectives of their education.

The children are ignorant of need for good or bad planning which can affect their future. If the children are made aware of intelligent planning in tenth class, the mistakes occurring in the selection of curriculum may be avoided. This can be done through systematic programmes of class discussions.

Every pupil should be helped in choosing the subjects. It is often done in terms of curriculum guidance. At this stage, curriculum guidance is the main function of educational guidance. If a pupil makes a right choice of curriculum, then he can make proper use of his potentialities and abilities.

In India, a provision of diversified curriculum has been made in the re-structured secondary system. This class begins from eleventh class. The aim of this diversified curriculum is that the pupils should choose the curriculum according to their abilities, aptitudes and personality qualities and may enjoy the benefits of their academic potentialities.

It is very important to collect the informations regarding educational potentialities of the pupils at the secondary and higher secondary stage, because on the basis of these informations guidance is provided to the pupils regarding the selection of the curriculum. Hence, it is important to make aware the pupils regarding the various aspects of the curriculum selection, such as

(a) To make pupils aware of nature and objectives of higher secondary school curriculum. Talks and hobby clubs can do it.
(b) To make aware of professional importance of various curricula.
(c) To make the pupils understand the philosophy of fictionalization at the + 2 stage.
(d) To provide informations to the school leaving pupils regarding polytechnic and university education.
(e) To provide information about those particular curricula not being taken up in the schools of that region.
(f) To provide help to the pupils in assessing their abilities, aptitudes, skills and interests.

It is being recognised now the importance of good study skills and remedial teaching. In a good programme of educational guidance, all these should be included. In the school studies, the development of proper motivation is essential. It is not so an easy task. Every school should explore its own motivational techniques. By clarifying the goals and objectives of education much can be done in this regard. In a way, all educational activities are guidance activities. In spite of these, the following activities should also be included in educational guidance at this stage-

(a) Cumulative record must be kept.
(b) Systematic development of interests of pupils.
(c) Systematic development of pupil's personality.
(d) Systematic development of proper profession motives in the pupils.
(e) Rectification of backwardness and problematic behaviour of the pupils through remedial methods.
(f) To provide counselling personally to the pupils when they face some specific problems.

Educational Guidance at Primary School Stage

Mental development of primary-stage pupils is not sufficient. Their mental powers are immature. Hence, the pupils are to face such situations at this stage, which seem to be very simple problems but these problems for the primary stage pupils are of very serious nature. Therefore there is greater need of educational guidance at this stage. The following can be the content of educational guidance at this stage

(i) Take care of every behaviour and every curiosity of the child.

(ii) Harsh behaviour towards children may create a permanent terror in them Hence, to control their harsh behaviour the children should be kept away from the terror.

(iii) There in no special and separate programme of educational guidance at this stage. It is the duty of every teacher.

(iv) At this stage, the handicapped children can be helped.

(v) The activities going on in the playground can be guided and these can be helpful in the adjustment of the children.

(vi) The teacher can provide help in the formation of good habits in the children at the primary stage.

(vii) Proper attitude can be developed by developing the ability of discriminating right and wrong in the children at this stage.

(viii) The teacher should provide help to the children in identifying their competencies.

(ix) The teacher must help the children in developing their talent at the primary stage.

(x) The teacher must help the children in their adjustment in the environment.

Hence, following are the functions of educational guidance at the primary stage—

(a) Assisting pupils to make a proper beginning—The teacher can assist the pupils to make a better beginning at the primary stage so that the children may not face any sort of frustration. For this, the help of various incentives can be sought.

(b) Aiding pupils to plan intelligently—The pupils should be made aware of various curricula. The knowledge of scope of various subjects should be provided. Only then the plan for future should be made.

(c) Aiding pupils to get the best out of their education—The intellectual abilities, health, aptitudes, interests, ambitions of parents, economic conditions etc. affect the academic progress of the children directly or indirectly. Hence, for the academic progress of the children, providing good educational guidance services can benefit them.

(d) Preparing pupils to enter the secondary school—The preliminary, educational guidance prepares the pupils for the entry to the secondary stage or helps them in this task.

In the guidance programme, the role of a teacher at the primary stage is central. The teacher functions as a guidance worker among the groups of the children and their parents or guardian and gives suggestions for the development of the children.

At this stage, a professional counsellor is also appointed from outside who is responsible for those guidance functions which are beyond the teacher's capacity or left incomplete due to lack of time. At this stage, the counsellor provides well-organised guidance to the children keeping in view their specific needs and their interests. Along with this, the counsellor imparts training to the school teachers regarding cumulative record and administration of the tests.

At the primary stage, the success of educational guidance programme depends upon the co-ordination among the principal, teacher, counsellor, parents etc. Only through their collective efforts the programme can be made a success.

At the primary stage of educational guidance programme, the following items can also be included -

(i) Making of categories according to the needs of the pupils.

(ii) Providing the opportunities to the mentally retarded and highly intelligent children according to their needs.

(iii) Helping the mal-adjusted and handicapped children.

On the basis of above description we conclude that the need of educational guidance at the primary stage is felt in the form of habit formation in the children in the form of preparation of the children for secondary education, and in the form of adjustment of the children in the school. When the children leave this stage and enter secondary and higher secondary stages, then the educational guidance continues irrespective of their form at these stages.

Educational Guidance at the College Stage

At the college stage, the personality pattern of the children gets matured. Some pupils visualize aims more distinctly. Some pupils start realizing their responsibility. Such pupils are very serious towards their studies and they understand the meaning of success and failure. But still there are some pupils who enter colleges without any prior thinking what the college education means. They enter colleges only because they don't know what they should do. But after entering a college, they have to face many difficulties. Such pupils do not understand the meaning of that education which they receive at the college level. They go to the college without any aim.

There should be a provision of paying attention towards the immediate needs of the pupils in the college guidance programme, such as, the pupils who are unable to make any progress in the college activities as a result of various reasons, and those pupils who fail to make use of facilities provided.

At the time of admission to the college, if educational guidance is provided to the pupils, many of them can be diverted towards more useful activities. This will reduce the burden on university education too. Guidance helps the pupils selecting their subjects of specialization, which help later on in choosing their vocation.

These pupils can be helped for the progress in their studies through well-organized tutorials and proper library facilities; It would be better if the pupils are made aware of scope, nature and aims of college education in the very beginning.

Often it is left with the pupils. This spoils their time. Every faculty of the college should start a comprehensive programme of educational guidance, such as extension lectures, tutorials, seminars and discussions etc. This type of education will not make the college education more meaningful, but it will raise the standard of college education also.

Hence, in short, the following activities can be included in the educational guidance programme at the college level—

(i) To introduce the pupils with the scope and aims of college education in the very beginning.

(ii) To pay attention towards the immediate needs of the pupils at the college level.

(iii) Initiation of educational guidance at the time of admission into the college.

(iv) At the college level, those students should be helped who could not make any progress in the college activities due to one or the other reason.

(v) Every faculty of the college should start a very comprehensive educational guidance programme for the pupils.

(vi) At the college level, educational guidance can be provided through tutorials extension lectures, seminars and discussions.

PRINCIPLES OF EDUCATIONAL GUIDANCE

The principles of guidance are those generalizations of rules which are kept in mind while helping the pupils through educational guidance. If these generalizations or principles are not cared for, then the process of educational guidance will not only be difficult but impossible. Hence, we should follow the following principles during the process of educational guidance—

(i) Principle of Relationship with School and Parents—In educational guidance, there should be a close relationship with the school and the parents. It is very essential. In the absence of this relationship, no guidance programme can be termed as complete because much desirable information can be sought from the parents and these informations prove very helpful during educational guidance to the pupils.

(ii) Principle of Guidance for All the Pupils—Educational guidance should not be meant for some selected categories only but it should be for the pupils of the capacity of every type and of every ability. Only then the process of educational guidance will succeed in achieving its objective. The necessity of following this principle is because of the fact that all the pupils don't have similar abilities. Every pupil feels the need or educational guidance at one or the other level of education. Hence, it should be for all the pupils.

(iii) Principle of Using Standardized Tests—In order to explore the educational problems of the pupils in the schools, various tests are to be applied. These tests are constructed either by the teacher or these tests are standardized. The results of these tests may predict the success or problems of the pupils in some curriculum. The results of the standardized tests are superior than the results of non-standardized tests. Hence, for educational guidance, only standardized tests should be used, such as aptitude, tests intelligence tests, interest inventories, adjustment tests, creativity tests etc.

(iv) Principle of Proper and Relevant Informations—For any type of guidance, proper and relevant informations are must, otherwise guidance process cannot take place. Improper and irrelevant informations may harm the guidance process. Such informations indeed I.Q., academic achievements, attitudes, interests etc. Guidance should be provided on the basis of these informations.

(v) Principle of Follow-up Study—It is important to evaluate the success of educational guidance. If it is not tested, the effectiveness of educational guidance cannot be known in-time. It would be like the wastage of-time and efforts. Hences after providing educational guidance, its success or effectiveness should be tested from time to time. It is known as 'Follow-up-Study.'

(vi) Principle of Problem Solving from the Very Beginning—The process of guidance to solve the problem should be initiated before it turns dangerous. As the problem becomes serious, the guidance process will not prove so much effective.

From the above-mentioned description it is very clear that without following these principles of educational guidance, the process of guidance cannot be so effective and advantageous. Hence, to follow these principles is very necessary.

TECHNIQUES OF IMPARTING EDUCATIONAL GUIDANCE

In order to impart educational guidance, it is essential to follow one or the other procedure. If it is not followed, the educational guidance programme will become a 'hatch-patch' programme. Hence, for convenience sake, we can start educational guidance programme in two situations. According to these two types of situations, the methods of educational guidance can also be divided into two types.

Techniques of Individual Guidance

In this category of methods, guidance is given by contacting personally. This enables to study physical, social, emotional, intellectual and individual problems of the pupils. For this, the following procedures or methods are followed -

Initial Interview: To study any individual pupil, first of all initial interview is conducted. In this initial interview, the educational guidance committee should collect all the relevant informations. The relevant informations include the following—

(a) About family circumstances,
(b) About educational and vocational plans,
(c) Leisure time activities.

There is another aim of initial interview to establish rapport between the pupil and the person who gives guidance.

Cumulative Record of the Students: It is important to keep the records related to the pupils for their educational guidance. These are called cumulative records. This cumulative record includes the following informations—

(a) Intelligence quotient.
(b) Interests.
(c) Aptitudes.
(d) Informations related to health and physical development.
(e) Special mental abilities.
(f) Educational achievements.
(g) Family background and economic conditions.
(h) About the parents of the pupils, friends and informations about neighbourers.
(i) Regarding the various aspects of pupils' personality.

These above mentioned informations can be collected with the help of questionnaires and socioeconomic status scales. The cumulative record of every pupil should be corrected from time to time because new informations about pupils are received from time to time.

Psychological Testing: For educational guidance, it is important to study the psychological aspects of the pupils. These can be studied by psychological tests. These tests can be as follows—

(a) Intelligence Tests—There are various intelligence tests for different age levels. By these tests, the intellectual level of the children can be explored. These tests can be administered individually or in groups.

(b) Aptitude Tests—It is essential to know the aptitudes of the pupils for every type of guidance. The knowledge of these aptitudes is possible by aptitude tests. By administering these aptitude tests we can know about those fields in which the pupils can gain success. Hence, through aptitude tests we can predict about the future success of the pupil while interest tests tell us about the present inclination of a pupil's mind.

(c) Interest Inventories—Through interest inventories, the interests of the pupils are discovered because the selection of curriculum, subjects and co-curricular activities depend upon the interests of the pupils. The role of interest is very important in educational guidance.

(d) Achievement Tests—In educational guidance, the facts regarding educational achievements of the children are collected by using achievement tests. For this, the scores obtained by the pupils in their monthly, three-monthly, six-monthly and annual examinations are taken into consideration.

(e) Personality Tests—It is important to know the personality of the children in order to provide educational guidance. In its absence it becomes impossible to provide guidance because in many activities, the characteristics of an individual's personality play a vital role. Various personality tests have been constructed for testing the personality.

Collecting Information regarding Schools or Colleges: After collecting informations regarding the various aspects of the pupil, it is essential to collect informations regarding the various aspects of the schools and colleges. This includes the informations regarding various subjects, curricula and other facilities existing in various schools and colleges. It is done because in this present scientific age, special schools or colleges are required to teach some specific subjects. For example, technical schools give technical education and agriculture schools give education regarding agriculture. Similarly, medical and engineering colleges give education in their respective subjects. The pupils get help in selecting curriculum, subject and school according to their capacities and abilities.

Techniques of Group Guidance

Sometimes such circumstances arise when we can give guidance to the pupils in groups. Group guidance methods are as follows

Orientation Talks: In order to provide guidance to the pupils in groups, the person who provides guidance explains the importance of educational guidance to them and encourages them to think about various educational problems in depth. Such talks are termed as orientation talks.

Psychological Tests: After orientation talks, various informations regarding the intelligence, interests, aptitudes, mental abilities and personality of the members of the group are collected with the help of psychological tests. These informations are collected by various tests such as aptitude tests, interest inventories and personality tests etc.

Collecting Information from School regarding Pupils: Educational guidance is not possible without collecting informations about various pupils, such as scores obtained in school examinations will tell about academic competencies of the pupils. Interviewing teachers, interests, habits, personality traits can know co-curricular activities of pupils etc.. Such informations cannot be sought from any other source. Much information can be sought from the cumulative records maintained in the schools hence; help can be sought from the teachers regarding various informations related to the pupils.

Collecting Informations from Families: During group guidance informations relating to the pupils of that group should be collected from the families of those pupils because their parents happen to be very close to them most of the time. They keep on observing them growing right from birth. Parents carry on discussions regarding their development. Hence, the parents of the children can explain in a better way about their habits, interests, aptitudes, personality and future educational and vocational plans. To know their ideas is must for educational guidance. All these informations can be collected by correspondence, or by going door to door and by contacting the parents.

Interview with the Pupils: When need arises, the group guide can interview the member pupils of that group. He records the interests towards various subjects, future educational and vocational plans etc. of each and every pupil. At the time of interview of the pupils, informations can be collected with the help of self-inventory.

Construction of Profile: A profile should be prepared on the basis of informations collected regarding all the pupils. It is just a sort of picture which depicts the various abilities of the pupils, their capacities and the results of other tests. Hence, a profile is a summary of all the informations related to the pupils.

Conference: A conclusion of the informations related to the pupils is derived from the profile. This conclusion is placed before educational guidance workers' group. On the basis of this conclusion, all the experts express their opinions and they reach at a decision acceptable to all. This phase is very decisive and is a phase of very careful discussion, because this decision is to affect the future of the pupils.

Report Writing: The group of educational guidance workers should prepare a comprehensive report keeping in view the decision taken in the conference. This report should be submitted to the parents or guardians of the pupils and school authorities. The pupils should act upon this report.

FROM SOCIAL POINT OF VIEW

Baqer Mehdi has classified the social needs of guidance into the following four areas. These areas are—

Guidance for Better Life

From social point of view it is essential to develop proper attitude towards family for better family life and for better understanding of the relationships of basic emotional methods. Actually family is a basic social unit. All sorts of adjustments should be linked with this social unit. Better family relations and better social adjustment in the family prove a better adjustment with the community. In families, there is a need to reform the relationships between the pupils and the family members. Bad mental health and delinquency are the results of maladjustment in the family. These problems will go on increasing if these are not curbed. It becomes essential to provide assistance of individual nature and this should include the parents, pupils and other relatives. In this effort, a good guidance programme may help properly.

Guidance for Good Citizenship

For good citizenship, an understanding of social values, social needs, social problems and the development of social attitudes and habits, learning of etiquettes and to imbibe them, loyalty and responsibilities etc. are essential. In democratic life, family and the school must shake hands in order to acquire social needs and moral objectives. But in India being illiterate the parents load the entire burden on schools. In order to achieve this objective, need of guidance programme is felt always.

Proper Utilization of Human Resources

By utilizing the human resources properly, individual expectations and social needs can be better fulfilled. For this act, an organized vocational guidance service is needed. Any vocation is not important from personal viewpoint but it is important from social point of view. From social viewpoint, a proper vocation is that which fulfills the society's immediate needs. At the time of selecting a vocation, an individual's abilities, skills, attitudes and personality characteristics are considered particularly. Hence, for utilizing human resources, guidance service is must.

Guidance for National Service

We have no way other than the protection of our values and life styles. The function of education is comprehensive like the functions of religion, family or industrial life. It is essential to prepare the persons for national service. It also includes the protection of social values. For this, military service is also included. A need for guidance is felt for national service and military service. In addition to these needs, following are the other needs according to sociological view point—

Today's civilisation is machinery based. Use of machines and devices is increasing day by day in all fields of life. It's reason is industrialization. This industrialization has caused the provision of sufficient time. Hence, in this mechanical age, guidance is required for using the leisure time and adjustment of the individual himself. Along with this development, old concepts are experiencing changes. In the context of these changed concepts, a person requires help from other persons in the form of guidance for adjustment. In order to understand new methods and techniques in the factories, guidance is required.

In this present age, the changing social and family status of women is being viewed as very important in the phase of social changes. These changes have proved that the women are not only for household affairs. Women are working today in all walks of life like men. Even, they are ahead of men. In order to consolidate their financial and family position, women are entering to various vocations. In such circumstances women too need guidance.

In India, joint family tradition was continuing. But after independence changes occurred very rapidly in the conditions of these families. Today, the structure of Indian joint families has changed. The main causes of this change in structure are unemployment, population explosion, industrialization etc. In search of employment, people are rushing from villages to cities. Due to the financial crisis in the families, blood-relations are getting damaged. In order to meet their demands, the family members of joint families are crossing the boundaries of their joint families and are scattering here and there. This change has mounted the tension in the families. In these changing family conditions, a person needs guidance so that he may face these situations.

In the present age, great changes in the social values too occurred. All the concepts, ideals and values got changed. Today all the selfish personalities are coming across in the society. This has intensified the tensions in the society. Such situation is a cause of worry for the nation. In the circumstances, a person can be made aware of the meaningfulness of old values through guidance service only. Hence, from this viewpoint, guidance service is must.

Many countries of this world could not avoid the adverse effects of population explosion. India is also one of them where population is continuously on increase. This explosion has caused imbalance in many national projects. Awareness in people is essential to control this population explosion. In this task guidance can contribute appreciably.

In the changing conditions today, urbanization is increasing day by day. Persons are leaving villages and rushing towards cities in search of employment. If a Person leads urban life, he cannot go for rural life. After acquiring higher education in cities, no body likes to work in villages. Our country's defective economic condition is responsible for this. Hence, for the solution of such problems, guidance service can prove advantageous.

As a result of machine-civilization people have to face the problem of proper utilization of leisure time, because due to sufficient time, a person spends his time by involving himself in improper activities. In such circumstances, guidance service can help the people by suggesting the proper methods of utilizing the leisure time.

Every person possesses one or the other capacity. It can be harmful to waste such capacities. We can control the wastage of these capacities with the help of new methods and techniques. We can succeed in this with the help of guidance service. For the progress of the society, it is necessary to assign the work to a person according to his abilities and interests so that he may enjoy mental satisfaction. It is possible through proper guidance services. After analysing a person's personality, we can place him properly after providing him training according to his interests and aptitudes.

FROM EDUCATIONAL POINT OF VIEW

Educational process is a very comprehensive process. This process can bring about important changes about in the behaviour of an individual. The present form of any nation or society is the result of its educational process. Hence, for the development of a nation and society, it is essential to make the educational process useful. In this educational process use of guidance service becomes essential for many reasons. From educational point of view, the need of guidance, becomes clear from the following description—

Imparting Education

The principle of individual differences has become universally accepted. Due to continuous population explosion, the effect of individual differences is visible to the maximum. The continuous population growth encourages various problems in the field of education, such as student unrest, indiscipline, shortage of trained teachers etc. From educational point of view, importance of individual differences is still more because all the children cannot acquire all types of education or they don't possess such abilities. In such circumstances children feel the need of guidance.

Choice of Relevant Curriculum

In this present period, many new subjects are floated. Many schools offer these subjects. All the pupils don't show interest and aptitude in all these subjects. Also all students don't possess the competence of studying all these subjects. From this point of view it is not necessary that if a student scores well in English, will also score so in Hindi too. Such variation is due to individual differences. Hence, the curriculum should be selected, keeping in view the individual differences. Guidance is required for such selections. For such selection of curricula, guidance requires the use of many standardized tests of psychology. On the basis of results of these subjects, pupils are helped in curriculum selection.

To Solve the Problems of Wastage and Stagnation

In Indian educational fields, the problem of wastage and stagnation has taken a very serious turn. Indian Government is trying hard to solve this problem.

For this job, many commissions have been organized and action has been taken according to the suggestions made. But not much success could be achieved. As a result of this problem, the pupils drop their education without completion or they stagnate for years at one level. These are known as wastage and stagnation respectively. For example, to fail repeatedly in a class is one form of stagnation. This problem is very serious at the primary level. It is at its extreme in urban areas. Many causes may be responsible for these problems, such as unsatisfactory school administration, untrained or undertrained teachers, appointment of incompetent teachers, neglecting individual differences etc. In some schools, teachers compel the pupils for tuitions by exploiting their academic weaknesses. Sometimes improper or difficult curriculum is also responsible for this problem. Hence, in order to save the pupils from the problems of wastage and stagnation, guidance services are to be provided. Only then this objective can be acquired.

By studying the above description, we can conclude what the place guidance occupies in educational field. It looks like mandatory to organize guidance services for each aspect of education.

To Maintain the Levels of Achievement

The existence of guidance services in the schools is must in order to maintain the higher levels of academic achievements. Guidance service can suggest the pupils how they can maintain their higher level of achievements. If they are not succeeding, guidance can pinpoint the causes of their failure. Guidance techniques can make the pupils aware of learning methods.

Problem of Indiscipline

In the field of education, indiscipline is a burning question. This problem has become a national problem. Everyday we hear and witness about strikes, lootings, dacoity etc. Such pupil-indiscipline is mainly due to the failure of education in making the pupils satisfying. Lack of solutions to the problems of the pupils in the educational institutions is also responsible for indiscipline. They need a person and a place where he can hear their problems and can provide help to the pupils. Guidance service can control the problem of indiscipline. By providing guidance to the students in order to curb student-unrest, they will get opportunities to exhibit their talent and hence they will undergo catharsis. By doing so, they will experience self-satisfaction.

FROM PSYCHOLOGICAL POINT OF VIEW

The knowledge of psychology, has disclosed many interesting secrets which cannot be discarded. From psychological point of view', all-round development of an individual is the main objective of our educational system. The process of an individual's development is very complex. The analysis of this developmental process and to understand it deeply is a very tedious task. Any error in understanding these complicacies may prove very harmful. A person's personality spoils when many complexes develop in him. If these complexes are not removed timely, then the person starts behaving like an abnormal. Many mental and emotional deformities start developing in that person. So in order to keep the person free from the effect of these complexes, provision of guidance looks very important. The following steps explain the need of guidance from psychological point of view—

To Develop the Personality

The concept of personality is very difficult and broader. It is not an easy task to understand it and to assess it because its characteristics are many. Each characteristic has its own importance in the life of a person. The measurement of characteristics is done by different methods and techniques.

In order to provide direction to the development of personality, help can be sought from guidance services. Through guidance services we can know whether a person's personality is developing properly or it is blocked somewhere. To know a person's personality is a technical job and its assessment requires trained persons. Hence, using the results of personality measurement is the job of a trained person. It is the responsibility of guidance to solve the problems related to the development of the personality.

For Emotional Development

There is one main part of a person's personality-emotional development. If a person lacks emotional development, he cannot be a balanced person. In such conditions, a person's personality becomes distorted and abnormal. Hence, emotional development is must for a person's personality. Many factors are responsible for emotional development, such as family, school, neighbourhood, community etc. The families where emotions are properly exhibited are better organized and enjoy strong background. The family members in such families enjoy and maintain rapport. On its contrary, we cannot think of rapport among the family members of those families where emotional situation is not sound. Such environment affects the child adversely. It is impossible to fulfil the psychological, social and personal needs of the children. In order to solve the problems of such pupils a special sympathetic attitude is needed. It becomes essential to honour the feelings of the children. After coming under emotional state, child becomes aggressive, frustrated, disappointed and neglected. They don't show interest in any task. They lack any co-ordination with their parents and guardians. The very same condition of the children living in the similar environment of school and neighbourhood prevails. An emotion of zealously can arouse after meeting prosperous children and can mount the tension. The teachers' irresponsible behaviour for the pupils can be responsible for the emotional state of the pupils in the schools. Adolescents face problems related to sex and love. In such problematic situations, if proper guidance is not provided to a person, his personality balance gets disturbed, which will be harmful to both, person and the society.

AS A BASIC NEED OF THE HUMAN BEING

Like other basic needs, guidance has also been considered a basic need of a human being. In the absence of guidance the development of a person may face many problems. As a person enters the various phases of development, his problems increase gradually and new situations are created. To understand these situations, to take advantage of opportunities and to fulfil the needs is only possible when we become competent for this. After acquiring these competencies, only then we can solve these various problems and only then the development can be speeded up. For doing so, guidance is needed at each step. Hence, guidance has been given the status of a basic need of the human being.

Hence, we see that how much the need of guidance is felt from psychological point of view. Without the psychological background, the work of guidance is not only difficult, but also impossible.

For Adjustment in Society

Adjustment is the basic need of a living being. Life of a person becomes unbearable without adjustment. For a person's adjustment it is essential to provide him opportunities for developing abilities and capacities. If a person is not provided with an opportunity for expression, his talents never get exposure. If there is a lot of difference between a person's school and family environments, then the adjustment of a person in such conditions becomes very difficult. The lack of such adjustment can be due to various reasons such as wrong selection of the curriculum, selection of incompetent teachers. In spite of this, if person does not get the occupation according to his interest and aptitude, he has to face the problem of adjustment. Such persons adopt that occupation due to compulsion but they never feel satisfaction and their progress is affected adversely. In such conditions, a person feels the need of guidance. He desires that he should be guided so that solution to his adjustment problems may be searched out.

Development according to Individual Differences

Psychological researches have emphasized individual differences. As these researches suggest two persons cannot be alike. Their personality shows differences in one or the other way. If we want to bring about essential changes in the behaviours of a person it is essential to give due importance to these differences. For example, in the field of education, the principle of child-centred education means the planning of educational programme keeping in view child's individual differences. It is a great contribution of psychology to the field of education. If these differences are understood very quickly, then the process of child development is not so complicated. Hence, knowing these differences is must. After knowing these differences there is need to provide proper direction to the development for this objective, help from guidance services can be sought. Hence, in this context, need of guidance services are felt.

FROM URBAN AREAS POINT OF VIEW

The need of guidance can also be described from urban areas point of view. In this context, the following is the need of guidance-

From Educational Point of View

As it has already been told, guidance is very important from educational point of view. If we study in detail the educational provisions and educational opportunities in the urban areas, no body can deny the fact that how much it is important and essential to provide guidance to the persons living in urban areas.

How benefit can be taken from the increasing educational opportunities in the urban areas? Due to lack of guidance in the urban areas, a person can follow wrong direction in the educational fields. He has to repent throughout life. Hence, people living in urban areas need guidance very much in the field of education.

From Recreational Point of View

As a result of modernisation and due to plenty of resources in the urban areas people and pupils have much spare time. Guidance is needed to utilize this time properly and from recreational point of view too. If this need is not fulfilled, people cannot be provided with opportunities of healthy recreation. Hence, guidance becomes a necessity here too.

From Women Point of View

In urban areas, women face many problems. Women have to face their educational, occupational, personal and matrimonial problems. In such circumstances women need a place where their problems can be discussed and solved. Guidance services can contribute to this very significantly.

From Labourer's Point of View

As a result of too much industrialization, labourers have to face many problems. Sometimes they become the target of exploitation by the industrialists and face many problems. In such difficult condition, if the persons are provided with guidance service, their many problems can be solved.

From Vocational Point of View

Due to multiplicity of vocations and due to their complexity, a person finds it difficult to select a vocation or placement in it. The person gets surrounded by many difficulties and sometimes faces this difficulty life-long as a result of wrong selection. Because the vocation is not selected according to a person's personality, his interests, aptitudes etc. this wrong selection may prove harmful for that person and his adjustment in the vocation. In such circumstances, it becomes very necessary to provide guidance to that person. For this many bureaux have been started in many universities so that immediate vocational guidance can be made available after the completion of education of the students. Guidance bureaux are also available in the district employment exchanges.

FROM RURAL AREAS POINT OF VIEW

Rural areas have their own needs and problems. These need guidance according to their needs.

From Economic Point of View

The persons belonging to rural areas have to face many problems related to the economic conditions. Due to lack of education and knowledge they don't know how to use their money properly and how to save the money. Urban areas exploit them on economic fronts. In order to make provisions of finance for their projects, rural people need guidance.

From Educational Point of View

Rural areas are still backward from educational point of view. These areas lack resources of education. If these facilities exist there, people are ignorant of them. They don't have the knowledge of new educational dimensions and also they don't know the importance of education. They stick to their traditional profession and they are deprived of the knowledge of modem facilities. Hence, in order to remove their problems, facilities of guidance should be necessarily provided from educational point of view.

From Political Awareness Point of View

Political awareness is highly significant in the present democratic set-up. Because it is the key to the success of democracy if every person becomes aware of his rights and duties in democracy. For this political awareness is must. In the rural areas, the provision for means of political awareness is very essential. Guidance programme can also be one of them.

From Social Point of View

Even today superstitions dominate the rural areas. Many people face various problems due to these superstitions. The main reason of these superstitions is the lack of education and scarcity of proper guidance. From this point of view, rural areas turned backward too much. Hence, in order to remove the superstitions from rural areas and to develop them socially, guidance is needed badly.

From Population Point of View

Population growth has become a problem in itself There is need of guidance to educate people and to provide knowledge of methods for controlling the population growth. Government has also made efforts to advertise the new methods and their advantages regarding the control of population growth in rural areas, but still guidance is needed.

From Health Point of View

In rural areas, health problems are also limitless. Diseases of children have turned horrible. The problems are very deep due to women diseases. Inspite of this, rural population is also unaware of new methods of cleanliness which encourage health problems. Hence, guidance has become necessity in order to remove health problems of these persons.

FROM POLITICAL CHANGES POINT OF VIEW

Like social, psychological and educational viewpoints, political viewpoint is also significant. For the development of political point of view, the following are the, reasons responsible for the need of guidance service—

For Developing Democratic Values

India has adopted democratic system after independence. Hence, all the plans of this country focussed the development of democratic system. The development of democratic system is only possible if the democratic values are given priority. From this point of view, the education system of this country is planned in such a way that the democratic values may develop. These values include our rights and duties along with the knowledge of methods of electing competent representatives who can constitute the government and can run the administration of the country. In the election of competent representatives, the feeling of impartiality and selflessness are alternatively termed as democratic values. For educating these values, the medium of guidance can prove very useful. Hence the need of guidance is being felt in this field too.

For the Security of the Nation

For the national security, it is very essential to provide information to the public of that country regarding internal and foreign destructive elements, because if such elements come into action in a country, that weakens the country. That country cannot protect its freedom. If the people are well informed regarding foreign interference in a planned way, they can be helped in their multiple problems. Some people join destructive forces after leaving their normal life. They do so after being failure in solving their problems. In such, circumstances, by making provisions of guidance service, people can be inspired in their home-coming to the main-stream of their life. Inspite of this, helping the national security forces in selecting the capable and competent persons by guidance service can ensure national security. Such contribution of guidance services will be highly appreciable. Hence the nation and the society need guidance service very much.

For Developing National Integration

If we wish an individual as well as society's progress, then it too is very essential that the nation must develop. In the absence of national progress or development, the individual or society can make no progress. The national progress depends upon the national feeling among the people of that nation. If the people lack national feeling that nation cannot make any progress. By inculcating national feeling we can produce, good citizens. The people can be alerted against anti-national powers. By establishing a balance and co-ordination among all the castes and religions of the nation, national feeling can be aroused. This also encourages communal harmony. In reality, the national feeling is based upon the communal harmony. For this, guidance service can contribute significantly.

GUIDANCE SERVICE

In 1953, Secondary Education Commission i.e. Mudaliar Commission emphasized guidance programme in the country. This commission also emphasized the extension of educational and vocational guidance and suggested some recommendations to the government in this regard. These recommendations are as follows;

(i) The education officers should insist on educational guidance.

(ii) In order to make the pupils familiar with the scope and importance of various industries, documentary films on industries should be exhibited and they should be made aware of real situations.

(iii) Some provision of career masters and other guidance workers should be made in all the educational institutions.

(iv) The Central Government should bear the responsibility of opening training centres for the training regarding guidance in all the states.

On the basis of above recommendations of Secondary Education Commission. Central Ministry of Education in 1954 established Central Educational and Vocational Guidance Bureau. This bureau has performed the following functions

(a) Provided guidance material to the educational institutes.

(b) The process of providing guidance started was based on Psychology.

(c) Prepared a guidance-manual.

(e) Established a close relationship between the vocational guidance and employment centres.

Objectives of Central Bureau

(i) To make progress in guidance by making the pupils aware of nature of guidance and its philosophy.

(ii) To encourage the development of guidance movement in India.

(iii) To strengthen guidance movement.

(iv) To provide leadership to the guidance programme in India.

In the beginning, Central Educational and Vocational Guidance Bureau remained attached to Central Institute of Education, but later on this was merged with National Council of Educational Research and Training (N.C.E.R.T.), But after sometime, the different departments of N.C.E.R.T. were re-organised. Its Guidance Department was merged with Psychology Department. Now, this department trains persons for educational and vocational guidance. Here, research work in guidance is also taken up.

Rehabilitation and Employment

The Directorate of Rehabilitation and Planning was established to rehabilitate the refugees from East and West Pakistan. This directorate is under the control of Central Labour. Rehabilitation and Planning Ministry. These days, all the employment exchange of the country are being controlled by this directorate. Various types of literature regarding guidance are published by this directorate. This department has published 85 employment pamphlets. The same directorate has started youth employment service during the second 5 year plan. This department also conducts research work regarding guidance. In spite of this department. Publication Department of the Union Government and other ministries also function in the field of guidance.

Vocational Guidance Association

This association is of national level. The main function of this association is to extend the ideologies of guidance programmes at the national level and to co-ordinate various guidance programmes. This association also publishes and distributes guidance literature. Also, this association brings out 'Journal of Vocational and Educational Guidance.'

3

Tests in Guidance

Tests are normally used in guidance to collect information about individuals, and use that information to appraise the individual. The guidance counsellor will use test and non-test data appraisal. A guidance counsellor should, therefore, have a good understanding of the general field of measurement.

Before we proceed to discuss in detail how tests are used in guidance, it is necessary for us to appreciate the need for testing.

Essentially, the need for testing in guidance is two-fold:

- Firstly, testing is supposed to be a more systematic, objective, precise and valid set of evaluations than is provided by the experience of an individual. Given test data, we can verify, reject or modify, previously held convictions about an individual.
- Secondly, testing provides new information about the quality of an individual's future performance in new situations, or information that is difficult for the individual to extract from prior experience. The overriding assumption in using psychological tests in guidance is that options appear for the individual, and the student must make his/her own decisions and live with them. It is hoped that testing may afford useful information that he/she does not already have, and which can be used in his/her decision-making.

Appraisal Using Test Score Information

Appraisal is crucial to the use of test score information in guidance. The guidance counsellor uses test score information to appraise his/her clients as follows:

- Guidance counsellors use tests and other data to determine each student's abilities, aptitudes, interests and other personal characteristics, in order to help the student gain self-understanding. Tests can also help each student increase the accuracy of self-estimates of achievement, intelligence and interests. Tests and other appraisal data can help the guidance counsellor to understand the student better. Such data can help the student to plan and make realistic decisions, because the individual understands his/her personal characteristics well. If guidance is conceived as a developmental process, then providing a student with the results of ability, achievement, interest and personality tests, followed by a discussion of these results with a counsellor, will ensure that the student is aware of his/her present standing and progress in these areas, and that he/she will be capable of putting himself/herself in a dynamic framework. He/she will be encouraged to think of life as involving making many decisions, some of which can be approached in a rational manner by weighing up alternatives based on accurate self-knowledge.

- A guidance counsellor uses appraisal data (test or non-test) to assist students in educational and vocational planning. Tests and other data can help the counsellor to understand a student's strengths and limitations with regard to personal characteristics. By using tests and interpretative devices like expectancy tables and 'regression equations', the student is helped to see the relationship between present levels of performance and educational decision, and his/her future chances of educational and occupational success.
- Guidance counsellors use appraisal data to diagnose students' problems. Such problems as reading disability, study skills deficiencies, and difficulties in relating to other people, may be identified more precisely, and solutions determined, with the use of test data.
- Lastly, tests are used to evaluate the outcomes of a guidance programme. It is important that any guidance programme be evaluated to find out whether the programme is achieving its objectives or not.

Student appraisal is frequently conceived in a very limited sense, as telling what someone is like from test scores. Appraisal is better seen as arriving at a systematic understanding of an individual's characteristics, within the context of his/her life pattern. Appraisal involves the ability to interpret information accurately. It is not merely the practice of measuring the presence or extent of human attributes or characteristics. It also calls for judgement of their strengths, desirability or unity.

The student appraisal services, as a part of guidance, are designed to gather and collate data about each student, for the purpose of helping him/her carry out his/her plans, and improve in areas where he/she is deficient, and to identify rapidly any difficulties which may interfere with the student's growth. This collection of data should never be intended to be used against the student, but rather for his benefit. A good appraisal service should be integrated, continuous and useful. An integrated appraisal means that it includes a variety of both test and non-test information, for example, the results of aptitude, intelligence tests and achievement tests, autobiographical information, questionnaires, interest inventories and occupational tests. The integrated information will enable the guidance counsellor to have a wider and more accurate picture of the student.

For appraisal to be meaningful, it must be continuous from year to year, recording the student's progress in school, the changes observed by the teacher, his/her attitudes, interests, etc. The data collected should be translated into some practical application—the useful aspect of appraisal. Data collected should be put to work for the benefit of the student. They should not be allowed to collect dust in the counsellor's office. A good appraisal programme is always student-oriented.

When putting the collected information to use, the counsellor must guard him/herself against indiscriminate release of the information to outside agencies, or others who have no interest in the student's welfare. The privacy of the appraisal information should be maintained. However, the counsellor can release information which is of an unrestricted nature, such as name, sex, age, race and school attended. Confidential information such as the psychological report, psychiatric evaluation or anything that is personal, should not be released to unauthorised persons. The counsellor must therefore have a clear understanding of what information he/she is entitled to release, and which information is prohibited or discretionary.

Guidelines on the Use of Information Gathered

Assuming that the guidance counsellor has safeguarded the privacy of information, how can he/she put it to a constructive use? How does he/she make it useful? The following are some guidelines:

- The guidance counsellor must evaluate the information as a whole, and never rely on a single piece of information. Any piece of information must be assessed in terms of all the information available.
- The guidance counsellor must use his/her interpretative skills in evaluating information instead of accepting it at face value. The counsellor may apply his/her psychological skills and insight in evaluating subjective information and statistical skills when evaluating objective test results.
- In sharing information with other members of the counselling team or school staff, the counsellor assumes full responsibility for the use made of information. In other words, the counsellor is the guardian of information on the student.

- The counsellor should attempt, in his/her interaction with student (clients), to integrate the information he has into the interview.

Despite the sentiments expressed by many that testing is just another instance of depersonalisation, testing is an integral part of the counsellor's specialised appraisal skills.

Although testing and evaluation are at times abused, they serve as an integral part of the counsellor's resources. Testing helps the counsellor to identify those students or clients who are most in need of help, remedial, or other forms of guidance.

Through testing, the counsellor is able to obtain information about his/her client that is inaccessible through a face-to-face interview, or consultation with teachers, parents and other interested parties.

MEANING AND PRINCIPLES OF GUIDANCE

What does guidance precisely mean? Let us first see what it does not mean. Lester. D. Crow and Alice Crow in "An Introduction to Guidance" have aptly stated that "Guidance is not giving directions. It is not the imposition of one person's point of view upon another person. It is not making decisions for an individual, which he should create for himself. It is not carrying the burdens of another life". If guidance is not all these, then what is it really?

To quote them again:

- "Guidance is an assistance made accessible through personally qualified and adequately trained men or women to an individual of any age to help them manage their own life behaviours, develop their own points of view, create their own decisions, and carry out their own burden".

Ordinary Meaning

Ordinary meaning of guidance is help, assistance, and suggestions for progress and showing the method. In that sense guidance is a life extensive procedure. Man needs guidance throughout his life. He needs it even from his infancy. When a child is born, the world for him is big, buzzing, blooming confusion and he knows nothing.

He learns everything from the society. From the mother, he learns how to stand on his feet, from the father, he learns to walk and from the teacher, he learns to seek knowledge and education, all learning takes lay through guidance. The society guides the individual to learn, to adjust oneself to the physical and social environment. To sum up we may say that guidance is a personal help rendered through the society to the individual so as to enable him to adjust to the physical and social environment and to solve the troubles of life.

Specific Meaning

Guidance in India, is comparatively a new field within the superior and more inclusive field of education and is used as a technical term as a specific meaning. It covers the whole spectrum of education, which starts from the birth of the child and continues till his death. This is a wide meaning of the term, which comprises all kinds of education such as formal, non-formal, informal and vocational, etc., which aims to adjust the individual in his environment in an effective method. There are usually three connotations attached to the word guidance:

- Guidance as a Specialised Service whose primary concern is with the individual and to help them to solve their troubles and take appropriate decisions in their choice-points;
- Guidance as a Common Service and is measured to be synonymous with education and educational processes; and
- Guidance as a Sub-Procedure of education in which developmental needs of the learners are measured the vital points.

Now let us look at some selected definitions of the term guidance in a bid to understand its conceptual and operational form: The term guidance symbolises the concept that is neither easy nor easily comprehensible due to the complexity of the human nature, the individual differences and personal-social troubles associated with changing environmental circumstances and cultural traditions.

- *Shirley Hamrin (1947) defined guidance as: "Helping John to see through himself in order that he may see himself through"*, is an easy and practical but demanding concept of guidance.
- *According to Jones (1951):* "The focus of guidance is the individual not his problem, its purpose is to give the growth of the individual in self-direction providing opportunity for self-realization and self-direction is the key-note of guidance."
- Downing (1964) points out towards a general problem in defining guidance that is one of keeping the definition short and sufficiently broad to be informative. He has attempted it through giving definition of guidance in operational conditions in two parts:
  - Guidance is an organised set of specialised services recognised as an integral part of the school environment intended to promote the development of the students and assist them towards a realization of sound, wholesome adjustment and maximum accomplishments commensurate with their personalities.
  - Guidance is a point of view that comprises a positive attitude towards children and realization that it is the supplement,

strengthen and create more meaningful all other phases of a youngster's education.

- Ruth Strang (1937) explains that guidance is a procedure of helping every individual through his own efforts to discover and develop his potentialities for his personal happiness and social usefulness.
- *Mathewson (1962):* Defines guidance as the systematic professional procedure of helping the individual through education and interpretative procedures to gain a better understanding of his own characteristics and potentialities and to relate himself more satisfactorily to social necessities and opportunities in accord with social and moral values.
- *Arthur, J. Jones (1963):* Thinks that guidance is the help given through one person to another in making choices and adjustments and in solving troubles.
- *Traxler (1957):* Considers guidance as a help which enables each individual to understand his abilities and interests, to develop them as well as possible and to relate the life-goals, and finally to reach a state of complete and mature self-guidance as a desirable member of the social order.
- Recently. B.L. Shepherd stated that:
  - The immediate objective in guidance is to help each pupil meet and solve his troubles as they arise; and
  - The ultimate objective of all guidance is self-guidance.

According to the Secondary Education Commission (1964-66):

- Guidance involves the hard art of helping boys and girls to plan their own future wisely in the full light of all the factors that can be mastered in relation to themselves and in relation to the world in which they are to live and work."

If we analyse the definitions of guidance, we will discover the following elements in it:

- Guidance programme is organised; it has a structure, system and personnel.
- It is an integral part of the school system.
- It consists of specialised seines of testing, counselling, educational and vocational information, placement and follow-up scheme.
- Its major aim is the promotion of student development.
- It helps children to develop and promote their skill to deal with their own troubles.
- It gives for the identification and development of talents and potentialities.

- The intangible elements of guidance are recognised as a point of view or as an attitude.

CLASSIFICATION OF TESTS

The goal of assessment is to help Counsellors to develop an understanding of the client or an individual. By using assessment and appraisal procedures, you will be able to gain understanding of the individual and in turn foster individual's understanding himself or herself. In this sense, you will appreciate that assessment and appraisal processes and procedures are the means of obtaining comprehensive understanding of students thereby fulfilling the goal of Counselling. It is essential that, you need to be familiar with the major tools and techniques of assessment, the purpose for which they are used and how the information provided by these can be used in understanding the individual. Psychological testing is one of the ways of assessment. The selection of any tool whether quantitative or qualitative depends on the type of information the Counsellor is interested in gathering. In most cases both are required to be used for holistic assessment an appraisal. In this unit, you will read about psychological tests, which are the tools for quantitative assessment.

Psychological tests are designed to assess the characteristics of people such as their abilities, attitudes, motivations, interests, needs and values and so on. Psychological test can be defined as a sample of an individual's, behaviour, obtaining under standard conditions and scored according to a fixed set of rules that provide a numeric score. In a standardised test, individual scores are compared with a norm or standard arrived at on the basis of performance of sample of individuals of the same age or grade level from around the country who took the same test when it was first developed. Good standardised tests are the result of years of research. Tests may take many forms. Usually, they comprise of a series of items/questions with well-defined correct answers such as in case of tests of intelligence or achievement, while others such as personality inventories, do not have right or wrong answers, but are designed to assess person's pre-dispositions, tendencies and preferences.

Tests can be used to compare the same individual on two or more traits and also compare two or more individuals on the same trait. Such an assessment is usually quantitative. Although most of the psychological tests provide relatively objective and quantifiable scores such as tests of intelligence abilities/ aptitudes. Some other tests may also provide descriptive and qualitative interpretations. A standard test has a manual which provides complete information of how the test was developed, evidence of its consistency, accuracy and objectivity. It also consists of detailed instructions for administering, scoring, interpreting the test, its uses and possible misuses. The test manual thus, provides you the requisite information to allow you to make an informed judgement as to whether the test is suitable for your use. Besides, the requirement to select the appropriate psychological test, a Counsellor needs to develop various skills in test administration, scoring, interpretation and communicating results to clients. The following part will describe some type of tests and the purpose for which they are used. Psychological tests are classified into different types depending on their content and the way they are administered. Tests vary in their content depending on the aspect of behaviour that is assessed, for example, some tests are designed to assess abilities, others assess motivation, personality characteristics etc. Psychological tests are also classified into individual and group tests, verbal tests and non-verbal tests and performance tests. Let us discuss one by one quantitative methods and techniques.

Intelligence Tests

Intelligence has been one of the most popular psychological terms used in identifying individual differences. It has helped to explain that people differ from each other in their ability to understand complex ideas or to learn from experience. Different theorists have tried to explain intelligence in different ways following different approaches. Theories by Binet, Weschler Spearman and Thustone are based on the psychometric approach where intelligence is considered as an aggregate of abilities.

It is expressed in terms of a single index of abilities. Howard Gardener's theory of multiple intelligences puts forth that intelligence is not a single entity and there exists multiple intelligences, each distinct from others. There are nine distinct intelligences that are relatively independent of each other. These different types of intelligences interact and work together to provide a solution of a problem.

The nine types of intelligences proposed by Gardener are briefly discussed below:

- *Linguistic Intelligence*: The capacity to use language fluently and flexibly, to express one's thinking and understanding others. Used in reading a book, writing a paper, a novel or a poem; and understanding spoken words. Poets and writers exhibit this ability.
- *Logical Mathematical Intelligence*: Thinking logically, critically, using abstract reasoning to manipulate symbols and solve mathematical problems.
- *Spatial Intelligence*: Abilities involved in forming, using and transforming mental images. Used in getting from one place to another, in reading a map, and is packing suitcase in the trunk of a car so that they all fit into a compact space. Pilots, sailors, interior decorators, surgeons, fashion designers generally exhibit this ability.

- *Musical Intelligence*: Capacity to produce, create and manipulate musical patterns. Used in singing a song, composing a sonata, playing a trumpet or even appreciating the structure of a piece of music.
- *Bodily-Kinesthetic Intelligence*: Ability to use one's body and muscle structure in a coordinated planned way. Used in dancing, playing basket ball, running a mile or throwing a javeline. Athletes, dancers, actors, gymnasts, sports person, surgeon exhibit this more than others.
- *Interpersonal Intelligence*: Used in relating to other people, such as when we try to understand another person's behaviour, motives or emotions, Counsellors, psychologists, politicians, social workers, religious leaders are shown to be high on this ability.
- *Intrapersonal Intelligence*: Knowledge of one's internal strengths and limitations and using that knowledge to relate to others.
- *Naturalistic Intelligence*: Complete awareness to our relationship with the natural world, useful in recognising the beauty of different species of flora and fauna and making a distinction in the natural world.
- *Existential Intelligence*: Can be defined as the ability to be sensitive to, or have the capacity for, conceptualising or tackling deeper or larger questions about human existence, such as the meaning of life, why are we born, why do you die, what is conscious-ness or how did we get here.

The multiple intelligences approach focuses on ways in which people can be intelligent. Theorists have also tried to explain intelligence in terms of information processing approach wherein the focus is on how an intelligent person thinks, acts and solves problems. Sternberg's information processing approach focuses on how solutions are arrived. The critical aspect of what constitutes intelligence is not necessarily the speed with which one arrives at a solution but the processes one uses. Processing information quickly does not mean it was done accurately or correctly. A relative rather than an impulsive style of problem solving has been associated with higher ability to solve problems. Jumping to conclusions without adequate reflection can lead to erroneous thinking.

The notion of emotional intelligence broadens the concept of intelligence and involves:

- Perceiving or sensing emotions,
- Using emotion to assist thoughts,
- Understanding emotions, and
- Managing emotions.

The concept of IQ dominated intelligence testing for a long time. With the emerging view of intelligence as multifaceted, the concept of intelligence as a single unitary ability or a composite of scores on different abilities is not considered valid. The concept of IQ has been found to be misleading. As Counsellors, the focus should be on a holistic assessment focusing on strengths and weaknesses of the client. This would help to plan remedial measures for intervention. The multiple intelligences approach is an alternative approach to assessment of intelligence. It emphasises a variety of abilities and skills (and not just an aggregate of mental abilities), which are required for success in life situations. As the meaning of intelligence differs from one culture to another there is a need to understand the cultural context for measuring intelligence. Even though tests of intelligence assist Counsellors and other personnel in providing a view of the clients abilities, the scores of these tests need to be used with caution.

Interest Inventories

In order to help students make vocational and educational choices, the Counsellor needs to know his/her interest for activities. The study of interest would help you as Counsellor to better understand the students in terms of his/her likes and dislikes. In this section, you will learn about the concept of interest and its assessment. You might have observed in your class that some students show more inclination to mathematics, while others in computers, some in literary activities, in paining etc. Interest is an expression of our likes and dislikes or our attractions or aversions. An individual chooses the most acceptable, suitable alternative out of many, go after preferred objectives, activities etc. and consequently desires satisfaction, success and happiness out of the activities selected. It is because of his or her natural liking fro these activities over others. Interest refers to activities that on individual likes to engage in enjoys.

Types of Interest

Interest can be classified in different ways.

Supper classified interest as:

- Expressed
- Manifest or observed and
- Measure or tested.

Interest testing is done to achieve some purpose such as:

- To provide teachers and Counsellors with information regarding the students preference and aversions which will help then acquire better understanding of students and their problems.
- To enable teachers, Counsellors and parents to assist the testes to prepare his educational and vocational terms consistent with his interest.

- To help in the selection of the right person for the right work, and thus same frustration, unhappiness and disappointment in the live of the individuals and increase productive capacity of individual.

We can use:

- Formal assessment techniques and
- Informal assessment techniques to discover a student's interest.

Formal Assessment Techniques

Interest inventories are formal techniques for measuring interests. They are considered more reliable at discovering on individuals interest than interviews as the inventories address a large number of questions representing a broad range of carriers. There are many inventories now in use and majority of them deal with occupational interest.

Interest Inventories

The Strong Vocational Interest Bank (SVIS) and Kuder preference Record (KPR) are significant milestones in the area of interest measurement and a number of revisions of the original forms have been undertaken. Both the interest inventories however better in terms of approaches in construction and purpose for which they are used. The SVIB is based on the assumption that a person who has the interest typical of successful people in a given occupation will enjoy and find satisfaction in that occupation. The KPR constructed by G. Frederic Kuder, assets preferences for specific activities. Each item contains three choices. The subject has to select one of the three choices as his first choice, and another as his third choice.

An example of the choices given in an item are:

- Build bird houses
- Write articles about birds
- Drawn sketches of birds.

This particular item aims to test three types of interests, namely mechanical, literacy and an artistic. The main difference in the two types of inventories is that in Kuder preference record the subject is forced to say which one of the three activities he likes best and which one he likes least, even though he may not like any of the that, hence it is called forced choice pattern type. In Strong Vocational Interest blank, the subject has to differentiate between L (like), I (indifferent) or D (dislike). Hence it is called category-response type of assessment. As Counsellor if you want a description of a persons so that inferences could be done regarding suitability for one of the very large number of jobs, Kuder Preference Record is your preferable tool of interest assessment. On the other hand if the purpose is to appraise the individually interest for a limited number of specific jobs, then strong Vocational Interest Blank is more useful. It is important to remember that the SVIB and KPR tell nothing about the ability or aptitude of an individual. These to be assessed by other methods.

Results of interest inventories or tests are particularly useful to the Counsellor as:

- The items of interest inventories are non-threatening and so the student is more likely to respond honestly.
- The student, with the assistance of the Counsellor, is helped to see the discrepancy, if any, between his/her view of one's interests and those assessed by the interest inventories.
- It also provides the counsellor a view into whether the clients expressed interests are shifted to what s/he is pursuing.

You have read about two distinct types of interest inventories. Besides, these two, some tools are available and used by the Counsellor and the individual her/himself.

Informal Assessment Techniques

It includes client's expression of interests and observation. The clients interviews regarding his/her interests provide the Counsellor a good beginning for understanding the client. For example, the books s/he reads, and the amount of time spent on reading provides on indication of clients interests on the kind of reading s/he does.

As Counsellors you can supplement this information by using qualitative techniques of assessment such as observation of the activities a client participates in or information gathered from anecdotal records and written works as sources informal information regarding client interests.

Cautions on the use of Interest Inventories

As Counsellor, you should keep in the following cautions in mind while using the results of interest inventories.

- Interest data of an individual provides a profile of the pattern of their interests (what they like doing) and should not be taken as the strength of the individual).
- Interest results tell us only about the likelihood of an individual finding enjoyment in a particular type of activity or occupation and not s/he is capable of.
- A high score on an interest inventory so should not be considered analogues to success in a career.

It is important to remember interests indicate the clients and not his or her strength. The emphasis of interest inventories is on self-exploration. One should know about one self and be able to relate this information to what one is doing. Thus the results of interest inventories should not be seen in an isolate manner but should be supplemented with information from other techniques such as observation, interview, informal talk etc., interest results are of little value themselves. They should be considered with achievement and aptitude scores to help individuals make educational and career choices.

APTITUDE TESTS

Aptitude is thought of as a natural tendency, special ability, or capacity or cluster of abilities. Often these natural abilities are looked at in relationship to a person's readiness to learn or their suitability for a particular career. For example, in order to be successful architect, one must possess the cluster of abilities such as a keen sense of observation, a sense of aesthetic visual memory, abstract reasoning, and an ability to sketch free hand. So, aptitude may be defined as a trait that characterises an individual's ability to perform in an area or to acquire the learning necessary for performance in a given area.

It presumes an inherent or native ability that can be developed to its maximum through learning or other experiences. However, it can not be expanded beyond a certain point, even by learning. Although that may be a debatable concept, it is stated here as a basis on which aptitude tests are developed. In theory, then, an aptitude test measures the potential of one to achieve in a given activity or to learn to achieve in that activity.

Aptitude tests may potentially be used by Counsellors and others because:

- They may identify potential abilities of which the individual is not aware;
- They may encourage the development of special or potential abilities of a given individual.
- They may provide information to assist on individual in making educational and career decisions or other choices between competing alternatives;
- They may serve as an aid in predicting the level of academic or vocational success on individual might anticipate; and
- They may be useful in grouping individuals with similar aptitudes for development and other educational purposes.

Types of Aptitude Tests

There are different types of aptitude tests. Some of them are single aptitude tests like tests of mechanical aptitude, clerical aptitude, teaching aptitude, musical aptitude and so on. Such tests covering a group of related abilities are necessary for performing in an occupation like becoming a mechanic, clerk, teacher, musician etc. Another type of aptitude test is work sample aptitude test. It requires the individual to perform all or part of a given job under the conditions that exist on the job. An example of a work sample test for the job of automobile mechanic is to repair a faulty carburetor. Besides this, there are differential tests Batteries as well. A commonly know Differential Aptitude Tests (DAT).

Bennett, Seashore and Wesman (1984) battery consists of eight subtests of verbal reasoning, numerical reasoning abstract reasoning, spatial reasoning, clerical speed and accuracy, mechanical reasoning, language usage, spelling, grammar, combination of such abilities is required for success in different occupations. Such test batteries can give comprehensive information about the relative picture of the students specific abilities.

Administration of total battery can prove to be costly in terms of time but one can make selective use of certain sub tests. For example, a student trying to explore whether s/he will have the required aptitude to go to engineering, may not be required to take tests like clerical speed, language usage, grammatical or verbal reasoning tests but may be required to take numerical abstract and spatial reasoning tests. Most of the batteries of tests available for assessment of aptitude at school stage are in the form of test batteries consisting of the underlying abilities required for success in different occupations rather than direct assessment of job aptitudes.

Caution in the Use of Aptitude Test Data

- It is important that Counsellors select and use aptitude tests carefully, keeping in view the student's/clients needs. If aptitude test data must be used, it should be used along with previous achievement data, present interests, leisure time activities and work habits etc., in order to guide the students into various occupational possibilities.
- The aptitude test samples certain abilities of the individual and helps to find what he/she can do now and how well it can be done further. On the basis of present performance, estimate of his/her future achievement is inferred which is in terms of probability only.
- It may also be kept in mind that aptitude tests score only provide leads or suggestions or to help in career planning and do not automatically match individuals to suitable courses or studies, and occupations. These are factors like willingness, hard work, that contribute to or one's success in a career which are not measured by aptitude tests.

ACHIEVEMENT TESTS

Achievement is what one successfully accomplishes in an area of study/ activity/domain. In the case of students, it may be conceptualised as successful learning of the assigned educational material. Such learning is usually demonstrated to teachers and others either through a verbal presentation or a written examination. An achievement test measures knowledge and skills attained by the student in a particular area, usually acquired after classroom teaching or training. In an educational system, achievement test scores are often used to determine the level of instruction for which a student is prepared, to indicate academic strengths and weakness, and to indicate the relative standing of the student in a group/class. Achievement test data, in combination with other data, is used to help guidance Counsellors plan students future educational programmes.

Types of Achievement Test

Achievement tests are of different kinds, each scoring a different purpose and providing different information on students' academic proficiency. These have been classified in various ways, and understanding of which helps the Counsellor to understand their functions.

- *Formative and Summative Tests*: Formative tests are used to measure progress made in knowledge and skills before and during instruction. Summative achievement tests are given at the end of course instruction, so as to assess the outcome of the instruction.
- *Progonostic tests*: Readiness or prognostic tests are used to predict how well an individual is expected to profit from training.
- *Diagnostic Test*: Diagnostic achievement tests provide information on performance of the students in different subjects and indicate their strengths and weakness in reading, arithmetic and language usage.

Achievement test can be either criterion referenced (CRT) or norm referenced (NRT). The two tests differ in their intended purposes, the way in which content is selected, and the scoring process which defines how the test results must be interpreted. Norm Referenced Tests (NRTs) are designed to highlight achievement differences between and among students and provide a rank order of students across a continuum of achievement from high achievers to low achievers.

These types of tests are used to help Counsellors/teachers to clarify students for remedial or gifted programmes. Criterion-reference tests (CRTs) determine the strengths of the test taker *i.e.,* what they can do and what they know, not how they compare to others. They report how well students are doing relative to a predetermined performance level on an specified set of educational goals or outcomes included in the school curriculum. An achievement test is designed to measure how much a person knows about a specific topic or area such as math, geography or science. Achievement tests can be standardised test or teacher-made tests.

Uses of Achievement Test Data

Data from standard achievement tests can be used for promoting, classifying, diagnosing or evaluating students. Counsellors can also use the achievement tests for:

- Helping clients in decision making. A Counsellor can use the achievement test scores to initiate decision on taking appropriate choices for a career.
- Assisting in diagnosis Counsellors can make use of achievement test data to diagnose problems faced by the students in different subject areas. Accordingly corrective remediation can be planned and carried out.
- Encouraging self-study. The student through achievement data, is able to gain insight into his/her strengths and weakness in different subjects which can motivate him/her to put in the desire effort.
- *Achievement test are used as learning measures of:*
  - The amount of learning,
  - The rate of learning
  - Comparisons with others or with achievement of self in other areas,
  - Level of learning in sub-areas, and
  - Strengths and workers in a subject matter area because of their extensive use and relatively easy task of identifying appropriate context measures.

Achievement tests of both kinds *i.e.,* standardised and teacher –made tests are based on the content taught and are considered valid. These are used to assess the level of overall proficiency to meet the entry requirements to certain/programmes or the proficiency in a particular subject. The informal classroom achievement test is suited to a select performance of a group of students. It is flexible and accommodates testing students on a local curriculum. The two types of tests can be used in a complementary manner.

Attitude Scale

Attitudes are expressions of how much we like or dislike various things. We tend to approach and seek out to be associated with things we like, we avoid, shun or reject things we do not like. Attitude represent our evaluations and performance towards a wide variety of objects, events, persons, and situations. The defining characteristics of attitudes is that they express evaluations along the lines of liking-disliking, pro-anti, favouring–disfavouring or positive–negative. By restricting the term attitude to evaluation, we distinguish attitudes from beliefs or opinions. Attitude includes certain aspects of personality as interests, appreciations and social conduct. Attitudes are learnt, they are adopted. They have aspects as directions, intensity etc.

Types of Attitude Scales

Attitudes need to be tested because our social life depends on some desirable attitudes. The success in certain vocations also depends on some attitudes. Attitudes can be tested through various techniques. Various scaling techniques have led to the development of different types of attitude scales which provide quick and convenient measure of attitudes. However, 'the method of equal appearing intervals' and 'method of summative ratings' have been extensively used in attitude or opinion research.

The attitude scales which are developed using these scaling techniques consists of a number of carefully edited and selected items called 'statements'. The method of equal–appearing 'intervals' was originally developed by Thurstone and Chave. The attitude score of an individual obtained by this method has an absolute interpretation in terms of the psychological continuum of scale value of the statements making up the scale. If this score falls in the middle range of the psychological continuum, the attitude of the individual is described as 'neutral'. If it falls towards the favourable end of the continuum, it is described as 'favourable' and if it falls towards the unfavourable ends, it is described as 'unfavourable'. In the 'method' of summated ratings developed by Likert, the item score is obtained by assigning arbitrary weights of 5, 4, 3, 2 and 1 for Strongly Agree (SA), Agree (A), Undecided (U), Disagree (D) and Strongly Disagree (SD) for the statements favouring a point of view. On the other hand, the scoring weights of 1, 2, 3, 4 and 5 are used for the respective responses for statements opposing this point of view. An individual's score on a particular attitude scale is the sum of his rating on all the items. There some more techniques, such as, Error Choice Technique, Free Response Technique, Paired Comparisons, Opinion Polling or Surveying, diaries, auto-biographic etc., are used for testing attitude. Attitude scales are used to measure the degree of positive or negative feeling associated with any slogan, person, institution, religion, political party etc. Attitude scales are also used in public-opinion surveys in order to make some important and crucial decisions. Educationists, for example, conduct opinion surveys to find out how people feel about educational issues.

Personality Test

Often by persons use the term personality to indicate the physical make up of an individual. The term 'Personality' however, signifies much more than simply the physical looks of a person and has a very broad meaning. It includes the emotional, motivational, inter-personal, attitudinal and even moral aspects of a person. some researchers have included intelligence also as part of personality. Personality refers to a unique combination of characteristics of an individual, which pre-disposes the person to behave in a particular and consistent way. Personality testing is necessary to achieve the following purposes.

- It helps the students in proper educational and vocational choice. Personality plays an important role in an individual, personal, educational and vocational adjustment and success. It is, therefore, important to diagnose the individual's personality pattern to see whether he posses the traits which are likely to contribute significantly to his adjustment to the course or career he is choosing.
- It helps the individual in resolving emotional conflicts. Personality diagnosis becomes essential when the difficulty the individual encounters in making proper adjustment with the educational and occupational choices, lies in emotional conflict about which the client has no knowledge. When the cause of the mental conflict is diagnosed, it may be possible for him to solve his problem in his own way.
- *It helps the clinical psychologist:* A clinical psychologist can use personality assessments to help choose the best therapy for his clients. Thus, personality assessment is important for educational, career, personal and social Counselling.

Techniques of Testing Personality

A number of techniques are used for testing personality.

The techniques are:

- Interview
- Observation
- Self-report Measures
- Checklists
- Rating Scales
- Situational Tests or Behavioural Tests
- Projective Techniques
- Anecdotal Records
- Autobiography
- The Daily Diary

Here we can discuss some of the techniques of assessment of personality like self-report measures, projective techniques and behavioural assessment.

Self-Report Measures

Self-report measures are personality scales that ask individuals to answer a series of questions/statements about their characteristic behaviour. When you respond to a self-report personality inventory, you endorse statements as true or false as applied to you. You indicate how often you behave in a particular way or you rate yourself with respect to certain qualities. The logic underlying this approach is simple. Who know you better than you do? A variety of personal characteristics can be measured through self-report inventories.

Projective Technique

Projective techniques focus on a composite picture of the personality as a whole. This method is called the projective techniques because the individual is stimulated to project his personality into the test exercises.

The stimuli used in projective techniques attempt to arouse responses that are a projection of the innerself or motives and personality traits that are usually hidden and often even unsuspected by the individual himself. The subject may be asked to respond to series of picture, inkblots or similarly ambiguous stimuli. The interpretation of responses requires a long period of training and should be done only by those who are specially qualified. The most popularly known projective technique is the Rorschach Inkbolts Test and Thematic Apperception Test (TA).

Behavioural Assessment

The manner in which a student/client behaves in different situations can provide you with meaningful information about his/her personality. Observation of behaviour, teacher reports, interviews, ratings and situations tests serve as the basis of behavioural analysis. The choice of a specific personality test is difficult but extremely relevant as different tests yield somewhat different, yet overlapping types of information. Some provide limited information while other provides a lot of information, some of which is very technical to understand. Of course, the more the information available, you may be able to help in more domains. You should choose a test that is relevant to clients. The test must have norms available. You should also be aware of the limitations of the test, particularly the conditions in which it may mislead the respondents or you. Even when a test is used the Counsellor may interpret and use the test scores along with non-test information, keeping in mind the age, gender, social group, culture, language of the client.

OBJECTIVES OF STATE LEVEL VOCATIONAL BUREAUX

(i) At the state level, the main objective of educational and vocational guidance bureaux is to provide assistance to the pupils to select courses of study and careers suitable to them. Such assistance is very essential.

(ii) To help the pupils in their adjustment in all areas of life and also in the maximum development of their abilities interests and personality.

(iii) To develop the guidance-mindedness in the staff members of the school or to make progress in guidance.

(iv) To make guidance an integral part of education and to explain the principals, parents and teachers about guidance, to know their interests and to seek their active co-operation.

(v) To make aware the general public and education-officers about the need of guidance services.

(vi) To develop better understanding about the basic philosophy of guidance its concept and principles by the guidance bureau. At present, the main cause of lack of popularity of guidance services is the occurrence of mis-conceptions regarding the nature and objectives of guidance.

(vii) To propagate by all the guidance bureaux that the guidance is more than assistance to the pupils at the end of school career and in the selection of vocations.

Till 1981, in 19 states and union territories of the country, there were educational and vocational guidance bureaux of the states. There are also some state level agencies which are responsible for guidance services. There were no such state level guidance agencies in ten states and union territories. There were three state level guidance agencies out of 19 as independent entities. These were headed by Directors of Education or these were controlled by a senior officer of directorate of education. These three bureaux are—Bureau of Psychology, Allahabad (U.P.), Institute of Vocational Guidance and Selection. Govt. of Maharashtra, Mumbai, Institute of Vocational Guidance, Govt. of Gujarat, Ahmedabad. There are 9 regional centres of Bureau of Psychology, Allahabad (U.P.). Other two have sub-bureaux.

Five state level agencies were integral part of the office of director of education. These were very small units. In 10 states and union territories, now the state level agencies are a part of State Council of Educational Research and Training (S.C.E.R.T) of State Institute of Education (SLE). In Madhya Pradesh. College of Educational Psychology and Guidance. Jabalpur plays the role of state level guidance agency. In this way we see that in each state, a state educational and vocational bureau was established. Mudaliar Commission recommended to the government for the establishment of these bureaux. Each state level bureau publishes related literature, manages testing of the workers and makes provisions for the guidance service in the schools. State level bureau also encourages research work in the field of guidance.

GUIDANCE SERVICES AT STATE LEVEL

In the third five year-plan, guidance was approved centrally sponsored plan and 13 bureaux were established for the development of guidance services in the states. As a result of efforts made by these bureaux, the pupils were provided with guidance through the counsellors and career masters in the schools. At the last stage of third five-year plan, guidance services were made available in about 3000 secondary schools of India. In these school, career masters used to provide informations.

The objectives of Central Educational and Vocational Guidance Bureau are different from those of such State Bureaux because Central Educational and Vocational Guidance Bureau is a central institution. The objective of central bureau is to develop guidance by creating sufficient awareness about the nature and philosophy of guidance in the pupils. Its other objective is to encourage the expansion of guidance movement in India and to strengthen it. The Central Bureau provides leadership to the guidance programme in the country. It is also necessary to pay attention towards the objectives of State Educational and Vocational Guidance Bureaux after considering the objectives of Central Bureau.

OTHER STATE LEVEL AGENCIES

There are many other agencies in addition to state level guidance bureaux in the state which conduct guidance work. These agencies are-

(i) Guidance Bureau of Universities
(ii) Planning Office
(iii) College of Teacher's Training
(iv) State Bureaux of Psychology

In some states some private institutes also conduct guidance services such as Parsi Panchayat, Y.M.C.A. etc.

PROBLEMS OF GUIDANCE IN INDIA

In India, guidance service is in its initial stage. It is yet to make progress. Continuous efforts are going on for its progress, but still much progress in this direction has not occurred. Its cause is - occurrence of various problems in the way of guidance. Due to these problems guidance services could not make much progress in India. Hence, it is very essential to control these problems. Following are the problems which come across in the field of guidance in India-

Traditionalism

In order to execute guidance programmes in India, it is very essential to disown traditionalism. Occurrence of traditionalism among teachers acts as an obstacle in the dynamicism of guidance programmes. Due to this traditionalism teachers are unable to exhibit interest and initiative for view experiments in education. This makes the latest programmes in the field of education a great failure.

Traditionalism does not exist in teachers only, but it also exists among the parents of the pupils or among "their guardians. Most of the parents or guardians are uneducated or less educated. They have not heard even the term 'guidance'. In the absence of knowledge about guidance, how parents, guardians and teachers can know about the importance of guidance service?

Even educated parents in India are under the influence of traditionalism. They force their children to select the profession according to their family traditions. They fail to experience the knowledge by dynamicism and practice. Hence, for the propagation of guidance service and its progress in India this traditionalism has to be eliminated education.

Lack of Training

Experts are required for guidance programmes. In order to prepare experts, a proper provision of training is essential. But our country lacks even the teacher-training facilities. In such conditions we can not expect the provision of training of the guidance workers. In the absence of training facilities, it is not possible to prepare experts for the guidance services. Handing over the responsibility of guidance to the untrained persons would mean to play with the lives of the persons or pupils. It would be better if guidance services are not started in the absence of trained persons. But it is not completely true that no attention is being paid towards this end in India. Some efforts have been made and still these are going on.

Lack of Standardized Tests

Standardized tests are essential in the guidance services. It is very difficult to collect informations about the pupils without these standardized tests. In India, many standardized tests are used but being in English, these cannot be used for the persons who don't know English because English is a foreign language. In India, too, many tests have been constructed in Indian language and more attempts are going on but there is still much more to do in this field.

Economic Condition

In India, most of the schools are economically weak. In some schools it is difficult to disburse even the salaries of the school staff. How we can expect to start guidance service and to follow guidance programmes in such schools under these conditions? It is very essential to strengthen economic condition for the guidance programmes: otherwise the programme can never be successful and developed.

Faulty Curriculum

In our country, it is a serious problem to determine a uniform curriculum due to variations. Due to lack of uniform curriculum in the schools, the entire education system looks faulty. No special importance has been given to guidance in the curriculum of Indian schools. The pupils are unaware of importance and utility of guidance. For this reason this service remained unfamiliar in the school. Due to lack of guidance, the pupil is unable to recognize himself and the guidance worker finds himself helpless in providing guidance. Hence, the guidance should be given proper place in the school curricula.

Information Collection and Analysis System

In order to make the guidance process effective and successful, there should be a sound system for collecting and analysis informations related to the pupils. But in India no such system has been developed at the school and state level. In the absence of such a system it is very difficult to know about the pupils. For such a system economic condition must be strong. In the absence of these informations, it is not possible to conduct the guidance service.

Un-employment

The problem of unemployment is getting nourished in most of the countries. In such countries, it is very difficult to run guidance service. The opportunities of guidance are created in the countries which lack vocations, especially vocational guidance. In the condition of unemployment, a person does not care for suitability or unsuitability, of the vocation. In such conditions, a person provides importance to the achievement of the vocation instead of guidance. Hence, in the condition of unemployment, it is very difficult to perform the guidance work.

Faulty Examination System

In our country many education systems got developed but none paid attention towards examination systems. The pupils pass the examination by following the cramming process but their interests, ideas, capacities, intelligence-level etc. remain unknown. In the absence of these informations, it becomes somewhat impossible to run a guidance programme.

Extra Work-Load on Teachers

In Indian schools, the teachers are already overloaded with work. Every citizen of the country expects more and more from the teacher. In schools, the teachers have so much work that they fail to make justification with the work. They are to teach 8-9 periods per day. They are forced to bear this load due to the fear of the service. In private institutions, such exploitation of the teachers has crossed all the limits. In 'such a condition, the teacher would be unable to take over the guidance work and to show interest in this work. It is all in vain to expect co-operation from the teacher in the guidance service in the over-crowded classes.

Lack of Co-ordination

Due to the lack of co-ordination between various agencies of guidance programme guidance programme becomes ineffective, such as school, psychology, community etc. have negligible, co-ordination in Indian conditions. The success of guidance programme depends very much on this co-ordination.

Lack of Research of Guidance

The guidance programmes in schools face various problems. To solve these problems, research work is needed, but in India, guidance services could not develop due to the lack of such research work. This research work includes research in various guidance systems counselling methods and methods of collecting informations.

4

Vocational Guidance

CONCEPT OF VOCATIONAL GUIDANCE

Vocational guidance according to DAW is that which have to be made well before the school leaving stage. Indeed with comprehensive education potentially offering a greater educational opportunity a good case for an increasingly important role for vocational guidance can be made. It is worthwhile to look at some of the concepts or frames of references that are fundamental to a consideration of occupational choice. Crites suggest that there are five sets of concepts that need to be considered. Firstly, how far is occupational choice the result of systematic behaviour as opposed to chance? Clearly the practice of vocational guidance is concerned with systematizing choice. Thus, vocational guidance is not only adjustment but also achievement and development of the individuals to the maximum extent to be successful in their chosen occupations to be satisfied and useful to the society. Let us discuss the objectives of vocational guidance:

- To assist the student to know about the characteristics, functions, duties of the occupations of his choice.
- To enable him to find out what are the specific criteria as skills, abilities, age, etc. are required for the occupations of his choice.
- To assist the student to know about his skills, abilities, interests for making wise choices.
- To assist the student to acquire the technique of analysis before making any final choice.
- To provide opportunity for experiences in school and out of school this may provide an idea of the work environment to the student.
- To help the student realize that all honest labour is worthwhile.

The recommendations of Education Commission set up by Government of India in 1964 indicated the aims and scope of vocational guidance. These recommendations suggest the following:

- The aim of guidance is not just to help student in making vocational choices but also be focused on the development of the child as good citizen.
- Guidance should be provided in solving learning difficulties, academic excellence, developing study habits and must be started at the primary stage itself.
- Guidance role is very crucial at the college level as at this stage student faces many problems related to educational vocational and personal. They should be make aware about the job market and how to make adjustment in it.
- Information may be provide about the training, competitive examinations and scholarships available.

NEED AND FUNCTIONS OF VOCATIONAL GUIDANCE

- Bringing individuals at par with the demands of the jobs: As we all know that individual differences exist among all and no two individuals can have the same abilities, skills and personalities. We can understand it with an example as a person can be skilled in doing a desk job while the other can be skilled in the field job so the skill differs and thus the demand for the job also different from different individuals. Thus here vocational guidance is needed for matching the right job with right individual.
- Assessing the right skill of an individual: The capabilities and the limitations of an individual should be known to him, *e.g.* a person may have interest in painting but may not have the skill to take it as a career. So here the work of vocational guidance comes to assist the individual in assessing himself and then accordingly choosing the right kind of job.
- Expansion of the world of work: Nowadays jobs are available at national as well as international levels. And it gives rise to many queries as how one can choose the best from several alternatives? How to know about the details of the occupation? How to apply? And many more all these are dealt with the help of vocational guidance.

Functions of Vocational Guidance

- Assessment of the individual in terms of his academic achievement, skills attitude, interest, limitations, etc.
- Assessment of individual's present environment such as financial resources, family background and family expectations, etc.
- Assessing the suitability of the individual with that of the job demands.

- Helping the individual to come at par with the job requirements.
- Counseling for the adjustment in the job.
- Follow-up services in the form of feed back from the individuals for further modification in the guidance programme if needed.

Factors Effecting Vocational Choice

- Personal Factors Affecting Career Selection
  - Aptitudes - What natural abilities do you possess?
  - Interests inventories - what gives you satisfaction?
  - Your personality - Do you perform best in low-pressure or high-pressure working environments?
- Social Influences on Career Opportunities
  - Demographic trends
  - Increase in working parents means more demand for food service and child care.
  - More leisure time means more interest in health, and recreation products and services.
  - Increased demand for further employment training creates opportunities for teachers and trainers.
  - Geographic trends
  - Where jobs are, salaries, and living costs. Economic Conditions affect career opportunities
- Trends in Industry and Technology affect career opportunities
  - Automated production methods have decreased the need for many entry-level employees in factories.

AGENCIES OF GUIDANCE AT DIFFERENT LEVELS

Different agencies, *i.e.* government and private at international, national and regional level have been doing significant works in the area of guidance. These agencies are working in training /orientation, career guidance services or development of materials for guidance workers/functionaries.

International Level

International Association of Educational and Vocational Guidance (IAEVG) is a worldwide guidance and counselling organization, whose mission is to promote the development and quality of educational and vocational guidance. IAEVG' s mission is also to ensure that all citizens who need and want educational and vocational guidance and counselling can receive this counselling from a competent and recognized professional. The objectives of the organization are as follows :

- To promote communication among persons and organizations active in educational and vocational guidance.
- To encourage the continuing development of ideas, practice and research in the field of guidance and counselling on each level, national and international, in developing and developed countries.
- To advise government and national or international organizations on the development of guidance systems and further the exchange of professionals and experts.
- To collect and disseminate information of interest in the field of educational and vocational guidance practice, study and research

The Mission of IAEVG is to:

- advocate that all citizens who need and want educational and vocational guidance and counselling can receive this counselling from a competent and recognized professional
- recommend the basic nature and quality of service that should typify the service provided to students and adults
- recommend the essential training and other qualifications that all counsellors in educational and vocational guidance should have
- urge governments to enhance, facilitate or establish an agency, institution, or office with responsibility to develop and maintain
- policies governing the provision of educational and vocaitonal guidance
- the provision of training and continuing education programmes for counselling and guidance practitioners
- the development and provision of appropriate and effective methods and materials for guidance
- the conduct of research and development to create new, more comprehensive, and better ways of conducting educational and vocational guidance
- the development of appropriate methods of evaluation af counselling and guidance

Cedefop, the European Agency to promote the development of vocational education and training, is the European Union's centre of expertise to support the development of VET and evidence-based policy-making. One important task for Cedefop is to provide guidance practitioners with advice, research, analysis and information. On Cedefop's web site European Training Village (ETV)there is an area with information on lifelong guidance (Choose lifelong guidance in the left menu). Here you will find information on European guidance projects, links to publications and research results, examples of good guidance strategies and practices and a live network for all the actors who have an interest in the field.

FEDORA is an organisation for those involved in student guidance in institutions of higher education in Europe. The FEDORA network has especially the focus on the higher student mobility across Europe and the challenges that gives to the guidance practitioners. FEDORA contributes to the further development of the guidance practitioners' competencies so they can better support, inform and guide the students on mobility issues. FEDORA organizes congresses, conferences and summer universities and each event takes place every three years. All types of events take place in different countries in the FEDORA member states each year. IAC (International Association for Counselling) wishes to encourage the exchange of ideas, research findings and personal experience in the field of counselling and guidance. This happens, among others, through organising conferences and publishing the International Journal for the Advancement of Counselling.

The International Centre for Career Development and Public Policy, ICCDPP, has the task to facilitate international sharing of knowledge and information concerning public policy and career development issues. ICCDPP has a base for knowledge and information which contains proceedings from international symposia, and reports and news provided to the site by the users and by other international contacts. ICCDPP is supported by OECD, the World Bank, and the European Commission, etc The Nordic Association of Educational and Vocational Guidance is a coalition of national associations for education and vocational guidance in the Nordic countries and the self-governing areas of Aaland Islands and Faeroe Islands. The aim of NFUE is to strengthen professional educational and vocational guidance in Nordic countries. NAEVG organizes seminars and conferences and develops cooperation with the Baltic countries. The European Lifelong Guidance Policy Network aims to assist the European Union Member States and the Commission in moving European cooperation on lifelong guidance forward in both the education and the employment sectors. The purpose is to promote cooperation at Member State level on lifelong guidance and to propose appropriate structures and support mechanisms in implementing the priorities identified in the Resolution on Lifelong Guidance (2004). The ELGPN was established by the Member States and the Commission has foreseen to support the activities of the network in 2007-2008 under the Lifelong Learning Programme.

International Labour Organization(ILO)

The ILO is the international organization responsible for drawing up and overseeing international labour standards. It is the only 'tripartite' United Nations agency that brings together representatives of governments, employers and workers to jointly shape policies and programmes promoting Decent Work for all. This unique arrangement gives the ILO an edge in incorporating 'real world' knowledge about employment and work.The organization publishes the results of research related to changing nature of work and employment which is important for policy makers and other users.

National Level Agencies

At national level the following organizations work in the area of guidance and counseling.

National Council of Educational Research and Training(NCERT)

The Department of Psychology and Foundation of Education(DEPFE), a Department under NCERT,New Delhi and Pandit Sunderlal Sharma Central Institute of Vocational Education(PSSCIVE) ,Bhopal a constituent of NCERT organize programme on guidance and Counselling.Some of the functions of PSSCIVE are:

- To advise and assist the Ministry of Human Resource Development, State Governments and Union Territory Administration in the implementation of the Vocational Education and Work Experience Programme.
- To function as the technical wing of the Joint Council of Vocational Education on all matters relating to Vocational Education Programme (VEP).
- To promote, supervise and guide the establishment of a comprehensive management system for VEP.
- To serve as a resource institution for both formal and non-formal VEP.
- To orient and train various key functionaries of VEP, including teachers.
- To evaluate and monitor VEP in States/UTs.
- To ensure uniformity and maintain quality standards in vocational teaching and learning.
- To provide guidance and counseling on Vocational Education and Training to the people at large.

DEPFE is the department of NCERT which coordinates guidance activities in the country. The department runs an International Diploma Course in Guidance and Counseling in collaboration with Commonwealth of Learning, Canada. This course is offered at the Department of Educational Psychology and Foundations of Education (DEPFE), NCERT New Delhi as well as five Regional Institutes of Education located at Bhubaneswar Bhopal, Mysore, Shillong, and Ajmer. Besides the department conducts training programme in the field of guidance and counseling. Central Institute for Research and Training in Employment Service (CIRTES) was established in October, 1964 under the aegis of Directorate General of Employment & Training (DGE&T), Ministry of Labour, Government of India. Later, in 1970 and in 1987, the Institute was expanded with the added responsibilities of developing career literature and to provide guidance for the promotion of self-employment. The Objectives of CIRTES are:

- Planning and conducting training programmes for Employment Service Personnel at State, National and International Levels.
- Conducting research into problems concerning the activities of the Employment Service.
- Development and publication of career literature and audio-visual aids for use in Vocational Guidance and Career Literature Programmes.
- Development of motivational material for promotion of self-employment.

There are four divisions of CIRTES, *i.e.* training division, research division, career study center and self employment guidance cell.

THE COMPONENTS OF VOCATIONAL GUIDANCE

The main components of vocational guidance include the following.

Analysis of the Individual

Self-appraisal of the student is a necessity. The student should have extensive knowledge about him/herself and match this information with such things as home background, school progress, work experience, personality, health, values, interests, aptitudes and achievement. The counsellor should assist the student to collect, analyse and use a variety of objective and subjective, psychological and social data about him/herself, so that he/she gains a better understanding of him/herself. The counsellor can administer interest and aptitude tests and provide occupational information.

Occupational Information

Occupational information is the publication and dissemination of facts on the nature and prospects for employment in different occupations. The data derived from selfappraisal enable the student to search for an occupation. For the student to have an intelligent match between him/herself and jobs, he/she needs knowledge of the occupational, industrial, and labour structure of the country, classifications of occupations, occupational requirements, entrance procedures, occupational distribution, training opportunities, and employment prospects, and occupational hazards. Self-employment is critical in an age when there are fewer jobs than the number of job seekers. Boys and girls need to be guided in assessing the resources around them, and exploring ways of making new products, and finding new sources of livelihood. In this regard, linkages between the guidance counsellor and science and technology should prove productive.

Consultation

The counsellor should give technical assistance to teachers, administrators and parents, and help them to be more effective. Personnel from a variety of occupations (e.g., medical, industrial), could be invited to speak to students.

Vocational Counselling

The major objective of vocational counselling is to assist the student to integrate the information about him/herself and the occupational world, and to develop a plan for career development. This involves a face-to-face encounter between a counsellor and a client. The student is assisted before any occupational selection is made, and measures are taken to meet occupational requirements. The student must possess an understanding and acceptance of her/his personality, interests, aptitudes, and background.

Placement

This is a co-operative enterprise which involves the services of the school, community and the student. The term 'placement' refers to helping the student obtain part-time or full-time employment. The term also includes giving the student work experience, and placing him/her in an appropriate vocational training institution. It involves record-keeping, vocational counselling, employment contacts, supervision, and follow-up.

Community Occupational Surveys and Follow-up Studies

The counsellor must conduct Community Occupational Surveys and Follow-up Studies of school-leavers, and procure data on local training and employment conditions, labour turn-over, and job opportunities. Such surveys should be conducted because the majority of workers find employment in their immediate environment or community. Follow-up studies on graduates should be made.

Evaluation

The counsellor should determine the impact of the vocational guidance programme on students, schools, and society, and find out how any deficiencies in the programme can be removed.

The Principles of Vocational Guidance

The provision of an effective vocational guidance service is based on the following principles:

- Vocational guidance is concerned primarily with the personal development of the individual.

- Human beings have a capacity for self-development, which is best encouraged through active involvement in the exercise.
- The primary way in which guidance is conducted lies through individual behaviour.
- Guidance is oriented towards co-operation, rather than compulsion, between the client and the counsellor. In other words, it is an activity based on mutual consent and trust.
- Guidance is based on recognising the dignity and worth of individuals as well as their right to choose.
- Guidance is a continuous educational process.
- Guidance demands that the counsellor should not be emotionally involved.

Exceptions to the Rule

The counsellor can apply the principles as he/she works with his/her clients. However, Miller gives exceptions to the rule. He is more specific in distinguishing between different guidance activities.

These are defined as follows:

- *Taking action or sponsorship:* leave it to the individual to act.
- *Advice-giving:* It will be appropriate occasionally to make suggestions to the client.
- *Structured learning experiences:* At times, clients may need an opportunity to learn through some form of instruction, such as role-playing.
- *Giving information:* The provision of reliable information, without any evaluation or judgement on the part of the helper, is an important part of guidance.
- *Counselling:* This enables the client to explore thoughts and feelings in a safe setting.

Occupational Information in Guidance

The dissemination of occupational information in guidance is carried out in the following ways:

- *General group guidance*: The counsellor collects information and makes it available to groups of students. The students also collect information on various occupations for themselves.
- *Teaching of occupations:* The counsellor meets a class and teaches them about different occupations.
- *Career day/week activities:* Lectures on different careers, career demonstrations, debates, and film shows, are provided by the school.
- *Trips and excursions to industrial establishments:* Students go out of school/ college to workplaces, to see things for themselves.

- *Career clubs*: The clubs can show films relating to careers, organise career quizzes, competitions, career conferences, dramas, and invite lecturers/employers to provide information on various careers.
- *Vacation jobs and work-study:* The school can assist students to obtain vacation jobs during the long vacation or provide work-study programmes.
- *Bulletin boards:* The school can display vocational, educational, and social information, on bulletin boards.
- *School subjects:* Teachers can relate their teaching of subjects to careers for which they are useful or applicable.

Kinds of Occupational Information Which Students Should Know

- *Employment prospects:* Are the employment prospects for this occupation expanding or diminishing?
- *Nature of Work:* What are the pleasant or unpleasant things workers have to do? What tools, equipment, or materials, are used? What are the hours of work? Are there any shifts?
- *Work Environment:* Is it hot, cold, humid, dry, wet, dirty, noisy, etc.?
- *Qualifications:* What are the academic and/or physical qualifications?
- *Aptitudes:* What are the I.Q. and other special aptitudes needed?
- *Interests*: What are the interests of people who succeed in this particular occupation?
- *Legal and professional*: Is a licence or certificate required?
- *Preparation*: What kind of education and training is needed?
- *Entrance*: Is it by examination, by application and interview, or by capital investment?
- *Likes or dislikes:* What are the likes and dislikes of the job?
- *Advancement:* What proportion of workers advance? And to what positions?
- *Earnings:* What are the earnings per month and year? How are wages paid?

APPROACHES TO CAREER GUIDANCE

Career guidance refers to services and activities which assist individuals, of any age and at any point throughout their lives, to make educational, training and occupational choices and to manage their careers. Such services may be found in schools, universities and colleges, in the workplace. It may take place individually or in group, and may be face-to-face or at a distance. It includes career information provision, assessment and self-assessment tools, counseling interviews, career education programmes. Guidance workers often encounter individuals having very little idea about the skills which they have and the career related to the skill. Sometimes, sufficient time devoted to the early stages of an interview, finding out about the individual. There are many approaches to career guidance as Computer-aided guidance.

Others are facial expression, especially glints in the eyes, can be used to know levels of interest in particular types of work. Often, the client will be interested in more than one. Individual judgement is required to look at likely interactions between traits, and selecting the appropriate one.

Holland's Theory of Career Development

The Holland Codes represents a set of personality types described in a theory of careers and vocational choice formulated by psychologist JOHN L. HOLLAND.Holland's theory argued that "the choice of a vocation is an expression of personality" and that the six factor typology he articulated could be used to describe both persons and work environments. His model has been adopted by the U.S. Department of Labour for categorizing jobs relative to interests. The Holland Codes are usually referred to by their first letters: RIASEC. He presents his theory graphically as hexagon. The shorter the distance between their corners on the hexagon, the more closely they are related. Holland's theory of career guidance is based on four basic assumptions. The first assumption is that most people can be characterized as one or a combination of six personality types. Second, the theory assumes that the work environment can be classified into the same six categories of personality. Third the theory assumes that people seek out environments compatible with their personality types. And, fourth, the theory holds that particular behavioural patterns emitted in any environment are determined by personality and environmental types. The six personality and work environment types described by Holland are as follows:

- *Realistic*—Working with your hands, tools, machines, and things; practical, mechanically inclined, and physical. *viz.* agriculture, computer engineer, basket ball player, chef, Gardner, martial arts, pilot etc
- *Investigative*—Working with theory and information, analytical, intellectual, scientific. *Viz.* lawyer, statistician, surgeon.
- *Artistic*—Non-conforming, original, independent, chaotic, creative. *Viz.* actor, writer,dancer.
- *Social*—Cooperative environments, supporting, helping, healing/ nurturing. *Viz.* psychologist, professor, social worker, physician.
- *Enterprising*—Competitive environments, leadership, persuading. *Viz* public relation, administration, journalism, marketing, management.
- *Conventional*—Detail-oriented, organizing, clerical. *Viz.* proof reader, copy editing, clerk, librarian.

VOCATIONAL AIMS IN EDUCATION

Bearing in mind the varied and connected content of the vocation, and the broad background upon which a particular calling is projected, we shall now consider education for the more distinctive activity of an individual.

An occupation is the only thing which balances the distinctive capacity of an individual with his social service. To find out what one is fitted to do and to secure an opportunity to do it is the key to happiness. Nothing is more tragic than failure to discover one's true business in life, or to find that one has drifted or been forced by circumstance into an uncongenial calling. A right occupation means simply that the aptitudes of a person are in adequate play, working with the minimum of friction and the maximum of satisfaction. With reference to other members of a community, this adequacy of action signifies, of course, that they are getting the best service the person can render. It is generally believed, for example, that slave labour was ultimately wasteful even from the purely economic point of view -- that there was not sufficient stimulus to direct the energies of slaves, and that there was consequent wastage. Moreover, since slaves were confined to certain prescribed callings, much talent must have remained unavailable to the community, and hence there was a dead loss.

Slavery only shows on an obvious scale what happens in some degree whenever an individual does not find himself in his work. And he cannot completely find himself when vocations are looked upon with contempt, and a conventional ideal of a culture which is essentially the same for all is maintained. Plato laid down the fundamental principle of a philosophy of education when he asserted that it was the business of education to discover what each person is good for, and to train him to mastery of that mode of excellence, because such development would also secure the fulfillment of social needs in the most harmonious way. His error was not in qualitative principle, but in his limited conception of the scope of vocations socially needed; a limitation of vision which reacted to obscure his perception of the infinite variety of capacities found in different individuals.

An occupation is a continuous activity having a purpose. Education through occupations consequently combines within itself more of the factors conducive to learning than any other method. It calls instincts and habits into play; it is a foe to passive receptivity. It has an end in view; results are to be accomplished. Hence it appeals to thought; it demands that an idea of an end be steadily maintained, so that activity cannot be either routine or capricious. Since the movement of activity must be progressive, leading from one stage to another, observation and ingenuity are required at each stage to overcome obstacles and to discover and readapt means of execution. In short, an occupation, pursued under conditions where the realization of the activity rather than merely the external product is the aim, fulfills the requirements which were laid down earlier in connection with the discussion of aims, interest, and thinking.

A calling is also of necessity an organizing principle for information and ideas; for knowledge and intellectual growth. It provides an axis which runs through an immense diversity of detail; it causes different experiences, facts, items of information to fall into order with one another. The lawyer, the physician, the laboratory investigator in some branch of chemistry, the parent, the citizen interested in his own locality, has a constant working stimulus to note and relate whatever has to do with his concern.

He unconsciously, from the motivation of his occupation, reaches out for all relevant information, and holds to it. The vocation acts as both magnet to attract and as glue to hold. Such organization of knowledge is vital, because it has reference to needs; it is so expressed and readjusted in action that it never becomes stagnant. No classification, no selection and arrangement of facts, which is consciously worked out for purely abstract ends, can ever compare in solidity or effectiveness with that knit under the stress of an occupation; in comparison the former sort is formal, superficial, and cold.

The only adequate training for occupations is training through occupations. The principle stated early in this book that the educative process is its own end, and that the only sufficient preparation for later responsibilities comes by making the most of immediately present life, applies in full force to the vocational phases of education. The dominant vocation of all human beings at all times is living -- intellectual and moral growth. In childhood and youth, with their relative freedom from economic stress, this fact is naked and unconcealed.

To predetermine some future occupation for which education is to be a strict preparation is to injure the possibilities of present development and thereby to reduce the adequacy of preparation for a future right employment. To repeat the principle we have had occasion to appeal to so often, such training may develop a machine-like skill in routine lines but it will be at the expense of those qualities of alert observation and coherent and ingenious planning which make an occupation intellectually rewarding. In an autocratically managed society, it is often a conscious object to prevent the development of freedom and responsibility, a few do the planning and ordering, the others follow directions and are deliberately confined to narrow and prescribed channels of endeavor. However much such a scheme may inure to the prestige and profit of a class, it is evident that it limits the development of the subject class; hardens and confines the opportunities for learning through experience of the master class, and in both ways hampers the life of the society as a whole.

The only alternative is that all the earlier preparation for vocations be indirect rather than direct; namely, through engaging in those active occupations which are indicated by the needs and interests of the pupil at the time. Only in this way can there be on the part of the educator and of the one educated a genuine discovery of personal aptitudes so that the proper choice of a specialized pursuit in later life may be indicated. Moreover, the discovery of capacity and aptitude will be a constant process as long as growth continues. It is a conventional and arbitrary view which assumes that discovery of the work to be chosen for adult life is made once for all at some particular date.

One has discovered in himself, say, an interest, intellectual and social, in the things which have to do with engineering and has decided to make that his calling. At most, this only blocks out in outline the field in which further growth is to be directed. It is a sort of rough sketch for use in direction of further activities. It is the discovery of a profession in the sense in which Columbus discovered America when he touched its shores. Future explorations of an indefinitely more detailed and extensive sort remain to be made. When educators conceive vocational guidance as something which leads up to a definitive, irretrievable, and complete choice, both education and the chosen vocation are likely to be rigid, hampering further growth. In so far, the calling chosen will be such as to leave the person concerned in a permanently subordinate position, executing the intelligence of others who have a calling which permits more flexible play and readjustment. And while ordinary usages of language may not justify terming a flexible attitude of readjustment a choice of a new and further calling, it is such in effect. If even adults have to be on the lookout to see that their calling does not shut down on them and fossilize them, educators must certainly be careful that the vocational preparation of youth is such as to engage them in a continuous reorganization of aims and methods.

THEORIES OF VOCATIONAL DEVELOPMENT

Ginsburg, Axelrad and Herma Theory

In Ginsburg's theory, the central idea is that vocational choice is a process which extends from late childhood to the end of adolescence. Nevertheless, it has been extended to be lifelong. The theory gives some guidelines as to how an individual develops, and may explore, crystallise, specify, and achieve, goals at different stages of his/her life. Thus, the counsellor notes the stages of development and helps the individual to achieve his/her goals.

Super's Self-Image Theory

In Super's theory, defining a vocational preference means making an occupational choice consistent with one's image of oneself. Therefore, the counsellor is no longer an expert in the accurate assessment of vocational choice. The counsellor is rather the person who helps the individual to discover who he/she is, and what he/she can become.

Holland's Theory

In Holland's theory, individuals and occupations are categorised according to the same scale of attributes. Vocational choice consists of choosing an environment which corresponds to one of the defined personality patterns emerging from the scale. Therefore, the counsellor's role is to help the individual make the best use of his/her skills, express his/her values, and take on roles which are gratifying.

Erikson's Theory

The central notion of Erikson's theory is that of identity, seen as the integration of emotions experienced during childhood. Each stage of development leaves its mark on an individual. For example, during adolescence, identity is stabilised through the formation of a set of ideals. Thus identity formation often implies resolving crises which had an impact on various stages of childhood. Hence the counsellor's role is less that of an expert who can best identify the occupation which best suits an individual (in particular an adolescent), but rather that of a specialist, who is there to aid people of all ages to achieve their personal goals. Thus, the counsellor helps people to become competent in their career development and concentrates less on their deficiencies.

Vocational Choice/Decision-making

A student makes a vocational choice if he/she expresses the intention to enter a particular occupation. A vocational choice results from a combination of factors. These include the student's opportunities to explore activities in the early school years, success in these activities, encouragement by others to continue, and later opportunities to fulfil the job demands for entry into the world of work.

General Principles of Vocational Choice

The following are the general principles on which vocational choice is based:

- *There are limits on your career options:* Entry into a particular occupation is not just a matter of choosing what you want to do, but you also have to persuade schools, colleges, and employers, to choose you for such a work. Therefore, your career options will be limited to some extent by your personality, abilities, financial resources, fluctuations in the economy, and the job market.

- *You have the potential for success in a variety of occupations*: People have considerable potential. There are thousands of different occupations to choose from. Therefore, do not expect to find one job that fits you perfectly and provides you with complete satisfaction, since you may spend your entire life searching for it.
- *Vocational choice is a developmental process extending throughout life:* It involves not a single decision but a series of decisions throughout life. A retired officer, for example, may consider the next vocational decision.
- *Some vocational decisions are not easily reversed:* Once you invest time, money, and effort, in pursuing a particular career, it may not be easy to change direction. This highlights why it is important for you to devote systematic thought and planning to making a vocational choice.
- *Vocational choice is an expression of your personality:* Holland asserts that we search for a work environment that fits our personality. He has identified the following personality types which he calls personal orientations: realistic, investigative, artistic, social, enterprising, and conventional. Thus, in the final analysis, vocational choice is the matching of your personal characteristics with an occupation. Hence the first step in systematic career planning is self-examination of your abilities and personality.

Decision-Making in Guidance

Tiedeman and O'Hara developed a Vocational Decision-Making (VDM) Model, which they named a 'paradigm of differentiation and integration' in attempting rational solutions to the problems of vocation. The problem-solving process is divided into two phases, called Anticipation and Implementation Adjustment, which distinguish between behaviour prior to, and after, making a decision.

In the anticipatory period, the problem-solving process is stimulated by experiencing a vocational problem and recognising that a decision must be made. Thus, the student should have a planning orientation. He must be aware of the need to make a decision before he/she consciously makes it. He should also be aware of the factors which should be considered when making decisions. He/she should also have a knowledge of the sources of information and of the resources which may be helpful. The anticipatory phase is sub-divided into four stages called Exploration, Crystallisation, Specification (or Choice) and Clarification.

Thus there are five major steps counsellors should consider in this VDM Model, namely:

- *Exploration*: This accounts for trial-and-error approaches whereby a number of different alternatives or possible goals are considered. A student, for example, may be engaged in exploratory behaviour, such as taking part in activities, reading, working during vacations, or after school. These activities often have vocational implications and help to crystallise vocational preferences.
- *Crystallisation*: Crystallisation describes attempts to clarify the order and pattern of goals. Goals are compared on the basis of competing demands, costs and returns, advantages and disadvantages. Thought about, the problem becomes more stable (less random), durable and reliable. Crystallisation results from exploration.
- *Clarification:* This stage, brought on by doubt experienced during the waiting period between choice and action, involves attempts to perfect the self-image. In thinking and talking about the information which the student has acquired, the consequences of decision become clearer. In this way decisions are then confirmed or rejected.
- *Specification or choice:* Choice involves commitment to one goal and, in turn, impels a person to act. The confirmatory experiences lead the student to a definite choice, which can be a preference or a choice which can be changed easily.
- *Implementation:* The implementation of a decision turns a preference into a choice. Some implementation acts are tentative but others are definitive.

5

Counselling

DEFINITION OF COUNSELLING

Counselling takes place when a counsellor sees a client in a private and confidential setting to explore a difficulty the client is having, distress they may be experiencing or perhaps their dissatisfaction with life, or loss of a sense of direction and purpose. It is always at the request of the client as no one can properly be 'sent' for counselling. By listening attentively and patiently the counsellor can begin to perceive the difficulties from the client's point of view and can help them to see things more clearly, possibly from a different perspective. Counselling is a way of enabling choice or change or of reducing confusion. It does not involve giving advice or directing a client to take a particular course of action. Counsellors do not judge or exploit their clients in any way.

In the counselling sessions the client can explore various aspects of their life and feelings, talking about them freely and openly in a way that is rarely possible with friends or family. Bottled up feelings such as anger, anxiety, grief and embarrassment can become very intense and counselling offers an opportunity to explore them, with the possibility of making them easier to understand. The counsellor will encourage the expression of feelings and as a result of their training will be able to accept and reflect the client's problems without becoming burdened by them. Acceptance and respect for the client are essentials for a counsellor and, as the relationship develops, so too does trust between the counsellor and client, enabling the client to look at many aspects of their life, their relationships and themselves which they may not have considered or been able to face before. The counsellor may help the client to examine in detail the behaviour or situations which are proving troublesome and to find an area where it would be possible to initiate some change as a start. The counsellor may help the client to look at the options open to them and help them to decide the best for them.

Models of Counselling

Although there is considerable consensus about the core content of a counselling course, there are nevertheless distinct methods of counselling. Most courses start from a theoretical base-typically humanistic, psychodynamic, cognitive or behavioural. Before enrolling on a course it is advisable to be aware of its theoretical emphasis and what that means in terms of the learning experience offered and the skills acquired.

Characteristics of Effective Counselling

Effective counselling is a two way street. It takes a cooperative effort by both the person receiving counselling and the counsellor. And it takes a commitment to make sometimes difficult changes in behaviour or thinking patterns. What you expect to achieve with your counsellor should be clearly defined as you begin your counselling. You and your counsellor should discuss realistic time frames for reaching your goals and agree on how you will measure your progress.

It's important that you and your counsellor establish a good relationship that allows you to be completely honest about your thoughts and feelings. Often, this requires an elusive "chemistry" between both of you in which you feel comfortable with your counsellor's personality, approach and style. If after the first few sessions you don't feel this chemistry, look for another counsellor with whom you feel more comfortable. Once you think you've found the right counsellor, how do you tell if your relationship is effective? Here are some signs to look for:

While you are responsible for making changes in your life, an effective counsellor can help pinpoint the obstacles in your way. If you have control over these obstacles, a counsellor can suggest behavioral changes to help you overcome them. If these obstacles involve factors outside of your control, your counsellor can teach you coping mechanisms that will foster your well being in trying circumstances.

An effective counsellor can identify negative thinking patterns that may be feeding feelings of sadness, depression or anxiety. By encouraging you to build upon personal strengths and suggesting skills that can overcome self-inflicted feelings of hopelessness, a counsellor can help you develop a more positive attitude.

A good counsellor can assist you in making positive changes in your relationships with others, helping you recognize behaviors that may be contributing to a troublesome relationship. Your counsellor can teach you effective ways of communicating, clearing the way for honest exchanges with people in your life who may be causing you emotional pain. You can determine whether your work with your counsellor is effective if you begin to obtain insights about your own thoughts and behaviors that may have eluded you before. Over time, you should be able to recognize patterns in the way you act, trace their sources and identify stumbling blocks to your happiness that you may have unwittingly created. The end result is personal growth that empowers you to control your life and enjoy positive, life-affirming relationships with others.

Objective

Primary Objectives: To provide a well founded Counselling Service, available to students and staff, in the university by:

- offering one-to-one counselling for personal and educational issues
- offering therapeutic group work
- offering a variety of personal skills training (e.g. examination preparation, assertiveness training) on a workshop basis
- developing awareness amongst staff of issues of concern to students
- contributing to providing training in tutoring and other skills relevant to staff in meeting their responsibilities to students

Secondary Objectives: To contribute to the creation of a positive environment for learning within the University by:

- using the knowledge gained through the nature of counselling to help the University identify and address areas of stress
- participation in policy making and policy implementation in areas directly related to student support

Objectives of Genetic Counselling

The results of a survey published in the Journal of Public Health suggest that, although purchasers, providers and users of genetic services are in broad agreement about the aims of such services, purchasers differ from providers and users in the relative priorities they assign to these aims. The study used the 'Delphi' technique to survey the attitudes of public health doctors and GPs (purchasers), clinical geneticists and genetic counsellors (providers) and users (outpatients and members of a support organisation). There was broad agreement that the five most important aims were to give information, give support, facilitate decision-making, enable risk assessment, and achieve understanding. However, purchasers assigned relatively higher priorities to facilitation of decision-making and risk assessment, while providers and users ranked giving information and support more highly.

Comment: There are several possible explanations for the difference between purchasers and the other groups, but at least on the surface it appears that those responsible for commissioning genetic services tend to value 'active' outcomes from these services, while those directly involved in the service, either as providers or users, value the more neutral aims of providing information and support. This difference may assume increasing importance as the potential range of genetic services widens.

Need Career Counselling?

What do you want to be when you grow up? Which one of us hasn't faced that question when we were younger? Most of us probably had an answer. Teacher! Fireman! Astronaut! The choices seemed endless then. But the question takes on a whole new significance for students fresh out of Class X or Class XII. In a world filled with career choices ranging from medicine to mass communications, engineering to event management, marine biology to information technology, the confusion teenagers face over which career to pick is understandable. A large number of students continue to choose a career based merely on the fact that their friends are doing the same thing or because their parents told them to do so. This, however, may not be the best way to go about it.

If you've just taken your Class X/ Class XII board exams, and are trying to decide on a profession, the first thing you need to realise is that every individual is different. Not everyone can be a doctor or an engineer (not everyone wants to be one!)—and that's okay!

Choosing a field of study that is not really suited to your interests or skills could prove disastrous. And that's where career counselling comes in.

What is Career Counselling?

Career counselling helps students discover their true potential and interest in various subjects in order to help them choose the right career. Several institutes, including schools and colleges, today offer career counselling through a series of aptitude and IQ tests. The tests usually have multiple-choice questions, which don't need to be prepared for in any way.

Then comes a face-to-face interview with a career guidance counsellor. The interview provides the student with the opportunity to clear any doubts or queries he/ she may have regarding career options and educational courses. It also allows the counsellor to further judge the aptitude of the student, thus building on the preliminary results of the written tests.

Varsha Rebello, manager and senior counsellor, Career Launcher India, says, "Career counselling is the guidance given to a student on the road he/ she should take to achieve his/her goals. The advice and counselling provided is based on three deciding factors — personality, aptitude and interest. The counsellor is trained in administering tests that determine the aptitude and skills of a child, his/her personality traits and subjects of interest."

CHARACTERISTICS OF A COUNSELLOR

Any counsellor has certain characteristics. These characteristics can be described under three headings. These headings are—

Personality Traits

Walter B. Jones has mentioned the following personality traits of a counsellor

Breadth of Interests—Each counsellor should have broad based interests i.e., the counsellor should take interest in the different types of persons, occupations and problems.

Farsightedness—The counsellor must have the farsightedness. He should understand the problems of teacher's. He should try to understand properly the problems of the pupils and have affection for them.

Feelings of Co-operation—The counsellor must possess the feelings of co-operation. He should co-operate all the workers and seek the co-operation from everybody.

Humble—The behaviour of the counsellor should be very humble towards the pupils and clients.

Magnetic Personality—The counsellor must have the magnetic personality so that he may win others confidence and may eliminate their tensions.

Training and Preparation

Myers has mentioned the following characteristics of the counsellor regarding his training and preparation-

1. He should have the knowledge of high-school objectives, curricula and methods.
2. He should have the knowledge of various activities about various occupations.
3. The counsellor should be equipped with the principles of guidance.
4. The counsellor should have received good education, such as, education of subjects like Sociology, Psychology, Economics, History, Geography etc.
5. The counsellor should have the full knowledge of organizing guidance services.
6. In the guidance services, the counsellor must have the knowledge of psychological tests.
7. The counsellor must have the knowledge of methods for providing occupational information.

The following educational qualifications for a counsellor have been prescribed—

(i) M.A. (Psychology or Education) or B.A., M.Ed. (With Guidance)

(ii) Diploma in Educational Guidance.

(iii) The counsellor should possess the knowledge of techniques for solving personality problems, testing, studying mental health and providing counselling.

Experiences

According to Smith, the counsellor should have the following experiences—

1. He should have attained the efficiency in the guidance programme. Such efficiency includes the following skills—
   (i) To understand the problems of children and pupils.
   (ii) To help in solving the problems of the client.
   (iii) To establish rapport with the children or clients.
2. To help in securing an occupation and to do correct actions.
3. Efficiency in interpreting every type of information.
4. Efficiency in using social means or resources.
5. To have ability to evaluate the counselling service.

Edward C. *Roebor* (1963) has also described the following characteristics of a counsellor—

Interpersonal Relationship—According to *Roeber*, the counsellor should have such an attraction that he may establish contacts very quickly with other persons, adolescents and youngsters. Such a counsellor is the owner of many qualities such as to understand youngsters sympathetically, fairness towards them, sincerity, ability to mix up with the persons, having interest among the persons and having interest in working with them, to be sensitive towards the attitude of others, patience, tactfulness, capability to win the confidence of others, social sensitivity, care of the people and their privacy, to pay more attention towards the attitude of others than own opinion etc.

Personal Adjustment—The counsellor has the capacity of personal adjustment. Personal adjustment includes the following—

(i) Maturity.
(ii) Emotional Stability.
(iii) Flexibility and Adaptability.
(iv) Sense of Humour.
(v) Knowledge of one's own Limitations.
(vi) Capability to Accept Criticism.
(vii) Self-respect and Self-confidence.
(viii) Capability of taking Advantage of Experiences.
(ix) Knowledge of Self
(x) Ability to Clarify the Things.

Ability of Leadership—An able counsellor must possess the ability of leadership so that he my win the hearts of others through his own behaviour.

Educational Background and Scholastic Potentialities—The counsellor should possess the higher educational background and scholastic potentialities. These potentialities may include the following

(i) Highly Cultured Social Interests.
(ii) Capacity of doing Work.
(iii) Intelligence.
(iv) Scholastic Aptitudes.
(v) Wide field of Knowledge and Aptitudes.
(vi) Regard for Facts.
(vii) Ability of making Good Decisions.

Philosophy of Life—The counsellor should have his own philosophy of life. This philosophy of life can be based on the following facts—

(i) Civic Sense.
(ii) Spiritualism and Religious Traditions.
(iii) Interests and Aesthetic Sense.
(iv) Faith in Human Nature.
(v) Good Behaviour and Healthy Philosophy of Life.

Health and Personal or Outer Appearance—The health and personal or outer appearance of the counsellor should be inspiring. This can include the following elements

(i) Physical Health.
(ii) Sweetness of Voice.
(iii) Attraction of Outer Personality.
(iv) Cleanliness.
(v) Other Behaviours of the Counsellor, such as, gestures, body movements or movements of body parts etc.

Professional Dedication—The counsellor must be dedicated completely to his profession. Only then he can be successful in his work. This identification of dedication, can be done on the basis of the following elements

(i) Professional Aptitudes.
(ii) Professional Attitudes.
(iii) Sense of Mission.
(iv) Loyalty and Enthusiasm for Educational Work.
(v) Interest towards the Employees appointed for the Welfare of the Students.
(vi) Strong Sense of Professional Ethics.
(vii) Professional Growth.

(viii) Will to Work Over Time.

(ix) To take Interest in Counselling Work.

According to Keller, the counsellor's personality should be impressive. He has considered the teacher equivalent to the counsellor. According to him, "The teacher is ideal whom the pupils follow". Hence, it is essential for him to create healthy and balanced beliefs and he should try to mould his personality according to them. In this way, Keller has considered the teacher's behaviour very important. Keller has emphasized the following characteristics of the counsellor.

Good Basic Intelligence—Good basic intelligence means the capability of using acquired knowledge through experiences and formal teaching. Hence, such capability is must for the counsellor.

Enriched General Knowledge—Inspite of the above mentioned qualities, the counsellor should also have the wide knowledge of vocational field. It will be helpful in his success.

Intensive Special Information—The counsellor's scope is very wider. He should try to collect special information for his specific task of the counselling. The counsellor should have the knowledge of future employment possibilities and essential qualifications for these employments and need of training etc.

Specific Skills—Each counsellor should have the knowledge of skills for using special technique, such as, interview technique, placement technique etc. In addition of these the counsellor should also know the techniques of collecting informations and tests of measurement etc.

Specific Personal Qualities—The counsellor should also possess the specific personal qualities, such as -loyalty for profession, sympathy, co-operation, objectivity and balanced behaviour etc. Inspite of this, the counsellor should be intelligent.

According to **Rogers** and **Wallen,** the counsellor should have the following qualities-

Belief in the Person's Capacity for Adjustment—The counsellor, is aware of the fact that most of the persons have the capacity of re-adjustment and adaptability. The counsellor should try to use this capacity.

Desire to help the Client Understand and Accept Himself—In the counselling process, it is very important that the client should be anxious himself to solve his problem. He should understand his problem properly and he should try to solve the problem with the help of the counselling. When the client gets assured that the counsellor is showing regard for the client's personality and his attitude is sympathetic, only then the client draws out his hidden feelings. In this role, the counsellor helps the client understanding him.

Respect for the Whole Person—The counsellor does not restrict his own role to the vocational placement only. The counsellor focuses on all the efforts of the person and anxieties or in short, focuses on the wholeness of the client.

Tolerance and Acceptance of the Client's Difference—The client has to search out the solution of the problem himself The counsellor cannot explain the description of the solution of the problem as a doctor can present the details of the medicines. The counsellor should exhibit his interest for the welfare of the client. In order to do so, the counsellor will have to bear the difference in the talks of the client. The counsellor should not consider the client according to his own norms or standards.

Respect for the Personal Autonomy of the Client—The counsellor should function in the light of the fact that the client has the freedom and right to take decisions about himself The client may refuse too to seek help from the counsellor. The client may make use of the suggestions made by the counsellor according to his own intelligence. In one sense, the client himself is responsible for his own life.

In the same way, **Steffler and Stewart** have also considered necessary some qualities for a successful counsellor. The qualities are as follows-

Ethical Behaviour—Possession of ethics is a compulsory condition for any counsellor. The counsellor also receives some confidential informations. To restrict these informations to himself is the duty of a good counsellor too. If the client has no assurance in this regard, the client will not believe the counsellor. Also, he will not exhibit himself freely. There will be no sound relation between the counsellor and the client. Hence ethical behaviour is must for the counsellor.

Intellectual Competence—Intellectual competence of a counsellor is very useful for a successful counselling process. He should have the ability to relate a person's behaviour and the current events. He should also have the ability of logical thinking.

Flexibility—The counsellor should never be traditional. He should be alert regarding the changes occurring in the attitudes or view-points of the client. He should control his behaviours in accordance with these changes. He should bring changes in his own behaviours by exhibiting his flexibility Only then he can prove himself as a successful counsellor.

Sensitivity—The sensitivity of the counsellor should be appreciable, i.e., he should be aware of honesty and duties. In the process of counselling the honesty and the awareness about the duty to make the role of the counsellor impartial contribute specially i.e., if the counsellor functions sincerely to perform his duties, only then this process happens to be successful.

Understanding—The counsellor should understand the client completely. In order to understand him completely, he should study him at the effective and thoughts level. The counsellor can link himself with both the levels.

Acceptance—It is the quality of the counsellor to accept everything of the client, because when the client approaches to the counsellor, he is surrounded by optimism, pessimism, doubts and fears etc. In such situations acceptance should be granted to everything of the client. In short, no one can be labelled as a successful counsellor by ignoring the facts regarding the personality of the client.

Under various researches, the qualities or characteristics of a counsellor have been enlisted. Cox has enlisted the following 24 characteristic of a successful counsellor—

1. Fairness.
2. Sincerity.
3. Personality.
4. Good Character and Wholesome Philosophy
5. Common Sense.
6. Health.
7. Emotional Stability.
8. Approachability.
9. Ability to get along with people.
10. Sympathetic Understanding of Youth.
11. Interest in People.
12. Understanding People different from Self
13. Flexibility and Adaptability.
14. Intelligence and Mental Alertness.
15. Social Culture.
16. Broad Knowledge and Interests.
17. Leadership.
18. Awareness of one's own limitations.
19. Professional Attitude.
20. Sense of Mission.
21. Interest in Guidance and Personnel Work.
22. Understanding of classroom conditions.
23. Understanding of Working Conditions.
24. Understanding of Social and Economic Conditions.

In the Indian conditions, no sufficient research has been done regarding the characteristics' of a counsellor. But some counsellors working in schools and counsellor have insisted on the following characteristic

1. The teacher should be a counsellor. He knows all the pupils and vice-versa. The pupils can well-explain about their problems.
2. The counsellor should be able to listen the client properly.
3. He should have the ability to initiate conversations with the client
4. The co-operation of the pupils and their participation are essential for a successful counsellor. If such co-operation and participation of the pupils are absent, then it would be difficult for the counsellor to help the pupils Sometimes, the client opposes such help. Counselling is considered as voluntary service.
5. The counsellor should respect the client. In turn, the client should also see the counsellor respectfully. In this way, the process of mutual respect goes on.
6. The counsellor should be honest in recognizing his training and limitations of the skills.
7. The counsellor should be able to attract the confidence of the pupils.
8. The counsellor should possess the ability of recognizing the merits of the client and encouraging them.
9. The counsellor should have the links with the client as a person and not as a symptom or as a problem.
10. The counsellor should be sensitive towards the problem. This sensitivity of the counsellor is his important peculiarity or characteristic.

Training Programme for Counsellor

The professional training of the counsellors is an important progress occurred in our country recently. In our country, there are very few institutes providing training programmes.

Most of the training programmes are short-term in which providing informations and vocational guidance are more insisted. In some institutes these are termed as 'Career Masters Course.' Then these are not termed as 'Training for counsellors'. In most of the teaching institutions, the counselling programme is going on at the following stage

(a) In schools and colleges, any teacher is assigned the additional work of the counsellor for part-time or full-time. Such a teacher is selected after considering his interest towards the counselling. Also, his ability to make the persons to follow him and ability to establish confidence with the pupils are also evaluated. These teachers do not have any preparation for this job, but they can perform the role of an advisor. In-service and short-term courses for such teachers can play an important and positive role in developing the skill of providing educational and vocational informations.

(b) The second stage of functioning the counsellor is to act as a full-time counsellor. It is impossible that a pupil comes with a pure educational or pure vocational problem. A full-time counsellor has proper training and hence, he is capable of solving all types of problems. Such counsellors use psychological tests and their interpretations. These persons select counselling as a specific area for training.

(c) Providing training to the counsellor for counselling at the Post Master's level is considered of the highest level. The highly educated counsellors can play an important role in planning and administration of counselling programmes. But in Indian conditions, such highly educated counsellors have no opportunity in schools and colleges.

American School Counsellor's Policy Statement has determined the following conditions for the training of the counsellors—

1. The school counsellor should be a graduate in education and have master's degree in counselling. In addition to this, he should have the certificate in counselling from the state where he is appointed.
2. Certificates of more than one stage or level should be awarded. For this, there can be a graduate study of two-years.
3. The following elements should be included in the school counsellor's education or training programme
   (a) Occupational study which should include the following—
      (i) Developmental and Educational Psychology.
      (ii) Counselling Theory and Procedures.
      (iii) Educational and Psychological Appraisal.
      (iv) Group Theory and Procedures.
      (v) The Psychology and Sociology of Work and Vocational Development.
      (vi) The Functions and Methodology of Research.
      (vii) The Legal and Professional Ethics of Counselling and Education.
   (b) To arrange the development of a background according to the specific needs and developmental stages of the pupil in the Humanities, Social Sciences, Behavioural and Life Sciences by the Counsellor.
   (c) Supervised experiences, such as- Laboratory, Practicum and Internship Work.
   (d) To arrange for the understanding of Psychological and Social environments of learning conditions and school curriculum in the school.

4. The educational programme of the school counsellor should be well-planned and according to the specific background of each pupil and his specific needs.
5. The educational programme of school counsellor does not cease to occur with the completion of the formal programme, but it continues till the counsellor's career.

Gilbert Wrenn, on the request of American Personnel and Guidance Association, with the help of his associates, has given the following suggestion for the training of the counsellors—

1. There should be two main subjects for the education of counsellors - the area of Psychology and areas of Social and Behavioural Sciences.
2. The following subjects should be included in the two-years graduation programme for the counsellor
   (i) Educational Philosophy and methods of school curricula.
   (ii) Supervised Experiences.
3. The trained persons of the related subjects should teach the counsellors such as, psychologist should teach the psychological curricula, social scientists should teach social science curricula.
4. Supervised experiences are necessary in order to award certificates at each level of counselling education.

In 1950, a committee set up by the Division of Counselling Psychology of the American Psychological Association has given the following steps for the preparation of the counsellor.

Personality Organization and Development—It includes the subjects related to the personality such as-theories of personality, methods of development, cultural determinants and their links with the personality etc.

Knowledge of Social Environment—It includes community, informations regarding social institutions etc.

Personal Therapeutic Experience—It has not been considered compulsory for the counsellor-education programme.

Research and Statistics—It is not expected from the school counsellor that he should conduct research for the whole day, but he should possess some knowledge of research methods and statistics.

Professional Orientation—In this, a pupil or a person is able to understand structural and administrative framework in which he is to function as a counsellor.

DIFFERENT TYPES OF COUNSELLING

With regard to the nature of the counselling procedure and the role of the counsellor, there are three following schools of thoughts in the counselling—

Prescriptive Counselling

Counsellor-centred counselling revolves around the counsellor. He tries to establish good relations through the friendship and assistance. In this, the counsellor is very active and he expresses his ideas and attitudes independently. He evaluates the expressions of the client. According to this view-point the counselling leads the interview. In this, the counsellor asks a series of standardized questions. Each question carries a short answer. The counsellor does not allow the development of client's expression and feelings. He leads as an expert, evaluates and gives suggestion or advice.

The chief advocate of this school is E.G. Williamson of the University of Minnesota. Hence, according to this school of thought, the counsellor owns entire responsibility of solving client's problem. In this procedure, the counsellor explores the problem and defines it, diagnoses it and tells about the remedy of the problem.

Steps in Directive Counselling

Williamson has described the following 6 steps of directive counselling—

Analysis: In this steps, data and informations are collected regarding the situation or the client which can be used in the counselling process as a valid and reliable base. For this counselling step, the following tools are used

(a) Cumulative records.
(b) Interview.
(c) Time distribution Form.
(d) Autobiography.
(e) Anecdotal Record.
(f) Psychological Tests.

For the integration of entire data, case-history method is used. It includes family-history, recreational interests and habits etc.

Synthesis: Williamson has defined synthesis as - "The process of summarizing and organizing of the data from the analysis in such a manner as to reveal the student's assets, liabilities, adjustments and mal-adjustments."

Diagnosis: Diagnosis consists of the interpretations of the data in terms of the problems indicated and assets and liabilities, the strengths and weaknesses of the student.

Diagnosis has the following main three steps-

(a) Identification of Problem.
(b) Discovering the cause.
(c) Prognosis.

Prognosis: This step can be a part of diagnosis and can be a separate step too. It depends upon the available specific information. Where the result of the problem or knowledge of the situation then the prognosis becomes the part of the diagnosis. Both, prognosis and diagnosis are cooperative processes in between the counsellor and the client.

Counselling or Treatment: It is that step when the counsellor helps the client. In this, various questions are answered. Client answers these questions for himself, such as, How I can make changes in self? What can be its alternate? If such goes on, how the progress will occur in future?

Follow-up: In this step, the evaluation of the effectiveness of the counselling procedure is alone and in this, it is observed what the client could achieve through counselling?

Basic Assumptions of Directive Counselling

According to Andrews and Willy, the following can be the basic assumptions of directive counselling—

Competency in giving Advice: The counsellor possesses the best training, experience and informations. He is more competent to provide an advice to solve the problem.

Counselling as an Intellectual Process—Any client's intellectual capability is not destroyed as a result of his mal-adjustment. Hence, counselling is primarily an intellectual process. It stresses upon the intellectual aspects of a person instead of his emotional aspects of the personality.

Counselling Objectives as Problem Solving Situation—The objectives of counselling, are achieved through problem solving situation.

Client's Incapability of Solving the Process—The counsellor assumes that the client does not possess the capability for solving the problem always.

Hence, we observe that the direct and explanatory methods are suggested. In such a counselling focus should be on the problem instead of the person and the client should cooperate in the entire process. The client is to act under the counsellor, not along with him. According to Williamson, the following are the assumptions of such type of counselling-

(i) The goal of the counselling is to help the person in his all-round development of the personality.

(ii) The counselling accepts the person's uniqueness.

(iii) The counselling is based on the desirability and not on forcing the counselling on a person.

(iv) The counselling should be provided only when the pupil faces some problem and when he himself fails to solve the same. From this point of view, counselling is remedial.

(v) In counselling, the mutual relations are neutral.

(vi) The counselling is focus on the self-assumption regarding the client's problem.

(vii) The counsellor respects the dignity of the client.

Hence, Williamson looks the counsellor as a teacher whose duties are to enable a person to understand his own capacities, attitudes and interests, self-motivation and identification of life-techniques etc.

Characteristics of Directive Counselling

1. The counsellor plays a vital role in the process.
2. It gives advice to the client.
3. In this process, the focal point is the problem, not the person.
4. The client is sub-ordinate to the counsellor, not at par.
5. The methods used in this counselling are direct, persuasive and explanatory.
6. Counselling stresses more on the person's intellectual aspect than the emotional' aspect of his personality.

Advantages of Directive Counselling

1. This method is useful from the time-consumption view-point. It saves a lot of time.
2. In this type of counselling, there is more focus on the problem and less on the person.
3. The counsellor can look the client directly.
4. Counselling focuses more on the intellectual aspect of the person than his emotional aspect of the personality.
5. In this process, the counsellor becomes readily available to help the client which makes the client very happy.

Limitations of Directive Counselling

1. In this process the client is more dependent. He is also unable to solve the new problems of mal-adjustment.
2. As the client is never independent of the counsellor, it is not an effective and best guidance.
3. Unless and until a person does not develop some attitudes through experiences he cannot make any decision himself This type of guidance always lacks such experience and development of attitudes.
4. The counsellor fails in saving the client to commit the mistakes in future.
5. There is scarcity of informations regarding the pupil which creates the possibility of wrong counselling.

Client centred or Permissive Counselling

The main advocate of non-directive or client-centred or permissive counselling is Carl R. Rogers. This principle was developed in many years. Hence, various areas got included in such type of counselling, such as, the development of personality, group leadership, education and learning, creativity, interpersonal relations and the nature of an entirely active person This theory was developed in between 1930 and 1940. This theory believes that the sufficient means of solving a person's problem are present within the person himself The function of the counsellor is to provide such an environment in which the client is independent to grow so that he may become what he likes to become. This school of thought gives importance to the emotional aspects of vocational and emotional problem and disapproves the diagnostic information as a part of counselling process. The client-centred counselling revolves around the client. In this, the client is encouraged to lead in conversation and to express his own attitudes, feelings and ideas. The counsellor mostly remains passive. He never interferes the client's ideas, thoughts, feelings, flow of expressions. The counsellor helps the client in completing his conversation. Basically" the counsellor makes his efforts to develop rapport and mutual feeling of confidence in both the parties.

In this approach, open-end questions are asked. These questions are loosely structured. In the answers of these questions, the person projects his own personality. The main concern of the counsellor is with the summarization of emotional contents told by the client.

When the client is answering, he should be encouraged to speak in detail through proper methods. The client feels that the counsellor really respects the client's ideas. He gets the impression from the types of questions which a counsellor asks from the client and the interviewer is taking interest in the client.

The counsellor does not ask the questions merely to explore the facts. In the non-directive counselling, every person has the right to be independent as a specialist psychologist. In such type of counselling, diagnostic instruments are used either infrequently or completely not used. This counselling is a growth experience. In this, the client can act with his own intellect or understanding. In this, emotional or affective aspects are more emphasized than the intellectual aspects.

Steps in Non-Directive Counselling

Carl Rogers has given the following steps of this non-directive counselling-

Defining the Problematic Situation—First of all the counsellor should define the problematic situation.

Development of Insight—The counsellor goes on thinking regarding the client's new feelings along with the development: of client's insight and he goes on classifying all those new feelings.

Free Expression of Feelings—After the first step, the client is made aware of the fact that he can express his feelings freely and the counsellor approves this.

Classification of Positive and Negative Feelings—After the free expression of feelings by the client, the counsellor identifies his negative and positive feelings and he classifies them.

Termination of Counselling Situation—The counsellor, looks for a point where he can terminate the counselling situation after all the above steps. According to this school of thought, either the client or the counsellor can suggest for such termination of counselling situation.

Basic Assumptions of Non-Directive Counselling

Tendency towards actualization—In the earlier writings of Rogers it was emphasized that the person's or client's growth and developmental capacity is that person's characteristic on which the methods of counselling and psychotherapy depend. Even after so many years, his this opinion got strength that a persons' inherent tendency includes growth, adjustment, socialization, freedom etc. This directional tendency is termed as 'Actualizing Tendency' these days.

Man is Trustworthy—Rogers considers the person basically good and reliable. He also knows that the person behaves in an unreliable manner too. A person is born with some urges which must be controlled if healthy personality development is desired.

Belief in the dignity of man—Rogers believes in the dignity of the man. He considers the person capable of taking decisions and he accepts his right to do so.

Man is Wiser than His Intellect—When some organization is functioning independently and effectively, then the 'awareness' is a very small part or component of the entire process. When the organization feels some difficulty in its system of functioning this awareness becomes more sharpened and focussed.

Snyder has also mentioned the following assumptions of non-directive counselling-

(i) The client has right to select the goals of his life.

(ii) If the client is given an opportunity, he will select those goals which may possibly provide him great happiness.

(iii) In the counselling situation, one should reach very quickly at a point from where the client may be able to start functioning independently.

(iv) Emotional disturbance inhibits a person's proper adjustment initially.

Limitations' of Non-Directive Counselling

1. This counselling is not so deep like psycho-analysis.

2. The client is allowed far the free expression of his present attitudes but it is not attempted to explain why these attitudes occur? There is no research regarding the past, no suggestion, no attempt of re-education.
3. This counselling has a drawback of lack of permission far flexibility to the counsellor.
4. This client-centred theory suffers the basic defect that it does not care how the behaviour is affected by the stimulus-situation and the nature of the environment.
5. Many counselling situations do not arise successfully in this client-centred counselling.
6. It is a time-consuming process. Once the client starts his conversation, he does not cease to speak. This makes the other's turn far seeking counselling impassible.
7. The client cannot depend on his resources, decisions and intellect.
8. All the problems cannot be salved orally or verbally or by talks.
9. It is not possible in all the schools because the counsellor has to attend many pupils.
10. Sometimes, due to the counsellor's passiveness, the client hesitates in expressing his feelings.

Characteristics of Non-Directive Counselling

1. It is a client-centred counselling.
2. It is based on the principle that a person has so much capacity and drive that he can grow and develop so that he may face the situations in reality.
3. In this school of thought, the counsellor is passive to the maximum.
4. A person is accepted in his originality and he is free-to express his any attitude.
5. Through this counselling, his psychological adjustment improves.
6. Its use reduces psychological tensions.
7. In this type of counselling, defensiveness falls dawn.
8. In this type of counselling, there is closeness between the picture of the self drawn by the client and a desirable or an ideal picture of his awn.
9. Client's behaviour is considered mare matured emotionally.
10. In his research **Axlines** (1947) has shown that the reading improvement speeds up as a result of client-centred play way-methods in the primary schools even if special reading instructions are not given.
11. The general aim of the counsellor in client-centred counselling is to bring changes in the functioning of the client and the organization.

12. This school of thought is just reverse to that of directive counselling
13. In this counselling, the entire responsibility is of client or the person.

Advantages of Non-Directive Counselling

1. The development of the problem-solving ability in the client through his school of thought is definite.
2. Being client-centred school of thought, other unwanted activities and tests can be avoided..
3. This school of thought shifts the person from his unconscious state of mind to the conscious state of mind and releases tension.
4. This type of counselling leaves its impressions for a longer period.

ECLECTIC COUNSELLING

Steps in Eclectic Counselling

Study of the Needs and Personality Characteristics of the Client—According to this school of thought, the counsellor investigates the client's needs initially. In this step too he gathers information regarding the characteristics of aversion's personality.

Seeking the Opinion of the Client and other related People—Opinion of the client and other related people are sought regarding the programme concerning counselling, other objectives and subjects etc.

Selection of Techniques—In this step, need-based techniques are selected and these are used in accordance with the needs of the person.

Application of Techniques—The selected techniques are applied in specific situations only. The utility of the selected techniques is observed in the context of the client.

Evaluation of Effectiveness—In this step, the evaluation of effectiveness is done through various methods.

Preparation for Counselling—Here, preparation is done for guidance and counselling.

Characteristics of Eclectic Counselling

According to Thorne, the following are the characteristics of eclectic counselling—

1. In this, objective and coordinating methods are used.
2. In the beginning of counselling, client-active methods are used and the counsellor remains passive.
3. In this, more importance is assigned to the job-efficiency and treatment.
4. In this, the principle of low expenditure is emphasized.
5. In such counselling, for the use of all the methods and techniques. The professional efficiency and skill in the counsellor are must.

6. Keeping in mind the need of the client, it is decided whether directive method or non-directive method should be used.
7. Making an opportunity available to the client is insisted so that he may find himself the solution of the problem.

Meaning

Sometimes, some counsellors agree neither directive counselling nor non-directive counselling school of thoughts. In such a situation, the counsellor succeeded in developing another type of counselling. This school of thought lies in between directive and non-directive counselling. This school of thought is known as Eclectic Counselling. In such type of counselling; the counsellor is neither active (Directive Counselling) nor passive (Non-directive Counselling). The chief advocate of this type of counselling is F. C. Thorne. In this type of counselling the needs of a person and his personality are studied by the counsellor. After this, the counsellor selects those techniques, which are useful for a person.

In this process of counselling, the counsellor may start with the directive counselling method and after some time, he can follow non-directive counselling procedure or vice versa as the situation demands. In this, the techniques should be according to the situations and the client. In this type of counselling, the main techniques used are reassurance, giving information, case-history, testing etc. Hence, in this eclectic counselling, both the counsellor and the client are active and cooperative. But they participate in Conversation turnwise and solve the problem jointly.

Limitations of Eclectic Counselling

1. Some people are of the view that this type of counselling is vague and opportunistic.
2. Both, directive and non-directive counselling cannot be mixed together.
3. In this, the question arises how much freedom should be given to the client? For this, there is no definite rule.

Inspite of this controversy, its practical value is very high. Hence, we see that the counselling is a learning process in which both the client and the counsellor learn something.

ROLE OF THE COUNSELLOR

E.G. Williamson has explained the role of a counsellor in detail in an edited book "Theories of Counselling". This book was edited by Buford Stuffier and W. Harold Grant. The summarization of role of a counsellor explained in this book is as follows—

The aim of the counsellor is to help the students in changing their behaviour through learning. The pupils also want to know maximum about their own characteristics, their abilities, their interests and their behaviours etc. They should also come to know what the importance or utility this knowledge of all these possess for the complete behaviour of the person. The client must know other alternate opportunities available for him. The counsellee should also know what the society can make available, the conditions imposed by the society presentation of awards and the possibilities to achieve them.

The client should know the methods to associate himself with the society. He should also learn what decision he should take? How decisions are, taken? How the decision making process can be made a continuous process.

The aim of the counsellor is to help the students in modifying their: behaviour through learning. From this point of view, the counsellor is just like a teacher. Effective counselling and effective teaching both depend upon the personal relationship between the teacher and life pupil. The content and the method both make the counselling effective. The content includes the single item of the behaviour or a few items of the behaviour. The content is different in every person. In the same person, the content is different, from time to time. Both, the counsellor and the client decide which behaviour is to be changed. They can also decide whether this changed behaviour is focussed on educational or vocational decision.

The counsellor, along with the client, collect the informations about the client and his surroundings. They think over the importance and utility of these informations. Also, they reject some of the informations and same are followed-up. Each item of the information can be a source of the botheses. The counsellor asks questions when he thinks it proper. The form of these questions are such that the counsellor can get the information to understand the client. These questions are also framed just to fasten the process of self-understanding. The counsellor should use these questions very carefully. Sometimes unintelligent and excessive use of the questions may be harmful.

Sometimes the counsellor listens only carefully. Rest of the time he remains busy in conversation with the client. He puts some general suggestions too. Sometimes general suggestions are given in the initial stage of the counselling and specific suggestions later on.

The counsellors also provide informations to the client. These informations are regarding the client, about social environment, about selected psychological concepts and regarding the decision-making process. Sometimes information's are gained in the form of figures from the test scores, school-record or other sources. At some occasions, the counsellor discovers the feelings, attitudes and values and presents the same information obtained from the client, to the client again. The client is unaware of such information. In addition to new data, the counsellor gathers those data too which the client knows.

The counsellor interprets the information about the counsellee or client. Undoubtedly this job is concerned with the organization of the data, but sometimes it is of different type of activity because in this, more attention is paid towards the client's reaction for such informations.

The counsellor makes available the informations about counsellee's social environment, such as, informations about employments, schools, economic sources, community facilities and services training programmes, directions of progress or responsibilities of citizens etc. These informations also include the prevailing attitudes in the community, social values, changes occurring in the attitudes and values or about the nations.

In the process of counselling, the counsellor goes on providing informations regarding the concepts of human behaviour. For example, the counsellor discusses about the concepts of trait and factor, with the client for a long time. The counsellor can help to make distinction between the ability of the pupil and his interests.

He can supply some such informations which make the pupils clear about their intelligence, academic ability, mechanical attitude, clerical aptitude etc. The counsellor can make efforts to provide informations about the nature of ambivalent behaviour.

Many pupils are very much concerned about the fact that they are unable to select that occupation towards which they are highly attracted and repelled too. The counsellor can help such clients. The counsellor can provide information about other psychological principles. Other persons are unable to understand human bisexual nature. This nature becomes the cause of anxiety. By providing informations about these principles the counsellor can help the client by interpreting such informations associating with other available data

The role of the counsellor also includes providing information to the client about decision-making process. He can review these decisions too in association with the client which have been taken earlier by life client. He can explain the client that the decisions are taken gradually. The counsellor should ensure the client that majority of the decisions will not be reversed. The counsellor can act as an advisor too. He can advise the pupil to delay the decision, to make tentative decision, to gather more informations, to discuss with others about the decisions or to take tests. Such an advice helps the pupil in making decisions at his own.

The counsellor can converse with other persons too confidentially in addition to the conversation with the client. This conversation would be the part of the counselling. The counsellor can talk to the parents, teachers, employers or friends. Such confidential talks are held so that effective functioning with the client may occur. The counsellor is also responsible for collecting informations about the counsellee in addition to the informations collected by others. The counsellor can give psychological tests to the counsellee and he can recommend him to those persons who perform such tests. The record of scores of these tests is collected. The counsellor can verify the school, health and work records and other informations about the counsellee.

The counsellor gathers informations regarding the relevant environment in which the counsellee lives or can live in future. He collects informations regarding schools, occupations and communities. If the counsellee belongs to such neighbourhood with which the counsellor is unknown, then the counsellor would try to learn more and more about that neighbourhood. The counsellor tries to know maximum about the school from which the counsellee comes. Out of the important tasks one important task of the counsellor is to collect normative data The scores collected from any test are meaningless if these are not compared with the scores of persons whose characteristics are known. Most of the tests have many norms. The counsellor is to decide which norm would be appropriate for comparison. But sometimes proper norms are not available. Then the counsellor is to decide how these norms should be achieved. The counsellor needs normative data not for tests only, but also for other behaviour indices.

Myers has also made references of main duties of the counsellor. According to him the following are the main duties of the counsellor—

(i) To set timings of meeting.
(ii) To arrange the meeting.
(iii) To prepare for meeting.
(iv) To hold meeting.
(v) To keep the record of the meeting.

Stewart has mentioned the following duties of the counsellor—

(i) To help the pupil to determine the value of his experiences.
(ii) To collect the base material concerning the person.
(iii) To understand the needs and problems of a person.
(iv) To hold a meeting.
(v) To establish coordination between the school and family, school and the class
(vi) To maintain coordination among the school activities.
(vii) To establish coordination between the progress in education and social contacts.
(viii) Group guidance.

ORGANIZATION OF GUIDANCE SERVICES IN SCHOOLS

Guidance in Second Level Schools

Guidance in schools refers to a range of learning experiences provided in a developmental sequence, that assist students to develop self-management skills which will lead to effective choices and decisions about their lives. It encompasses the three separate, but interlinked, areas of personal and social development, educational guidance and career guidance.

Counselling in Second Level Schools

Counselling is a key part of the school guidance programme, offered on an individual or group basis as part of a developmental learning process and at moments of personal crisis. Counselling has as its objective the empowerment of students so that they can make decisions, solve problems, address behavioural issues, develop coping strategies and resolve difficulties they may be experiencing. Counselling in schools may include personal counselling, educational counselling, career counselling or combinations of these.

The Aims of Guidance and Counselling

The guidance and counselling process aims to help students to develop an awareness and acceptance of their talents and abilities; to explore possibilities and opportunities; to grow in independence and to take responsibility for themselves; to make informed choices about their lives and to follow through on those choices. In this document, the word *guidance* is used to describe the activities provided by the *guidance and counselling* services identified under *support services* in paragraph 2 of the Education Act 1998.

The Importance of Guidance and Counselling

Significant changes are taking place in economic and social structures in this country which have important implications for the education system and for the students who are its principal focus. The value of guidance and counselling in responding to these challenges is widely recognised in Government policy statements and by other national and international bodies:

- The National Development Plan (NDP) 2000-2006 states that the provision of guidance and counselling in second level schools is vital to enable each pupil to gain the maximum benefit from the education system. The NDP identifies the school guidance service as a social inclusion measure within the education sector. The New Deal 1998 also supports this theme, it states that guidance plays a *major preventative role in helping young people at risk to stay within the formal education system.*

- The importance of lifelong guidance is emphasised by the White Paper *Learning for Life - 2000,* which lists it as a key support *necessary for successful access and learning.*
- The Commission on the Points System states that *good quality, comprehensive guidance can contribute significantly to broadening the views of second-level students and their parents on diverse pathways to careers. The Commission supports the need for an effective and comprehensive guidance and counselling service in schools and considers that the provision of such a service should be viewed in terms of the right of a student to access to an appropriate level of such services.*
- The Organisation for Economic Co-operation and Development (OECD), which carried out a comparative review of national policies for career information, guidance and counselling services in 14 OECD countries, including Ireland, describes guidance within education systems as having an important role to play in laying the foundations for lifelong career development, *including knowledge and competencies regarding self-awareness, the world of work, and making decisions and transitions. It defines guidance services as services that assist individuals, of any age and at any point throughout their lives, to make educational, training and occupational choices and to manage their careers.* It stresses that effective advice and guidance on educational and training options and on links between these options and later occupational destinations *can help better match individuals' learning choices to their interests, talents and intended destinations.* In the OECD's view, this can help to reduce early school leaving, improve flows between different levels of education and improve transitions from education to the labour market. It states that *these outcomes help to make better use of educational resources, and to increase both individual and social returns to investments in education.* A report of the review was published by the OECD in 2004.
- European Union Presidency Conclusions on the importance of guidance throughout life in supporting and furthering the Lisbon Agenda10, issued after the informal meeting of the European Ministers for Education and the Commission of the European Union in Dublin on 28/29 April 2004, stress the importance of all European citizens having access to guidance services at school level and at all later life stages, as appropriate and reflecting local circumstances. The need for particular attention to be paid to early intervention with individuals and groups at risk of not completing their schooling and at risk of alienation from society is highlighted as well as the need for provision for persons with special educational needs.

- In May 2004, a Resolution1 was adopted by the Council of Ministers of the European Union on Strengthening Policies, Systems and Practices in the field of Guidance throughout life in Europe. The Resolution highlights the need for guidance provision within the education system, especially in schools. Guidance has an *essential role to play in ensuring that individuals' educational and career decisions are firmly based, and in assisting them to develop effective self-management of their learning and career paths*. The Resolution stresses the role of guidance services in:
  - o the prevention of early school leaving
  - o the empowerment of individuals to manage their own learning and careers
  - o the re-integration of early school leavers into appropriate education and training programmes.

PLANNING GUIDANCE PROVISION IN SCHOOLS

Guidance as a Whole School Responsibility

The development and implementation of the school's guidance plan is a whole school responsibility. It should involve the guidance counsellor/s in the first instance, as well as all other relevant members of management and staff of the school. Parents and students must be seen as an essential part of this process and representatives of the local community, especially local business, NEPS and other relevant agencies should also be consulted and actively involved as appropriate.

The Role of Other Members of Staff

While the guidance counsellor/s has/have primary responsibility for the delivery of the school's guidance and counselling programme, other members of staff have important and worthwhile contributions to make to the planning NAME and delivery of many aspects of the programme.

These activities begin with the induction of incoming students into second level education. Some students may experience this transition as a traumatic time in their young lives and may need continuing support well into the first term. The more familiar incoming students are with the second level school, the easier will be their induction into the new system. Activities such as exploratory visits to the second level school, taster classes for students and information sessions for parents can contribute to dispelling doubts and uncertainties as well as helping the development of the confidence of the incoming students.

It is important that students and their parents are clear about the role and functions of the various members of staff concerned with aspects of student support, such as the guidance counsellor/s, chaplain, class tutors/year heads, Home School Community Liaison (HSCL) co-ordinator etc (some of these titles may vary between schools). It can help if the names and the different roles of support team members are explained to incoming first year students and their parents. This contributes to the elimination of confusion and helps to ensure that both students and their parents know who to approach for information, support or help when needs arise. The principal and /or deputy principal and teachers of first year students together with the guidance counsellor should endeavour to participate as far as possible in contacts between the school and the primary schools from which their students come.

Every effort should be made by schools to draw on the knowledge, experience and contacts of all staff members in providing the best possible guidance programme for students, for example:

- subject teachers are best placed to provide students with information and expertise on both the content and demands of their particular subject(s) syllabus
- subject teachers have a key role to play when students are choosing subjects and levels for the Junior and Leaving Certificate examinations
- subject teachers may also be in a position to indicate to senior cycle students the content and study commitments of particular subjects in further and higher education courses
- the expertise of the subject teachers, learning support teacher and/or resource teacher, guidance counsellor/s and programme co-ordinators can combine to assist students in choosing the most appropriate, for them, of the educational programmes offered by the school
- teachers with special ICT skills and responsibilities may have opportunities to collaborate with the guidance counsellor/s in assisting students to use QualifaX and other guidance software packages and in enabling them to access the most up-to-date career information via the Internet
- teachers may have close links with community agencies and local businesses and, therefore, may be well placed to help individual students benefit from contact with these bodies for activities such as work experience or working with their local communities, as part of their guidance programme.

Guidance in Second Level Schools

The Importance of School Guidance Planning in Identifying Student Needs: The school, through the planning process, makes decisions regarding the provision of guidance using the professional expertise of management, guidance counsellor/s and other members of staff and taking into account the views of students, parents and other partners. It is important that the school guidance plan should balance the needs of all junior and senior cycle students in a sequential, developmental and comprehensive way, including those with special educational needs, those from minority ethnic groups, members of the Traveller community, those at risk of early school leaving, Post Leaving Certificate (PLC) students and those on Vocational Training Opportunities Schemes (VTOS).

Choosing Educational Programmes

Schools should ensure that students and their parents are informed of the benefits to be gained from the programme options available. In addition to the Junior Certificate (JC) and Leaving Certificate (Established) (LC), such options are likely to be:

- Junior Certificate School Programme (JCSP)
- Transition Year Programme (TYP)
- Leaving Certificate Applied (LCA)
- Leaving Certificate Vocational Programme (LCVP)
- Post Leaving Certificate (PLC) courses.

Students also need to be made aware of how the choice of programme can have a bearing on future career options.

Appropriate Guidance

Following on from the identification of student needs in the planning process, schools will be in a position to define the principal activities to be included in the guidance programme. These will include providing students with:

- clear information concerning subject choices. This includes information about the consequences of subject choice and level taken for future educational, training and career options
- opportunities to explore their interests and subject choices and how these link to further education, training and career areas
- an awareness of the content and the syllabus demands of particular subjects
- assistance in the choice of educational programmes offered by the school
- assistance in identifying their own most effective learning styles and in developing effective study and note-taking skills, examination techniques and time management skills
- objective assessments of their aptitudes and achievements and feedback on these assessments

- guidance on the educational, vocational and career options available, including career progression routes and lifelong learning opportunities
- encouragement to explore a wide range of educational and career choices, including non-traditional careers
- the integration, as far as is practicable, of career themes and information into relevant aspects of the curriculum
- oportunities to develop information-seeking skills, including the use of ICT, with particular reference to career exploration and planning
- guidance in developing individual career plans based on the individual's achievements, ambitions, interests and personal circumstances.

The most up-to-date course and career information is to be found on the Internet. The planned connection of all schools to broadband will provide schools with greater access to multimedia applications and will facilitate more efficient use of the Internet to obtain up-to-date information on educational and training courses. In view of this, schools should work towards ensuring that students have regular and adequate access, for guidance purposes, to web-based information sources.

Given the nature of some aspects of the work of the guidance counsellor, schools should be cognisant of the need to ensure that adequate physical facilities are available for guidance purposes. Individual work with students requires appropriate surroundings and equally, work with small groups and classes requires suitable facilities. Space for the storage and display of guidance materials should also be provided to the extent possible.

Personal and Social Education

It is recommended that staff members involved in Social Personal and Health Education (SPHE) and Religious Education (RE) as well as HSCL co-ordinators should work together with guidance counsellors and others involved in guidance provision, since they share the objective of promoting the students' personal development and growth.

The particular contribution of guidance to SPHE is in facilitating students to:

- recognise their own talents and achievements and to identify their strengths and weaknesses
- develop coping strategies to deal with stress, personal and social issues and the challenges posed by adolescence and adulthood
- cope with the demands of school programmes, study and examinations
- organise the management of time for school, study, sporting and leisure activities
- develop interpersonal skills and awareness of the needs of others

- establish good patterns of decision-making and to learn how to make informed choices
- make successful transitions from primary to second level and from second level to further or higher education, training or directly into employment.

Where young people have serious learning, personal and social difficulties, these may need to be addressed by the relevant professional/s, such as the learning support teacher, guidance counsellor and/or NEPS psychologist or health services personnel, before the student can begin to make educational and career choices. Such young people may require ongoing learning and guidance support in order to enable them to participate fully in the education process.

6

Counselling Skills in Training

THE SKILLS OF COUNSELLING

Listening

It is the process of hearing the other person.

- During listening it is important to show that the counsellor is listening through the 'minimal prompts' such as head nods, yes, no, etc. They indicate that 'I am with you'. Overuse of these should be avoided.
- Behavioural aspects of listening - (SOLER)
  - S - Sit squarely
  - O - Openness
  - L - Leaning
  - E - Eye contact
  - R – Relax

Aspects of Listening

- Linguistic aspects - words, phrases, figures of speech
- Paralinguistic aspects - timing, volume, tone pitch, 'ums' and 'errs', fluency
- Non-Verbal aspects: facial expression, gestures, touch, body position, and proximity to the counsellor, body movement and eye contact.

Attending and Showing Receptiveness

It is the act of truly focusing on the other person. It involves consciously making ourselves aware of what the other person is saying and of what they are trying to communicate to us.

Observing Body Messages

Non-verbal aspects of communication refer to body language. The way the client expresses through the use of their body. They offer clues about the client's internal status beyond the words. Morris calls it 'Man Watching'. Body language depends on context in which it occurs, the nature of the relationship, individual's personal style, personality of the person. Therefore avoid assuming what person is saying with their body languages.

Listening Blocks

- Attraction: Attention is focused on what you are feeling rather than what client is saying.
- Physical condition: Sick/tired, without realizing it you tune out certain things client is saying.
- Concerns: Preoccupied with you own concerns.
- Over-eagerness: Listen to only a part and respond.
- Similarity of Problems: Same as your own problem. Your mind wanders.
- Differences: Different experiences of yours and client. Distracting.

Effective Listening

- Attention focuses outward
- Suspension of judgement
- Attention to the behavioural aspects
- Avoidance of interpretation
- Development of free-floating attention

Communicating

It is the exchange of ideas and opinions between two or more people through speech, writing or signs. The communication included physical setting as well as psychological predispositions of the receiver.

Communication = thoughts and feelings

Factors Involved in the communication:

- Purpose: Specific
- Distribution:
- Environment
- Timing
- Feedback
- Follow-up

Causes of Communication Breakdown:

- Lack of consideration of the other person's feelings and personality
- Use of technical language
- Not thinking about other, how they get affected
- Lose human factor

- Clarification: To get definite information through this to help clarify the client's thinking without pressurizing.
- Concreteness: Using clear language to describe the client's life situation. It promotes clear insight in clients life and provides counsellor with a fuller sense of the uniqueness of the clients experiences.
- Restatement: Enables the counsellor to let the counselee realize that he is being fully understood and accepted. Counsellor exactly repeats as said by the client. Client thus gets a rest and a chance to collect his thoughts before going forward.
- Paraphrasing: The counsellor summarises. He chooses/selects those ideas and feelings which seem most important and relevant and feeds them back to the client in a more organized form.

Ways to Impede Communication:

- Counsellor's predispositions
- Premature advice giving
- Lecturing
- Excessive questioning
- Story telling

COUNSELLOR TRAINING PROGRAMME IN INDIA

In India, the counsellor-training programme may include the following subjects—

1. Theory of Guidance.
2. Measurement in Guidance.
3. Statistics in Relation to guidance.
4. Counselling Theory and Techniques.
5. Practical Work - In this, preparation of individual tests and their application are taught.

Limitations of Counselling

Pravin Thevathasan: Counselling is a vitally important aspect of medical practice; many an experienced GP has commented on the fact that a patient's wellbeing may respond more through the art of counselling than through the science of medicine. Perhaps this art is in danger of being downgraded in an ever growing culture of evidence-based practice.

However, experienced counsellors recognise that counselling has its limitations. It is useful in only certain given circumstances. Their view compares to a widely held belief that any sort of counselling is bound to do some good. "If you have been affected by any part of this programme, you may wish to ring this number for some confidential counselling". As long as someone is seeing or listening to a counsellor, it is said, things are bound to get better.

How many counsellors does it take to change a light bulb? Only one, but the light bulb must wish to change. This joke is now a little over-mature but it does contain a grain of truth. There are certain personalities who simply do not have the built in mechanism to learn from the counselling experience. The histrionic person may be delighted to be told that he has been referred to a counsellor after several visits to his local hospital with various instruments attached to his person. He may proceed to wear down many a counsellor with detailed descriptions of his past medical 'career'; but he is unlikely to gain insight from his counselling experience. The dependent person may indeed make great strides during the counselling process. But when the counsellor starts talking of ending the sessions, he becomes distressed. For him, the counsellor has become a sort of human benzodiazepine. The sociopath does not have the built in mechanism to learn from his past experiences. The classic paedophile, for example, has a pathological need to control others and little insight into his problem behaviours. He has a limited desire to change. Counselling by itself may prove a disaster as others around him may feel that "at least something is being done". The less experienced counsellors may not be able to offer an adequate screening process prior to the counselling sessions.

Assuming that counselling is deemed to be of help, ought a Catholic see a Catholic counsellor? If she needs to see a counsellor because of a fear of spiders, it really does not matter. If she wishes to discuss feelings of guilt after an abortion it would surely help her to see someone who understands her spiritual perspective. In this latter case, seeing a non-directive counsellor is unlikely to prove beneficial. There needs to be a moral framework to guide the counselling process. She is rather like a passenger on board a plane who is unlikely to have much confidence in a non-directive pilot-even if the said pilot shows lots of empathy.

One hears of counselling in certain schools. This may be entirely appropriate if, for example, a child has been bullied, but what happens when a young person wishes to see a counsellor because he is confused about his sexuality? If you have a facilitator counselling a group of young people, he is likely to impose his own set of beliefs on them either consciously or unconsciously by means of group dynamics. Although the facilitator's role is supposed to be value free, that in itself introduces a new dogma.

There is no right or wrong. What is good for you may be bad for me. The mature deliberation is never that clear.

The facilitator first creates the appropriate environment for change. His task is to create doubts about previously held perspectives. This may be done by techniques such as role playing, whereby difficult dilemmas are presented. By enhancing a person's self-esteem, it is possible to make him believe that the old rules are unlikely to work now. "An actualised" person evolves into a more flexible and more "affirming" person. As has already been stated, self-esteem programmes are entirely appropriate in certain circumstances. However, it needs to be said that they are wholly inappropriate in most circumstances and may promote the values of ethical egoism and a general preoccupation with the self. St Gregory wrote of the "rottenness of wretched self gratitude". Of course he probably never had the benefit of attending a self-esteem seminar. Counselling has its uses. Like any other therapeutic intervention, it has side-effects and contra-indications. There is a generally held view that improving a person's self-esteem is bound to promote authentic values. This view needs to be challenged.

TYPES OF COUNSELLING

There are three main types of counselling or support. These are:

- Individual work with one counsellor and either one client, a couple or some members of a family.
- Group work where a counsellor leads or facilitates the group.
- Self-help groups where there is no leader. Members attend on an equal basis for mutual support.

A group called a *support group*may have a counsellor as a leader or facilitator, or it may be a self-help group without a leader. Some self-help groups follow the 12 step programme developed by Alcoholics Anonymous. No one has found an approach to counselling that will work with everyone in every situation. Some will work better for you than others. You need to find a counsellor with beliefs compatible with your own. Self-help groups usually have some common beliefs about the issue they share. The 12 step groups, for example, share common beliefs about the causes of addiction and the steps necessary for recovery. No matter how much knowledge a counsellor has, if she can't listen to you and understand you she won't be able to help you. In fact, some women believe that the personality of the counsellor is more important than technical skill or training.

A counsellor may have trained in a particular style of counselling but use other types as well. Very few of the training courses for counsellors include training in cultural awareness or working with an interpreter. A counsellor's training may not have challenged her racism or sexism or prejudices about lesbians or women with mental illnesses.

Some counsellors are trained to use the medical model and only look at what is happening within you, your body or your mind. They ignore things that are happening to you and the ways you're affected by other people. For example, you may be very stressed by your family situation in which you're being abused or not getting enough support. You may be told that 'it's just your nerves' and only be given pills to take. You may have been diagnosed as having a mental illness but find that it is treated as purely a physical problem when you also need to talk about traumatic experiences you've had. You need to ask each individual counsellor about her work.

People Who Offer Counselling

Counsellors: People with many different backgrounds work as counsellors. The name is not used to refer to any one type of training or qualification. There are many training courses in counselling skills.

Psychotherapists

Psychotherapists have a variety of qualifications. They have usually been in counselling or psychotherapy themselves and can work on personal change at a deeper level.

Community Health Nurses

They are qualified nurses who have completed extra training in community health which includes some counselling skills.

Family Therapists

They have a variety of qualifications. Members of the Victorian Association of Family Therapists (VAFT) have at least two years additional training in working with individuals and families.

Feminist Counsellors

There is no specific qualification in Victoria in feminist counselling. They have an awareness of the specific experiences and pressures on women. You need to ask each individual what she means by feminist counselling.

Psychoanalysts

They can train in several ways which are regulated by the Psychoanalysts Association. Some are medical doctors. They use a specific process to explore buried feelings from childhood. It can involve several sessions per week and take many years. 'Support groups are good later on, particularly with incest the secrecy means that it is incredibly threatening to start doing that in a group it's very exposing. Later on it's great and what you get is understanding and not feeling isolated and validating your own experiences.' 'I was on medication prescribed by a psychiatrist, but another doctor said that it was bad for me and took me off it.'

Financial Counsellors

They are trained to help sort out finances and renegotiate contracts and other financial obligations.

Social Workers

Social workers have a degree in social work. Some of them do counselling and they use a variety of approaches.

Psychiatrists

They are medical doctors with extra training in psychiatry. They deal with the diagnosis and treatment of mental illness. They can prescribe drugs. Some of them use other approaches as well.

Psychologists

They have university qualifications in psychology. Some with extra training are registered psychologists. They counsel people in a variety of settings using a range of techniques. They do not prescribe drugs.

IMPORTANT VALUES OF COUNSELLING

At all times counsellors must show a commitment to:

1. Human Rights and dignity.
2. Supporting and alleviating personal distress.
3. Appreciating the differences in culture and human experience, and remaining non-judgmental.
4. Providing adequate counselling services whilst ensuring the integrity of the client/counsellor relationship.
5. Maintaining client confidentiality and ethical principles.

Personal Qualities of an Effective Counsellor

All the counsellors are not alike. They differ in various ways. Their personal characteristics, as well as, their personality differ quite substantially. A number of research organisations have tried to ascertain the personal qualities of a *counsellor*, which are essential to bring about therapeutical transformation in another person (i.e. the client). Three researchers namely Carkuff, Truax & Carl Rogers came up with the under mentioned characteristics, which are as follows:

a) *Empathy:* The empathic behaviour is the ability of a **counsellor** to stand in the shoes of the client i.e. to see the things from the point of view of the client. The quality of empathy is a must for the counselling process to succeed. Empathy calls for 'forgetting oneself so that the **counsellor** surrenders himself completely towards the client. The process of empathisation is never total or complete, which leaves a lot to be desired, for the counselling process to succeed. Several empathy enhancing activities helps in enhancing the quality of empathy in a **counsellor**.

b) *Genuineness:* Rogers as well as Truax considered genuineness, as a very important part of counselling. The employees of various public services are well trained to meet the public at large, in a very cordial and friendly manner. "Genuineness" is synonymous with good or honest intentions. A genuine interest in the client is a must for the counselling process to succeed.

c) *Warmth:* Personal warmth or being warm is a controversial issue. There is a hairline difference between being warm or being dubbed as 'sickliness'. The quality of being warm refers to a situation, where a person shows interest in other individual/group. 'Cold' individuals rarely become good counsellors. A word of caution here, a too warm **counsellor** may lead towards the development of over-dependence on the part of the client. The ideal feeling of being warm is the one which demonstrates that the **counsellor** is non-judgmental and is honestly interested in his/her client. Care should be taken to see that the **counsellor** does not try to dominate the process of counselling.

d) *Concreteness:* It can be termed as a type of skill. It is an ability to listen, to what is being said by the client, instead of what is being implied. Concreteness in counselling is essential, if the counselling process has to succeed. A **counsellor** possessing the skill of 'concreteness' does not go for details (regarding psychological explanations) of what the client is speaking about, but instead tries to understand what the client is trying to express. Any quick, preconceived or initial judgment about what the client is saying will not be particularly helpful. In fact, it will be counterproductive. The concept of concreteness almost integrates all the important elements of the counselling process. A concrete **counsellor**, invariably, listens to and accepts what the client is saying and does not quickly make his judgments.

e) *Unconditional Positive Regard:* Rogers came up with a term called, 'unconditional positive regard' to refer to 'necessary and sufficient conditions for therapeutic change' in the counselling relationship. Rogers emphasized that the counsellor's positive feeling for the client must never be conditional in nature. He further suggested that the **counsellor** should feel warmly disposed towards the client, irrespective of the client's feelings or emotions, which is almost impractical or unreal. This is impossible. Further, it is important that a **counsellor** is broad minded and initially non-judgmental. Also positive general disposition towards the client is a must for the counselling process to succeed.

f) *A Tragic Sense:* In order to get involved with a client's problem a 'tragic sense of life' must be developed. All human beings have some limitations. A tragic sense helps the **counsellor** to remain humble. It also inducts a sense of humanity in him. Counsellors are not people with better brains, but are the people who readily listen to the problems of their clients.

g) *A Sense of Humour:* A sense of humour comes quite handy, in rescuing most of the sensitive or delicate situations. It does not means that a **counsellor** should resort to a comedian's tactics. It also does not mean that a **counsellor** should start taking the conversation during counselling session lightly. But, it means to help a client to regain the sight of the larger picture of a problem. It helps in calming down the tense atmosphere, that builds up because the clients generally blow the things out of proportion. Even subjects dubbed as 'taboos', can be easily confronted with the help of a sense of humour.

h) *Self-awareness:* It means to being aware of oneself i.e. to be aware of one's own limitations and strengths. It means to explore oneself. It is a realistic attempt of comparing oneself with other people. It means to explore one's own life situations.

A MAN is literally what he thinks, his character being the complete sum of all his thoughts.

The Concept of Roles and Functions in Counselling

The terms role and function have been used almost synonymously in the literature and in most counselling discussions. It is only recently that writers are beginning to look at the terms separately with a view to highlighting their specifications. Role, according to Shertzer and Stone (1981), is viewed as a set of complementary expectations that result In behaviour. This view looks rather loose usage that writers have suggested a more prescriptive and definitive approach.

From a perceptual approach to role definition, Shertzer and Stone (1980) stated that to identify the role of school counsellors, an examination of their perceptions by those they serve i.e. the students, teachers, principals and parents should be carried out. Using a specification and expectation approach, Ipaye (1986), stated that a role is a part of function assumed by someone, a specific set of responsibilities assumed by a professional worker, or s set of perceived duties or such a professional in a given setting or organisation. Durojaiye (1976) simply Refined a role as a part one plays in any given position, social situation or social relationship. From these views, it seems that a role may be perceived as a concrete set of expected behaviours. What then is a function? Ipaye (1986) stated that a function refers to the activities assigned to a role. According to Wrenn (1973), the distinction between a role and a function may be conceptualised as one of purpose (role) and process (function) or as one of ends (role) and means (*functions*). In this paper, therefore it is assummed that in carrying out a role, an individual 'is also carrying out a set of activities (*functions*).

Who should determine counsellors' roles and *functions*? If a role is a set of expected behaviours, it is expected that, apart from counsellors themselves, employers or consumers would have an input in defining counselling roles through their various expectations. Thus, would expect that in Nigeria, employers of counsellors such as the Ministries of Education, Schools Boards, and private school governing is may be involved in defining counsellors' roles because they are responsible for hiring counsellors for specific set of well defined tasks.

They should state their (counsellors') expected roles very clearly as well as determine what their consumers (i.e. students, teachers and parents) should expect from their employee-the *counsellor*. On the other hand, if *functions* are seen as the activities in which professionals are engaged in performing their roles, then judgement of the *functions* to be performed remains the prerogative of the professionals as long as they fulfil appropriate culture and institution-bound expectations of the role.

This writer believes that the professional body of counsellors (e.g. CAN) should play a major role in defining *counsellor* functioning because it ensure that counsellors are trained to exercise judgement in determining how best to utilise their skills and qualifications as well as to conform to the varying settings where their specific *functions* match the existing situations. It is expected that the *functions* of counsellors would differ from setting to setting, i.e. the function of a *counsellor* in a school would differ from that of an industrial *counsellor*; and that within a given setting, e.g. in the schools, individual counsellors may function differently according to the school's characteristics. Thus, it is also expected that the approaches and procedures employed by counsellors in the same setting may differ to suit individual client needs and the collective institutional needs.

The questions of what should be counsellors' identities (their roles) and how they should best do it (their *functions*) have continually surfaced in most counselling circles seeking solution: As obscure as answers to these questions may seem, it is clear that counsellors' roles and *functions* go hand in hand and that counsellors themselves should have some responsibility in defining their roles and specifying the services or *functions* they provide such that it is different from, and cannot be mistaken for, those provided by other professionals. However, this does not presume that all *counsellor* will work in the same way under all conditions. Afterall, *counsellor* themselves are not the same: they differ in their personalities motivations and levels of experience. Any documentation of *counsellor* functioning thus serves as general guidelines for professions practice with the proviso that it is flexible enough to allow for each counsellor's individuality, the job setting and his/her level of experience.

THE USE OF COUNSELLING SKILLS IN GROUP TRAINING AT WORK

Group or One-to-One

Most of the time we talk of 'counselling at work' as taking place in a one-to-one format. Working over a limited number of sessions, issues are addressed that affect people's performance at work. In that setting the counsellor uses his or her specialised abilities to facilitate clients being able to understand and deal more effectively with their specific issues. What is less talked about is the use of counselling skills in-group training workshops. In this context, too, the use of counselling skills can have a significant and positive impact on the intended outcome.

Training can be damaging to your health! When you look at the non-technical areas those much training addresses–communication, personal effectiveness, team building, presentation, etc–you can see that all these areas touch on people's self-esteem, value and confidence.

In unskilled hands participants can finish a training feeling undermined and unsupported. And this is often why companies shy away from 'touchy-feely' training that they fear won't really make things better. The counselling skills are essential to good training and it is required to all of facilitators to have some background in the use of counselling or psychotherapy skills. By this we are not talking about group therapy, which by its very nature needs to be facilitated by counsellors or psychotherapists. We mean the sort of courses run by the various institutes: structured, active trainings, with delegates participating in a variety of processes and exercises.

However, experience shows that the use of counselling techniques in training makes for a better outcome. Just about any interactive workshop situation can benefit from the use of counselling skills. Good training is viewed as personal development, not just a place to learn new tools and techniques.

Similarities between One-to-One Counselling and Group Work

Part of the purpose of counselling is to facilitate clients developing their ability to cope with stress and deal more effectively with difficult or challenging situations as they arise. As esteem and confidence are increased, individuals have a greater capacity to change their behaviour in healthy and appropriate ways. So, too, with good people skills training.

These kinds of workshops should not be places where participants are 'trained' in the 'right' way to communicate, to present, and to lead others. Unfortunately, that is often what happens: participants are given rigid rules and regulations which can be demotivating and can shut down their creativity and enthusiasm for finding their own solutions. When counselling skills are used in training, delegates' esteem and capabilities are dramatically increased. As a consequence of this, their capacity to take in new information and integrate it is far greater.

"You didn't try to change me, but let me find my own way."" This is also what counselling is about: not changing the person, but helping them to become more authentically themselves.

There are the obvious transferable Counselling Skills such as:

- Creating a safe environment so that people are more able to take risks
- Setting effective boundaries so that delegates know where they stand and what's expected of them within a workshop format
- Using active listening and responding skills, which allow participants to feel heard and understood
- Working in a non-shaming way so that people can disclose some of their concerns
- Allowing participants to work at their own pace
- Not pushing or forcing delegates to do things they don't want to do
- Letting people find out what works best for them
- Allowing people to find their own solutions rather than giving advice or answers, while at the same time offering a range of options for them to practise
- Understanding that there will be issues of transference and projection during even the shortest training session

Workshops are just that: Places for delegates to explore different options and practise new ways of behaving where there are no career limiting consequences, mirroring the exploratory nature of counselling. They may experience unusual or even uncomfortable feelings, but they will also discover not only what works best for them but also what they know they'll be able to put into practise in the 'real world' outside the training arena. Good counselling is flexible rather than fixed to a rigid structure: the counsellor sees what a client needs and is able to provide that flexibility. People skills training also needs to be flexible and attuned to the needs and capabilities of the group rather than sticking to a fixed, prepared structure. Having counselling skills enables a trainer to change that structure when they see what else might be needed.

A less obvious skill is the ability to deal only with what delegates bring into training, rather than what else the facilitator may see is going on. Effective counselling creates the space for clients to realise that there may be deeper issues that need tackling.

But counsellors who 'move in' too quickly when they are aware that there is more going on than the presented problem(s) are in danger of undermining a client's trust and pushing them beyond where they are ready, willing or able to go. In turn, there can be a great temptation amongst trainers to 'show off' how good they are at noticing what people need. They often confront delegates and comment on their behaviour, motivation or feelings when it is inappropriate to do so. They will lose the delegate's trust and may be entering territory outside the workshop remit.

The use of counselling skills in this type of situation is having the awareness that there may be other issues going on for the delegate, being capable of dealing with them if they do arise, but having the patience and humility to leave them be if they don't. One of the surest ways of creating trust, building confidence and boosting self-esteem is for people to really feel seen for who they are.

We know that when we run trainings at work, we are privileged to be dealing with very capable, intelligent and willing delegates. Even if people are resistant, having been sent on a training rather than self-enrolling, they will be of a high caliber in terms of their ability to understand relatively complex ideas and concepts. Respect for which the delegate is, is fundamental to our work; as well as trusting that they will know what is best for them. By working with the skills, talents and abilities delegates already bring to the workshop and developing those, we can help them see that some of the recurring difficulties they have are usually triggered by certain people or situations. This is far more effective than telling people what their problem is and what they're doing wrong that gets them into difficulties.

Pointing out what's wrong and trying to fix it is a lot harder on both the facilitator and the delegate and is ultimately de-motivating and de-skilling. Yet time and time again we hear about training that does just that. We have even heard people being told the cringe-making phrase: getting criticism may not feel good, but remember, there's no gain without pain. Counsellors who give their clients a run-down of their faults and say, 'Now we'll work on fixing those' will soon find themselves without much of a practice! Counsellors see and support the best in their clients in order to then be able to address the difficulties and areas that most need attention.

Differences between One-to-One Counselling and Group Work

Having looked at the similarities between counselling and use of counselling skills in work groups, there are also many areas where the dynamic created in one-to-one formats simply cannot be used in-group settings. Training courses are of finite duration and the relationship between a facilitator and delegate can rarely have the depth and breadth as that of a counsellor and client. Delegates also have to share the time and attention that a facilitator gives to them and issues of transference aren't generally addressed in people skills trainings.

This means that there won't always be the time available during a training to deal in any depth with other issues that arise. Personal disclosure of delegates may be limited and certain subjects simply cannot be dealt with during a training session. Interventions that might be normal practise in a counselling session require more skill and time than is available in a training session.

Even more importantly, the whole area of confidentiality is open to serious question. Many training organisations have people sign or agree to confidentiality 'contracts'. In theory, this practise is laudatory. However, our experience is that it is almost impossible to guarantee confidentiality no matter how well intentioned everyone's agreement is. People inadvertently gossip; they might mention in strictest confidence to their best friend or spouse what happened during the workshop, in front of other people they might refer to a process or game and what it was like.

Although some training organisations offer a follow-up 'service' there are many times when issues arise after a workshop is over where delegates are often left to their own devices to get the support they need. Unfortunately that doesn't always happen as effectively as it could.

What can be done in a Group that can't be done One-to-One?

There are also certain areas that can be dealt with in-group training that can't be done in a counselling format. The most obvious is the fact that a workshop is a shared experience. People come because they want to address similar issues and will often be surprised that other people in their workplace have concerns that mirror their own. Participants are also able to see themselves in relation to other people, which adds a dimension to the work unavailable in one-to-one. The reality of group dynamics provides more choices and increases awareness.

A training programme will often have a section where delegates bring in scenarios where they felt their people skills weren't as effective as they could be. In this setting people get a chance to practise with others different ways of behaving that will create more positive outcomes. This also means that participants actively support each other and have an opportunity to 'play' in ways that stretch their capacities. Finally, delegates can practise something new, find it doesn't work, try something else, find it doesn't work, try a third thing and find that it does; all within the safe confines of the workshop environment. They experience immediate results. Even if they don't practise these new ways of behaving right away in the 'real world' they have the knowledge that they are capable of doing something different when and if they choose.

The use of counselling skills is growing: in their traditional format of one-to-one settings, in group therapy, in personal development and people skills training, in everyday life. The more they are used, the better people are able to communicate with each other, cope with stress, deal with difficult situations and feel much better about their own capabilities.

SKILLS NEEDED IN COUNSELLING

Several skills need to be brought into a one-to-one counselling session. *These include*:

- Attitudinal skills;
- Listening skills;
- Verbal communication skills; and
- Giving leads.

Attitudes

There is probably nothing which has a greater impact on the outcome of a counselling session than the helper's attitude. Attitudes can be positive or reactive. Attitudes are included in this unit on skills because good attitudes can be learned and practised.

They include the following:

- Respect
- Guidance/congruence
- Unconditional positive regard
- Empathy
- Self-disclosure
- Confrontation

Respect

It is one of the most important human attitudes required. It normally begins with respecting one's self, so that others respect you in turn. It is having good intentions and warm regard for students. Respect the students and avoid imposing your values on them. Avoid judgment. Many times, respect demands praising the individuality of each student, supporting each one's search for him/herself, and structuring the counselling to the needs, capacities and resources of the individual student. The teacher needs to ensure that the student accepts the problem and the solution as his/her own.

Genuineness/Congruence

Genuineness is at times referred to as congruence. It is the consistency or harmony between what you say, and what you are, as a teacher. This condition reflects honesty, transparency, and trust. This element is basic to a counselling relationship. Once it is established, open communication, warmth and respect for the client gradually develop.

Unconditional Positive Regard (Warmth)

You may have experienced situations where a student approached you with a concern, and you blamed the student, or acted as if the student bothered you. These are negative attitudes which are ineffective in counselling. Unconditional, positive regard makes students feel welcomed and valued as individuals.

An example to illustrate this warmth is the following:

- 'Hello, Jane. Can I help you?'

Not:

- 'I am sorry, I am very busy. I prefer you to be very brief.'
- 'Hello. Can I help you? I am sorry I am very busy and prefer that you be brief.'

Empathy

Empathy is your ability, as a teacher, to understand what your students experience, and communicate this kind of feeling. Carl Rogers, defined it as perceiving the internal frame of reference of another person. Gerald Egan, explains it as entering the private perceptual world of the client, and being sensitive to his/her feelings, whether good or bad. As a teacher, you need to be empathetic. You need to be responsive to both the content and the feelings expressed by students. This attitude helps you to assess students' concerns and understand them better.

Self-Disclosure

Self-disclosure helps your student to communicate easily. It is one of the attitudes that helps your student to reveal something about him/herself. It helps to create mutual trust, and disarm the student, so that he/she feels free and talks openly. This is equally important for both parties in the counselling session. It promotes a relationship through increased communi-cation and better understanding of the student. It also helps the student to understand him/herself better, and help him/her get rid of the burden of guilt. This is a first step in behavioural change. Opening with self-disclosure helps the student to talk about his/her problems more concretely and realistically, and allows him/her to act accordingly. Disclose only what is necessary.

Confrontation

This is when you use your student's behaviour, or words, to point out inconsistencies between what is said and what is done. When handling a response, confrontation, or challenging attitudes, is a healthy development in counselling. For example, a student may say he/she hates a particular teacher and, in another instance, may say that he/she likes her. This is inconsistent. You could draw the attention of such a student to such inconsistency by saying, 'You said that you did not like the teacher. Now you are saying that you like her. What exactly do you mean?' Remember to bring this out in a 'feeling' and not in a threatening way. You will, in this way, initiate action in your student.

Listening

Effective listening is more complicated than it seems, since it involves a teacher's own level of self-awareness, as well as his/her awareness of the spoken and unspoken cues of the other person. Furthermore, a teacher needs to be able to respond to the student in such a way that he/she feels understood. Being a good listener entails receiving and sending appropriate messages.

In counselling this is important, because it means meeting the needs of the students. Listening to students is not just a matter of receiving what they say, but also receiving how they say it. Sometimes how they communicate is much more revealing that what they actually say, which may be more concealing than revealing. Listening skills are basic to all human interaction, whether the purpose is for getting information, conducting in-depth interviews, or offering informal help. Listening is considered to be the most important counselling skill.

Verbal Communication

The use of words in counselling is a skill which, like any other skill, requires practice to master. Verbal communication takes place first in the literal or content phase. If inappropriate vocabulary is used, rapport and understanding will be hindered. When this happens, miscommunication occurs. Even common words can be misunderstood due to the multiple meanings they carry. Look up any common English word in an unabridged dictionary, and you will find several different definitions of this word. So the potential for miscommunication is great.

In addition to the literal phase of verbal communication, there is also the emotional phase. This refers to other attributes involved in vocal interactions, such as volume, the emotional edge, and other non-verbal cues such as gestures. A student saying, 'I don't care' while angry, or while indifferently walking away from you, or while weeping with his head in his hands. Although the words are the same, the message conveyed is vastly different. As helpers, we must be sensitive to both the literal and emotional phases of verbal communication. In addition to the two general phases of communication that we have just discussed, there are five more levels of communication. Each of these levels is valuable in different contexts.

The five levels of communication are:

1. Cliches;
2. Facts;
3. Beliefs;
4. Emotions; and
5. Intimacy.

Cliches

This is a French word which has been adopted by English speakers to mean a trite, well-worn phase. A universal example is the greeting, 'How are you?' 'I'm fine. How are you?' In some African languages, a formal greeting may take ten minutes and yet nothing new is communicated. Everybody is always *good* or *fine,* because that is the pattern the greeting takes. This is communication at the most superficial level, but an important social obligation is met.

Facts

Facts are pieces of information that we pass on to others. They include comments on current events like, 'The morning news mentioned that the President is coming to town tomorrow,' or making conversation on the weather e.g., 'Those clouds look as if they could bring rain this afternoon.' The communication of facts may transmit valuable information from one to another, but little interaction takes place.

Beliefs

Beliefs include any part of an individual's value system. They may communicate insights and choices, or facts which are value-laden. The sharing of one's person begins at this level, and the risk of rejection increases. The sharing of beliefs may include subjects which are considered 'forbidden' in some cultures, such as sex, politics, or religion.

Emotions

Emotions include communicating personal feelings. 'I am thrilled that I was invited to the party', or 'That teacher is rude, he annoys me'. Communication at this level is difficult for most men and women. It requires a great deal of vulnerability to share feelings with someone else, and more so when feelings about another are shared.

This is the optimum level for counselling to take place. If the student talks to the teacher at an emotional level, and the teacher responds at the level of facts or beliefs, counselling may be derailed. A miscommunication may occur. Guidance may take place at the facts or beliefs level, but effective counselling rarely does.

Intimacy

Although sometimes used as a euphemism for sexual intercourse, intimacy is more accurately defined as the intercourse of the soul. At this level, the self becomes united to another person. This is a level of communication that many individuals never experience. Indeed there is some debate as to whether such a level is even desirable, since the self may be compromised. In counselling, this is an inappropriate level, since it may encourage the dependency of the student on the helping teacher and thereby inhibit the student's personal growth.

Leads

Leads may be defined as statements that counsellors use in communication with the clients.

Leads have been classified into categories of techniques, namely:

- Restatement of Content: Attempts to convey understanding by repeating or rephrasing the communication.
- Questioning: Seeks further information and asks the person counselled to elaborate a point.
- Reflection of Feeling: Understanding from the client's point of view and communicating that understanding.
- Reassurance: Serves as a reward or reinforcing agent. It is often used to support the client's exploration of ideas and feelings or test different behaviour.
- Interpretation: Explains meaning behind the client's statements.

Example

A statement by a client immediately after seating herself in the counsellor's office. The counsellor had not met the student before. Different leads or counsellor responses are given and classified. 'Miss Musonda told me to come down here to talk to you. I don't know why. She said I couldn't go back to class until I have learnt to stay awake. I work at a restaurant until one o'clock every morning in a part-time job, and I am tired. Anyway, who could stay awake in there? She bores you to death!' Among some of the responses the counsellor could make are the following:

- 'You were bored and fell asleep, and Miss Musonda asked you to leave the class.'
  - Restatement of content = understanding
- 'What does she do that you find boring?'
  - Questioning = investigating
- 'You feel put off.'
  - Reflection of feeling = understanding
- 'I am sure that something can be worked out between you and Miss Musonda in this situation.'
  - Reassurance = supporting
- 'Do you think that you might be disowning responsibility for what has happened?'
  - Interpretation = interpreting

UNDERTAKING AN ANALYSIS OF SKILLS, KNOWLEDGE & BEHAVIOURS TO DEFINE LEARNING NEEDS

There will be occasions when the HR or training professional is invited to provide professional guidance on the learning and development needs of professionals or teams. Often this involves identifying the skills, experience, knowledge and behaviour needed of people in the role. In this article Sarah Cook provides practical tips on how to go about undertaking such a learning needs analysis.

The Starting Point

The need for a Learning Needs Analysis to be undertaken is often triggered by the performance review cycle. Alternatively more often than not it is prompted by the discovery of underperformance or potential change within the organisation. Imagine that you are a Training and Development Manager for a medium sized organisation. You have been asked by a line manager to help identify the learning and development needs of two individuals within their team. One of the two individuals is new to the team, having been there three months. They are new to the organisation and have not worked in this particular function before.

The other individual is someone who has been with the team for the past eighteen months. Prior to this they have worked for five years in another part of the organisation. The line manager is keen that they progress and develop. However, being relatively new to the line manager role themselves, they have never undertaken a learning needs analysis before and have requested your help.

You have offered to work alongside the line manager to undertake the analysis and to offer coaching to them so that they will be able to undertake the LNA (learning needs analysis) themselves with other members of staff. The organisation has bi-annual and annual performance reviews from which each individual creates a Personal Development Plan.

The Purpose of the LNA

Before starting the LNA, it is useful to remind yourself and to clarify with the line manager the function of the learning needs analysis. This is to identify the attributes of the individual?s performance that constitute a shortfall between the actual and desired levels. The resulting shortfalls can then be addressed via a learning and development intervention.

The New Starter

In your role as advisor there are potentially different approaches you would take to completing the Learning Needs Analysis for the new starter rather than the individual who has been in the role for eighteen months. Essentially what you are trying to identify is the skills, knowledge, experience and behaviours that are needed for a person to do their job efficiently and effectively both now and in the future. Next, you will need to ascertain what are the levels of skills, knowledge, experience and behaviours that the individuals currently demonstrate and where are the gaps. Finally you will make recommendations on how these gaps can be addressed.

Desired Skills, Knnowledge, Experience, Behaviours Versus Current Skills, Knowledge, Experience, Behaviours

The first part of the investigation that the Training and Development Manager needs to undertake surrounds the desired levels of skills, level of expertise and behaviours. In the case of the new starter, there are some fundamental building blocks that will help you to define these expected levels. Before speaking to the individual, ascertain from the line manager a copy of:

- The individual's job description
- The job specification used to advertise the position
- Relevant competency framework and with permission of the individual:
- Their performance review, if they have had this.

Job Description

The job description will outline the role and responsibilities of the person in their function. It will also set out who the individual should report to within the organisation. The job description is an important document to help you understand the role of the individual. Once you have a copy of this document, find out from the line manager who are the individual's internal and external customers and who they interface with in their role. This will give you a greater understanding of the function that the individual plays within the organisation.

Job specification

Refer back to the job specification that was developed for the new incumbent. Job specifications set out the requirements of people in the role. A job specification sets out the essential skills, knowledge and experience needed in the role as well as the desired.

Example of Job Specification

Essential:

- Minimum three years' experience in the field of training and development
- Good interpersonal skills
- Effective presentation skills
- Minimum of two years' experience of working with senior and middle managers

Desirable:

- Experience of delivering interpersonal skills training to senior and middle managers
- CIPD qualification.

Relevant Competency Framework

Many organisations utilise a competency framework to help identify the competencies or skills needed for someone to fulfil their role. In this case, if the organisation had such a framework, your job will be made far easier. Competency frameworks are usually designed with various families of skills in mind. Each 'family' shows the different levels of competence needed. Here for example is one organisation's competency framework for the competency family of 'customer service'.

Level 1:

- Listens actively to customer requests
- Demonstrates willingness and enthusiasm to meet the needs of customers

- Applies knowledge of service standards and processes to meet customers' needs.

Level 2:

- Provides solutions to a wide range of customer requests
- Deals effectively with customer complaints
- Puts themselves in the customers' shoes and manages win-win outcomes.

Level 3:

- Achieves customers' goals by proactively working through others
- Deals with complex grievances satisfactorily, maintaining a relationship with customers and gaining trust and respect
- Actively seeks feedback from customers.

Level 4:

- Shapes customers' attitudes
- Champions customer service excellence and acts as a role model for others
- Continually improves the service offered to customers.

When an organisation uses a competency framework it is able to plot the desired level of competency against each job role. Competency families are usually presented at different levels, so the higher the level the more skill and competence the person needs to demonstrate. A competency framework is a very useful tool to the person undertaking a learning needs analysis as it allows them to pinpoint the desired level of performance.

Performance Review

Another useful tool is a summary of the learning needs identified as part of the individual?s performance review. If the Training Manager has permission to view or discuss the individual?s Personal Development Plan, they should also be able to identify not only the desired performance but where there are any gaps.

What if some or all of these tools are missing? On a practical note, you may find that some or all of these documents are missing. You may wish to supplement this analysis with your own observations, interviews, questionnaires or focus groups. The idea is to consult the individual, their line manager and / or team leader, colleagues and customers to help identify learning and development needs.

Observation

Observing someone at their place of work can provide objective evidence of the skills, knowledge and behaviours that are required in the job. So for example, you could decide to observe the new individual to find out more about their role. Be careful of two things however if you decide to do this. Often someone's natural behaviour can be altered just by the mere fact that they are being observed. Also, if you observe just one person, you only see one version of the job role. Particularly if the person is new to the role, it would be helpful to observe other people as well. Effectively what you are doing is 'shadowing' the person in their work. This will involve sitting apart from what they are doing and watching the normal transactions of their work. It does not mean that you comment or become involved in the person's job. Of course, observation is best carried out with the permission of the individual undertaking the role. It should be preceded with a discussion with the individual so they know:

- The reason for your observation
- What you are looking for
- What you will do with the results.

What are you looking for? Establish with the individual their principle job responsibilities. Find out who are their internal and external customers, who they interface with on a day to day basis. Ask them what level of experience or expertise they believe they need to do their job well. Establish what knowledge they need to be competent in their role. Identify what skills they need in their job - these could be both technical skills such as ability to process an application as well as 'soft' skills such as negotiation skills for example. Probe to see what behaviours are valued in their role. Be careful to focus on behaviours rather than 'attitude'. It is easy to say for example 'This role requires someone with a positive attitude'. How do you measure positive attitude? You can see this in the behaviours a person demonstrates. For example, the degree of enthusiasm and energy they bring to their work. You may also want to make reference to the organisation's values or guiding principles if they have them. So, if a business says that it values Team Work, Openness and Honesty and Innovation for example, you would expect to see these values reflected in the way that the person undertakes their job role.

The following is an example of a summary of the skills, knowledge, experience and behaviours observed during a day spent with a sales executive in the financial services industry. The sales team were expanding and taking on new starters. They did not have a formalised development programme. The purpose of the shadowing days was to identify the development opportunities that could help individuals become high performers in their role. The day consisted of observing the person in their office environment and then shadowing them on several sales calls. The organisation in question did not have a competency framework. However, it did have a set of values for the organisation.

7

Group Guidance and Counselling

Group guidance can deal with problems people have in common. A group member has the opportunity to spend time with other professionals facing similar challenges on the job, for example, which helps him realize that he is not the only one dealing with these issues. He has the opportunity to share his story with other group members, who listen to what he has to say and can try to help him solve his problem.

He also has the opportunity to listen to the similar stories of his peers. For example, attending a seminar on time management might help a busy professional realize that he's not the only one that struggles with finding enough hours in the day to complete his work. Others in the group can suggest ways he can work to balance his priorities.

SOCIALIZATION

Spending time with a diverse group allows people to be exposed to a variety of new situations, circumstances and opinions. Group members must learn to listen to others and to modify their behaviors in a manner that is socially acceptable, out of respect for their peers. They also must learn to appreciate and tolerate the opinions of other group members, even if they don't agree with them. For example, employees from different groups may be selected to work on a project together. Everyone in the group may have a different idea on how the project should be completed, and when they all listen to each other's thoughts in a respectful manner, they can choose the best option.

Facilitate the Sharing of Information

It is much more efficient for a supervisor to share information with an entire group of people at once than having to talk with each person individually.

This is appropriate in situations where the information shared is not a private matter and is relevant to everyone in the group. Examples are situations such as new hire orientations, training seminars and department meetings.

Monitor Interactions

Group guidance can help a manager see how employees interact with others. An employee may behave one way toward the manager when the two are alone together and act in an entirely different manner when placed in a group setting. Observing an employee in a group guidance situation allows a supervisor learn more about the employee's interaction patterns. This can help the supervisor better understand problems an employee may have getting along with his co-workers or completing his work on time. It also can assist the manager when preparing employee performance reviews.

GUIDANCE AND COUNSELLING

Teachers as helping professionals have to come across many situations which demand guidance and counselling help from them. Students require counselling and guidance. Now a day the guidance and counselling is an integral part of teaching. In this lesson we will discuss meaning, types and importance of guidance and counselling.

GUIDANCE

Guidance is a personalised assistance made readily available by a sympathetic, mature, experienced and personally qualified person to a needy person. A variety of definitions are available for guidance.

"Guidance is a process of helping individual's through his own efforts to discover and develop their potentialities for personal happiness and social usefulness" - Moris

"Guidance as kinds of help given by one person to another in developing ability, making adjustments and problems that confront him in attainment of his goals" - Jones

Guidance is an 'umbrella term' involving several functions such as publications, information, institutions, testing, counselling services, etc. Guidance is not carrying others burden, but enabling them to carry their burden themselves.

TYPES OF GUIDANCE

Educational Guidance

Educational guidance is aimed to help students to solve their problems related to education at different levels of education – from primary to university. Good C. V in his "Dictionary of education" regards educational guidance as 'guidance concerned principally with matters relating to schools, courses, curricular and school life, rather than vocational social or personal matter". Its functions are to help the students to:

a. Selection of course.
b. Adjustment with the institution and course.
c. Ensuring achievement in the course.

Vocational Guidance

Vocational guidance is the process of helping the individual to choose an occupation that fits him best. The General Conference of International Labour (GCILO) defines it as "Assistance given to an individual in solving problems related to occupational choice and progress with due regard for the individual's characteristics and the relations to occupational opportunity." Its functions are to help the students:

a. To select a career
b. To adjust with the career
c. To enhance and fulfil his potentiality in the career.

Personal Guidance

Personal guidance refers to the guidance to students to enable them to adjust themselves to their environment so that they become efficient citizens. Its functions are to help in solving:

a. Personal problems
b. Familial problems.
c. Occupational problems
d. Problems in attaining fulfilment and success.

Steps in the Organisation of Guidance Programme:

1. Formulation of a guidance committee.
2. Organisation of the guidance bureau.

Guidance bureau organises the following programmes.

a. Career Corner – availed periodicals, employment news and bulletins.
b. Career Talks – on teaching, banking, Indian defence services, Indian administrative forces, etc.
c. Career Conference – supplementing information. A number of successful persons explains the vocations in which they work and answer questions about their job. Occupational orientation covers the following points.
    i. Nature and importance of work.
    ii. Conditions of work.

iii. Minimum qualification necessary for receiving training.

iv. Different aspects of training.

d. Placement programme – provide help to secure a grade, a place or a job.

e. Testing programme – administration of tests or assessing traits and aptitude of peoples.

f. Film show – arranged to give educational and vocational informations.

g. Visits – visit to institutions relevant to occupational choices.

h. Exhibitions – organised to disseminate information regarding modern courses and occupation.

i. Diagnostic programmes – for identifying physical disabilities, mental ill health and mal adjustment

j. Guidance service centres – like – employment guidance bureaus.

COUNSELLING

Counselling is a process of enabling the individual to know himself and his present and possible future situations in order that he may make substantial contributions to the society and to solve his own problems through a face to face personal relationship with the counsellor.

"Counselling is a unique relationship in which the counsellors' job is to hold up a mirror for the client to see himself or herself in. we all have experiences in which we can't see things about ourselves without a mirror."

Counselling is a process by which a troubled person (the client) is helped to feel and behave in a more personally satisfying manner through interaction with an uninvolved person (the counsellor) who provides information and reactions. These stimulate the client to develop behaviours which enable him to deal more effectively with himself & his environment. A theoretical definition of counselling, widely accepted by the educators and counsellors is given by Carl Rogers. According to him, *"counselling is a series of direct contacts with the individual which aims to offer him assistance in changing the attitudes and behaviour".*

Other popular definitions regarding counselling are as follows:-

Ruth Strang – "It is a face to face relationship in which growth takes place in the counsellor as well as the counselee"

Webster's Dictionary – "Counselling is "Consultation, mutual interchange of opinions deliberating together".

Smith (1955) defines counselling as "a process in which the counsellor assists the counselee to make interpretations of facts relating to a choice, plan or adjustments which he needs to make"

Counselling also has been defined by *Hahn and MacLean*as "a process which takes place in a one-to-one relationship between an individual beset by problems with which he cannot cope alone and a professional worker whose training and experience have qualified him to help others reach solutions to various types of personal difficulties".

Pepinsky and Pepinsky (1954) state that counselling is that interaction which (1) occurs between two individuals called counsellor and client, (2) takes place in a professional setting, and (3) is initiated and maintained to facilitate changes in the behaviour of a client.

Patterson (1959) characterizes it as "the process involving interpersonal relationships between a therapist and one or more clients by which the former employs psychological methods based on systematic knowledge of the human personality in attempting to improve the mental health of the latter".

Blocher (1966) explains it as "helping an individual become aware of himself and the ways in which he is reacting to the behavioural influences of his environment. It further helps him to establish some personal meaning for this behaviour and to develop and clarify a set of goals and values for future behaviour".

PURPOSES OF GROUPS

The following are the goals and purposes of groups:

- To grow in self-acceptance and learn not to demand perfection.
- To learn how to trust oneself and others.
- To foster self-knowledge and the development of a unique self-identity.
- To lessen fears of intimacy, and learn to reach out to those one would like to be closer to.
- To move away from meeting other's expectations, and decide for oneself the standards by which to live.
- To increase self-awareness, and increase the possibilities for choosing and acting.
- To become aware of choices and to make choices wisely.
- To become more sensitive to the needs and feelings of others.
- To clarify values and decide whether, and how, to modify them.
- To find ways of understanding, and resolving, personal problems.

FORMING A GROUP

Where to Begin: Formation of the Group

In forming a group, the place to start is by clarifying the rationale for it. It is well worth devoting considerable time to planning, for if planning is done poorly, and if members are not carefully selected and prepared, groups can flounder.

Announcing a Group and Recruiting Members

If you are successful in having a proposal accepted, the next step is to find a practical way of announcing it to prospective participants. How a group is announced influences the way it will be received by potential members, as well as the kinds of people who will join the group. Personal contact with potential members is one of the best methods of recruiting members. The leader can, through personal contact, enthusiastically demonstrate that the group has potential value for someone.

Screening and Selecting Members

The group leader conducts a pre-group interview with each prospective member for the purposes of screening and orientation. He then selects group members whose needs and goals are compatible with the established goals of the group, who will not impede the group process, and whose well-being will not be jeopardized by the group experience.

Some questions that can be productively explored in a half-hour interview with each candidate are these:

- Why does this person want to join the group?
- How ready is the person to become actively involved in the process of self-examination that will be part of the group?
- Does the candidate have a clear idea about the nature and purpose of the group? Does he, or she, have a view of what is expected?
- Are there any indications that the person might be counter-productive to the development of cohesion in the group? Might this group be counter-productive to the person?

Some Practical Considerations in Group Formation

In selecting members for a given group, there are some basic factors to keep in mind.

How Large should the Group be?

The ideal size of a group depends on the age of the members, your experience as a leader, the type and purpose of a group, and whether you have a co-leader. For instance, a group with elementary school children might be kept to four or five members, while a group of adolescents might have eight to ten. The group should be big enough to give ample opportunity for interaction, and small enough for everyone to feel involved in the group.

How often should a Group Meet, and for how Long?

With children and adolescents, frequent short meetings may suit their attention span better. If the group is taking place in a school setting, the meeting times can correspond to regularly scheduled class periods. For a group of well functioning adults, a two-hour weekly session might be preferable. The frequency and duration of a meeting should suit your style of leadership and the type of people in the group.

Where should the Group Meet?

Physical arrangements and setting contribute to, or detract from, the climate of a group. Privacy and freedom from distractions are essential. Group leaders sometimes think that meeting outdoors is a good way to promote informality, but generally such a setting lacks privacy and is a source of distractions.

Will Membership be Voluntary or Involuntary?

Although it is ideal to have a group composed only of those who want to be part of the group, some groups consist of clients who are required to attend. Attending a group because one has been ordered to go by someone else greatly curtails the chances of success. The key to successful participation lies in carefully orienting members, and preparing them for being a part of the group, as well as in the leader's belief that the group process has something to offer to prospective members.

Should the Group be Open or Closed?

An open group is one characterized by changing membership, while a closed group adds no new members during the lifetime of the group. Closed groups have some distinct advantages, as trust can be developed and work accomplished. If membership changes from week to week, as in some open groups, productive work as a group may be difficult to achieve.

Conducting a Pre-Group Session

Once the members have been screened, and the group formed, it is useful to conduct a preliminary or pre-group session with all the members selected. The pre-group meeting can be an extension of the individual screening process, for it is an ideal way to present basic information, help members get to know one another, and help them decide whether to commit themselves to the group or not. Depending on the nature of the group, certain ground rules will have to be established early on. For example, the following ground rules could be presented to most types of groups at the preliminary session, in the form of a written contract that members can sign.

- Members are not to use drugs during the session, and are not to come to a session under the influence of drugs, or alcohol.
- Members are expected to come to the sessions on time, and be present at all the meetings, since absences affect the entire group.
- Members must avoid sexual involvement with others in the group throughout its duration.
- Members may not smoke during the group sessions.
- Members must maintain the confidences of others in the group.
- Members are not to use physical violence in group sessions, nor are they to be physically or verbally abusive of others in the group.
- Members will be given a list of their rights and responsibilities, so that they know what is expected of them before they join the group.
- For groups of children or adolescents, written consent must be given by parents or guardians.
- If members decide to leave the group; they are expected to bring this up for discussion with the group before they go. Abrupt departures can be detrimental to the member leaving as well as to the others.

GROUP COUNSELLING POPULATION

Groups offer particular advantages for working with a variety of people, for groups can be designed to meet the needs of children, adolescents, young adults, middle-aged persons and the elderly.

Children

In the school setting, group counselling is often suggested for children who display behaviour problems, such as excessive fighting, chronic tiredness, violent outbursts, extreme withdrawal, inability to get along with peers, and a neglect of appearance.

In small groups, children have the opportunity to express their feelings about a wide range of personal problems. Children frequently experience learning difficulties in school as a result of inner turmoil. Some of these children suffer from anxiety over broken homes and disturbed family relationships. If the group is structured properly, these children can receive psychological assistance at an early age, and will stand a better chance of dealing effectively with the tasks they face later in life.

Adolescents

For most people, adolescence is a difficult period. It is characterized by paradoxes. Adolescents strive for closeness, and yet fear intimacy and often avoid it. They rebel against control, and yet want direction and structure.

While they push and test the limits imposed on them, they see limits as a sign of caring. They are not treated as mature adults, and yet are expected to act as though they had gained complete autonomy. They are typically self-centred and pre-occupied with their own worlds, and yet are expected to deal with social demands and expand their horizons. They are asked to face and accept reality and, at the same time, many avenues of escape are available in the form of drugs and alcohol.

With adolescence come some of these conflicts: dependence/independence struggles, acceptance/rejection conflicts, identity crises, the search for security, pressure to conform, and the need for approval. Because of the stresses of the adolescent period, these years can be lonely, and it is not unusual for an adolescent to feel that there is no-one who can help. Group counselling can be useful in dealing with these feelings of isolation, because it gives adolescents the means to express conflicting feelings, explore self-doubts, and realise that they share these concerns with their peers.

A group allows adolescents to question openly their values, and talk freely about their deepest concerns. In the group, adolescents can learn to communicate with their peers, benefit from the modelling provided by the leader, and can safely experiment with reality and test their limits.

A unique value of a group is that it offers adolescents a chance to be instrumental for one another's growth and change. Because of the opportunities for interaction in groups, the members can express their concerns and be genuinely heard, and they can help one another gain increased self-acceptance.

Adults

A wide variety of special interest groups can be developed for adults of all ages. For example, groups can be formed for couples, single parents, parents who want to explore problems they have relating to their children, middle-aged people who return to college or change careers, and adults who want to explore developmental concerns, such as the search for identity.

On college campuses, groups have become increasingly popular as a way of meeting the diverse needs of students, who range from young adults to the elderly. Such groups can be created for relatively healthy students who experience a developmental crisis, or students who want to talk openly with others about their concerns. The purpose of these groups is to offer participants an opportunity to explore ways of changing certain aspects of their lives.

In group situations, college students of all ages deal with several different issues. They may include issues regarding career decisions, male/female relationships, the need for, and fear of, love, sex-role identity issues, educational plans, the meaning of life, challenging one's value system, and the meaning of work. There are also issues regarding feelings of loneliness and isolation, learning to form intimate relationships, exploring marital conflicts, and other concerns related to becoming a self-directed adult.

The Elderly

As people grow up, they face feelings of isolation, and may struggle with the problem of finding a meaning to life. Some of these older persons may resign themselves to a useless life, for they see little in their future. Like adolescents, the elderly often feel unproductive, unneeded, and unwanted by society. Another problem is that many older people have uncritically accepted myths about ageing.

Themes that are more common to the elderly than other age groups, include loneliness, social isolation, losses, poverty, feelings of rejection, the struggle to find a meaning to life, dependency, and feelings of uselessness, hopelessness and despair. There are also fears of death and dying, grief over another's death, sadness over physical and mental deterioration, depression, and regrets over past events.

Older people have a need to be listened to, and understood. Respect is shown by accepting them.

Acceptance can be through listening to their messages, and by not patronizing them.

These individuals need support and encouragement, and the chance to talk openly about what they feel, and about the topics which concern them.

A counselling group can do a lot to help the elderly challenge the myths they may have that limit their lives. It can also help them to deal with the developmental tasks that they face. Like any other age-group, they must be able to face them in such a way that they retain their selfrespect. Groups can assist the elderly to break out of their isolation, and encourage them to find a new meaning in life.

CHIEF GOALS OF COUNSELLING

Emotions play and significant role in determining the goals and direction of human activities. The goods qualities latent in and individual can be fully realized only if he harmonizes all his reactions with his logical insight, by utilizing all his innate capacities.

The following are the significant goals of the counselling

1. To give individual information on important matters leading to his success.
2. To gather relevant information about the person and to make him aware of this with a view to help him solve his problems.
3. To help the individual to plan appropriate steps and work these out for shoving his problems and difficulties.

4. To assist the person knows himself better – his interests, abilities, aptitudes and opportunities.
5. To encourage and develop special abilities and right attitudes.
6. To inspire successful endeavour toward attainment.

Thus, the goal of counselling is problem clarification and self directed needs. The counselling officer helps the person to understand the problems and helps the individual to assist himself. The role of the individual is objective self – assessment of the situation and the role of counselling officer is to formulate the decision making process and to act as the stimulator of insights and sensitivities of the person. Counselling does not solve the problems but only helps in solving it. If solution is not possible it helps face challenges and to live with them.

Scope of Counselling :

- Intended to help the individual to realize his potentialities.
- It helps the persons to solve his problems.
- It provides assistance to teachers.
- Aimed at enabling students to acquire abilities, which promote self-direction and self-realisation.
- It is a centred round the needs and aspirator of students.

THE MAIN APPROACHES IN COUNSELLING

There are mainly three types of counselling they are*Directive counselling, Non Directive counselling and Electric Counselling.*

Directive or Prescriptive or Counsellor –Cantered Counselling

E.G Williamson is the chief exponent of this viewpoint. Such type of counselling involves six essential steps.

1. *Analysis*: Collecting from a variety of sources the data needed for an adequate understanding of the student.
2. *Synthesis*: Summarizing and organizing the data so that they reveal the student's assets, liabilities, adjustments and maladjustments.
3. *Diagnosis*: Formulating conclusions regarding the nature and the cause of the problems exhibited by the student.
4. *Prognosis*: Predicting the future development of the students' problems.
5. *Counselling*: The counsellors taking steps with the student to recurrence of the original problem and determining the effectiveness of the counselling provided to him.
6. *Follow-up*: Helping the student with new problems or with recurrence of the original problem and determining the effectiveness of the counselling provided to him.

Here the counsellor plays the major role he does that entire he can to get the counselee to make a decision in keeping with his diagnosis. He tries to direct the thinking of the counselee by informing, explaining, interpreting and advising.

A considerable use of interpretations and direction by the counsellor has led to this type of counselling being described as directive or counsellor centred or active approach technique.

Non-directive or Permissive or Client-centred Counselling

In this type of counselling, it is the client – the counselee – who is the pivot. Carl R Rogers is the chief exponent of this viewpoint. The client takes an active part in the process of therapy. He gains insight into his problem with the help of the counsellor. It is he who takes decisions as to the action to be taken. The counsellor's role is passive. This type of counselling is a growth experience. The goal is the independence and integration of the client rather than the solution of a particular problem. The principal function of the counsellor is not to cultivate self-understanding in the client but instead, to create an atmosphere in which the client can work out his own understanding. The emotional elements or the feeling aspects are stressed rather than the intellectual aspects and the counselling leads to a voluntary choice of action.

Eclectic Counselling

Eclectic counselling is defined as the synthesis and combination of directive and non directive counselling. F.C Thorne, is the chief exponent of this view. In electric counselling, the counsellor is neither too active as in the directive counselling, nor too passive as n the non-directive counselling. He follows a middle path between these two extremes. The process of eclectic counselling proceeds somewhat along the following lines:

1. Counselling may be preceded by an intake interview.
2. During the opening phase of counselling, the counsellor tries to establish rapport and may have to do structuring so that the client understands what to expect of counselling.
3. Often a tentative diagnosis is made which may include the collection of a case history and a plan for counselling is formulated.
4. To enhance the client's self-understanding, information, about him and his background may be gathered from various sources. The client needs to be helped to assimilate this information.
5. Educational, occupational and social information, if needed by the client, may be supplied to him.

6. The client achieves emotional release and insights.
7. During the closing phase, the client makes decisions and plans, modifies behaviour, and solves his problems.
8. There may be follow up contacts, if needed.

Group Counselling

It is an empowerment of person in formal group situations with the leadership of trained facilitator. Here problems are of more on subconscious and unconscious level of the mind. Group counselling has the advantage of having feed backs by participants and less resistance from the clients as feed backs are given by co-participants.

PARTICIPATORY TRAINING

Objectives and Characteristics

The main training objectives are; a) to improve the economic and social conditions of the poor; b) to assist the beneficiaries to become active and productive group members and leaders; c) to encourage group promoters and other supporting staff to adjust their standard training to meet the needs of the rural poor; and d) to stimulate all project participants to develop adequate training contents, methods and also materials.

The essential training characteristics are: 1) participatory; every trainer is a trainee and vice-versa; 2) on-going: the training is conceived as a continuous process and is designed and carried out within the context of any project action to improve the production. income and social conditions of the beneficiaries; 3) pragmatic and problem solving: the training is based on solving immediate and recognized problems; 4) in-service, on-the-job, on-site training, learning by doing; 5) self-learning: individually but also group-or team-wise; 6) reality-exposure: both trainers and trainees are to be exposed to the realities of the rural people and their living areas; and 7) dialogue and cooperation on equal terms; no we-they dichotomy between staff and beneficiaries.

Conventional training has a top-down approach, is entirely pre-planned and uses mainly the classroom (teacher-pupils) method. Instead participatory training is based on the felt needs of the trainees, recognizes that the poor can also be resource persons, stresses learning from each other, facilitates building of team work and links knowledge much more directly with action and problem-solving.

The innovative training approaches include: 1) stimulation of farmer-to-fanner and group-to-group training to attain self-reliance; 2) the trainees are not passive recipients and objects, butsubjects of training; 3) training in specific technical fields is not exclusively given to group leaders (whose workload often hinders proper dissemination of the know-how obtained) but also and preferably to group members selected by one or more groups. This will enhance shared leadership, inter-group cooperation, self-reliance and farmers becoming informal grassroot extensionists.

Moreover, an accounting system of payment for services rendered could be developed by the beneficiaries themselves in order to decrease over-dependence on outside aid, while the delivery system could gradually obtain adequate cost recovery.

Training Target Groups, Personnel and Committees

The main "target groups" are: a) the intended beneficiaries; b) the project staff, including the participation agents; and c) supporting government and NGO staff such as line agency and other (field) officers, but also local leaders and influentials. The trainers must have practical experience. They include: the group promoters and other project staff, technical officers of the delivery system, experienced farmers/fishermen and also successful groups which enlighten, train and motivate other ones.

A small training committee which would include interested technical officers, group promoters and beneficiaries, could be very useful to assist in the planning, implementation and evaluation of feasible training programmes.

Beneficiary Training

The types of topics are the following:

a) Certain general subject matters which aim at enhancing beneficiary participation through efficient group formation and action and should be given to all intended beneficiaries. These matters include group dynamics, shared leadership, planning of group activities, savings and credit, accounting, cooperative management, monitoring and evaluation as well as negotiating and bargaining. In some projects certain basic issues like fostering thrift habits and overcoming bad customs such as irrational spending, drinking, gambling, etc. are also very much stressed.

b) Specialized training is to be given according to the type of project as well as to the specific, felt group needs. For example, in crop production, small livestock development, soil and water conservation, small-scale fishery, aquaculture, forestry, group marketing, etc., but also in non-farm activities such as (agro-)processing, weaving, tailoring, pottery, production of house-building materials or of artisanal items in wood, bamboo, metal, leather, etc., as well as maintenance and transport.

c) Training could furthermore be given in: home life and community development, in particular for women: health, sanitation, first aid, nutrition, child care, etc., but also management, leadership, village development, etc.

d) Other very useful training subject matters include: legal and procedural matters, e.g. land reform, tenancy rights, mortgaging, wages, employment (rural works programme, etc.), the use of banks, and of local administration etc. Pragmatic information on these topics is frequently not or badly communicated to the poor

e) Functional literacy for adult women and men, which help them to analyse their problems, plan actions and also to reduce their dependency upon literate villagers or group members.

The training opportunities include: 1) short courses, preferably given at field (village) level; 2) advice and consultation between group members, group promoters and technical officers; 3) information given by knowledgeable successful farmers or fishermen; 4) exposure media: audio-visual aids, radio (rural broadcasting programmes), films, slideshows, public meetings, etc.; 5) demonstrations organized jointly with group members for improved crop cultivations, livestock rearing, aquaculture, handicrafts, etc.; 6) written extension materials; 7) simple newsletters prepared together with the beneficiaries; 8) initial and successive field action workshops; 9) inter-group exchange visits; 10) (inter-)group evaluation exercises; and 11) where appropriate, role playing and socio-drama. Training equipment and materials. Each group needs at least extension materials, a blackboard and elementary stationery. Each cluster of groups needs a flannel or black board, a camera, folding exhibition boards, transistor radios and possibly a slide-projector and a video-tape recorder. The local production by the groups of simple training materials is to be encouraged.

Training of Participation Agents (Group Promoters), the Project Coordinator and Other Project Staff

This training, a central project operation, aims at: a) introducing the field workers into the approaches and procedures of participatory development; b) fostering adequate attitudes, motivations and team-spirit; c) experimenting innovative ways of poverty eradication; d) teaching basic technical topics which are needed for group guidance and are also taught to all group members; in particular: philosophy and methods of participatory development, group dynamics, savings and credit, accounting and monitoring and evaluation); and e) stimulating group self-learning and self-development of training contents, methods and materials.

The group promoters must obtain in particular management training consisting of: project planning, methods of production planning and implementation (group enterprise management), transfer of appropriate technology, marketing, communication techniques, leadership, team-building, record keeping and report writing.

Also the project coordinator needs of course, to be trained as early as possible by the implementing agency and FAO (or another agency) in all the aforementioned topics. The initial orientation training of group promoters should be well structured and sufficiently long. It should mainly consist of familiarization with the objectives and operational aspects of the project.

An inception training workshop for group promoters and other project staff is to be given for at least three weeks in or near the project area with not more than 30 participants including the candidate group promoters (half of whom female), the project staff and selected key officials of the delivery system. It is recommendable to invite twice as many candidate participation agents as needed initially in the project in order to obtain a reserve pool of these field workers. The curriculum should be pragmatic and include work experience presentations by the participants and course evaluation exercises. "Sandwich" type training (classroom and field experience combined) is very recommendable.

The group promoters need thereafter initial field training of 2-3 months which is at the same time the starting period for their field action in the project area. They will learn team-wise, among others, to prepare and carry out village and household surveys, to solve work and living problems met in the field, to cooperate with the delivery system and to plan the project initiation workshop.

The follow-up training of participation agents includes: a) periodic (preferably monthly) review and evaluation meetings for group promoters and other staff to evaluate team performance, to identify and solve work problems and to prepare workplans; b) field action workshops; c) refresher courses in such subjects as new rural development policies and programmes, innovative income-raising activities and credit schemes; d) issue of a periodic (project) newsletter; and e) exchange visits of group members. group promoters and officials between different areas of their own and similar participatory projects.

Training of Government and NGO Staff as well as Local Leaders

This training aims at familiarizing those involved in the project with the approach and procedures of the project and its participation efforts, the handicaps of the poor to have access to the delivery agencies and the roles of the latter to help solve the problems of the rural poor. In many instances, the above mentioned officials and leaders need to be to a certain extent "de-trained" and then re-trained to perform well their participatory roles. Ongoing exchange of experiences and views particularly in field workshops, is crucial in this learning process.

The training opportunities for the government and other staff consists mainly of their participation in: 1) training courses for group promoters and other project staff; 2) field workshops; 3) briefing sessions with the use of promotional materials; 4) project coordination committees; 5) the programming, provision, and evaluation of beneficiary training; 6) intra- or inter-country seminars related to the objectives and issues of the project; and 7) inter-group and/or inter-project exchange visits.

AUDIO-VISUAL AIDS IN EXTENSION

The term audio-visual aid refers to anything that an extension agent uses to help to convey the message when communicating with farmers. The spoken word is the agent's main communication tool, but, whether the agent is speaking to a large village meeting or discussing a problem in a field with a group of farmers, its impact and effectiveness can be greatly increased by the use of suitable audio-visual aids. When selected and used properly, audio-visual aids can help in the following ways:

- The interest of the audience can be maintained if the agent varies the mode of presentation. It is difficult to concentrate for long on what someone is saying; but if the agent refers to a wall chart, or illustrates a point with some slides, his audience's attention can be maintained.
- When information is presented to more than one sense (sight and touch, for example, as well as hearing), more is taken in and it is better understood and remembered.
- Processes and concepts that are difficult to express in words alone can be explained. The procedure for applying for a loan, for example, may sound confusing, but a simple chart or diagram can make the process clearer. Again, the life cycle of a crop pest can be explained by showing a series of slides or drawings.
- The effects of decisions and actions that farmers might take can be shown. Photographs of a cattle dip or a model of a cooperative store can give farmers a clear idea of just what it is they might be considering.
- Pictures can have a more immediate impact on our emotions than words. Photographs of a heavy crop, for example, are likely to arouse interest more effectively than details of yields read out by an extension agent.

The Range of Audio-visual Aids

Extension agents often use sophisticated audio-visual aids which require electricity and complex machinery such as projectors or television sets. But there are many simple aids that the agent can make locally, and these have several advantages. They do not require a power source or heavy equipment, they do not cost much to produce and they can be made to suit the precise needs of the agent. Between these two extremes lies a wide range of more or less sophisticated aids. The distinction between a mass medium and an audio-visual aid lies only in the way it is used. All the mass media described earlier can be used as audio-visual aids. A film is a mass medium, in that it is shown to large audiences in many different places; but for an individual extension agent who uses it to increase the impact of a talk, it is an audio-visual aid. Many of the principles of media use discussed earlier also apply to audio-visual aids. The audio-visual aids available to the extension agent can now be examined.

Objects: A real object is often the most effective aid. It enables the audience to understand exactly what the extension agent is talking about. Equipment and tools can be shown, samples of diseased plants and insect pests displayed and different seed varieties and fertilizers handled by farmers.

Where an object is too large to be shown, a model of it can sometimes be used as a teaching aid. This applies particularly to buildings and other fixed structures. The construction of a poultry shed, for example, or the installation of a dip tank can be demonstrated by using a model, which can be taken to pieces in front of the audience.

Photographs offer another substitute for real objects. They can be passed around an audience or displayed by the agent. If a photograph is being taken to use as a visual aid, just the right amount of detail should be included for the audience to recognize it. Too much detail confuses and distracts, while too little prevents recognition. Photographs of people doing things are more likely to interest the audience than photographs of objects alone.

Chalkboards: Blackboards are widely available in schools, rural training institutes and extension offices. They may be fixed to an inside wall or supported on a freestanding easel which can be moved around. They are useful for setting down the main headings of a talk, for sketching simple drawings and diagrams, and for noting points raised in questions and discussion.

If using a blackboard, the agent should practice writing on it, if necessary by drawing horizontal chalk lines for guidance. He should make sure that the writing is large enough for someone at the back of the audience to see clearly and that the headings and phrases are kept short. There is not much space on blackboards and the agent will lose the audience's attention if he spends a lot of time with his back to them while writing.

Whiteboards have a smooth, shiny surface on which coloured felt pens can be used, but it is important to use only pens with water-soluble ink.

Whiteboards are easier to use than blackboards from both the agent's and the audience's point of view. The pens flow smoothly over the surface and the colours are much clearer than chalk on a blackboard.

Newsprint, which is an inexpensive paper, can be obtained in large sheets and fixed to a blackboard or to the walls of a building. It can be used in the same way as a blackboard but it is more versatile. Text and drawings can be prepared on several sheets, before a meeting, to avoid having to write while speaking. Paper and pens can be given to small discussion groups to note their conclusions. These conclusions can then be displayed around the meeting-place and discussed by others. Suggestions and ideas from the audience can be added to enable farmers to see their decisions taking shape. Used sheets can be kept for future reference. At a planning meeting with a group of farmers, for example, the agent can take away the sheets to guide him in preparing a written record of the decisions taken.

Posters: Posters are useful for highlighting the main theme of a talk and wall charts can be used to show complex processes. Although they are used mainly in class-room teaching where they can be left on the wall for future reference, they can also be carried by the extension agent to help him to convey ideas to farmers.

Flip charts: Flip charts contain a series of pictures, with or without words, fastened along one edge between two sheets of thin wood or thick cardboard. The two covers can be opened and folded back so that the flip chart stands in front of the audience. Each picture illustrates one point in the extension agent's talk and he simply turns over each one when he moves on to the next point. As well as helping the audience to understand and remember they remind the agent of the structure of his talk without the need to refer constantly to his written notes.

Many extension agents will already have access to printed posters, wall charts and flip charts, but they can also be made locally with large sheets of paper and coloured pens. When making flip charts, the following points should be noted.

- Lettering should be large.
- Diagrams should be simple.
- Information on each sheet should be limited.
- Pictures from posters and magazines can be cut out and stuck on by those who cannot draw.
- Pre-testing is important for all home-made visual aids.

Flannelgraphs: A flannelgraph is made from rough textured cloth, such as flannel or a blanket, which is hung or supported almost vertically. Figures, words, and symbols cut from cardboard, which are backed with similar cloth or sandpaper, are attached to it. A cheaper backing is obtained by putting glue on the back of the cut-out and then dipping it into fine sand. The backing holds the cut-outs firmly on the cloth surface. The cut-outs are prepared beforehand and can be used repeatedly.

The flannelgraph can be used very effectively to build up a story or an explanation. Unlike a wall chart, which can confuse an audience by presenting a finished diagram at the start of a talk, a flannelgraph can be used to present in turn each part of the diagram until it is complete.

The cut-outs can be placed in different positions to show alternative outcomes. After showing the process of wind erosion, for example, the effect of wind-breaks can be demonstrated by placing cut-outs of trees between the wind direction and a field. Arrows representing the wind can then be deflected, and the general effect shown by putting back soil symbols on the surface of the field.

A modern alternative to flannelgraphs is the magnetic board. Cutouts are backed by a magnetic strip, that holds them firmly to a metal board. They can be used in windy conditions when flannelgraph cut-outs would blow away, but they are cumbersome to transport. On the other hand, flannelgraphs, which can be made in a variety of sizes and designs can be folded into an agent's bag or rolled up and tied to a bicycle.

Projected aids: Films, colour slides, filmstrips and overhead projector transparencies are useful as teaching aids, bringing colour, variety and interest to an extension talk. However, they all require specific equipment and electricity. Extension agents are, therefore, more likely to use them in training centres and schools, although some slide projectors can be adapted to work from a 12-volt car battery. Films, filmstrips and slides are best used at night or in a room with curtains drawn or shutters closed. Daylight screens can be used for small groups. Overhead projectors can be used in daylight, provided the sun is not shining directly on the screen or wall on which the image is projected.

Colour slides can be selected and put in a suitable sequence by the extension agent. He can produce his own slides to suit his purposes, provided he has access to a camera, film and film processing facilities. A slide set can easily be modified or updated by replacing one or more slides. If they are kept dry and free from dust and fingerprints, they will remain in good condition for many years. An agent can either provide his own spoken comments on the slides, or a commentary can be recorded on an audio cassette. With synchronized equipment, the tape can be modified so that slides automatically change at the appropriate point. Filmstrips contain a sequence of slides in a single continuous strip of film. They are shown on a slide-projector fitted with a filmstrip carrier between the projector body and the lens. They cannot be modified easily and the sequence is fixed, but individual frames cannot fall out or be put into the projector the wrong way round. They are useful when a fixed message has to be presented many times. Overhead projectors are usually only found in class-rooms. Diagrams and texts are put on to a sheet of transparent acetate with special felt pens; the acetate is then placed on a flat glass platform through which a light shines, projecting the contents on to a vertical screen. The agent can write on the acetate while facing his audience, or he can prepare it beforehand.

USING AUDIO-VISUAL AIDS

Audio-visual aids are only effective if they are appropriate to the situation and are used properly by the agent. Unsuitable aids or ones that are not used properly can at best distract and at worst mislead the audience. When selecting suitable audio-visual aids, the agent will be limited to what is readily available or can be made. Within that range, some aids are more suited to a particular objective than others.

For example, if accurate detail is needed, a photograph, slides or a careful drawing may be more appropriate. If, on the other hand, the agent simply wants to highlight the structure of a talk or the main conclusions of a discussion, a blackboard or newsprint will be suitable. The agent should also consider where the aids will be used: indoors or outdoors, with or without electricity, at a large meeting or with a small group. All these factors will influence the choice of audio-visual aids.

Proficiency in using audio-visual aids cannot be learned from a book; it comes only with practice. The following principles may, however, be useful, whatever audio-visual aids an extension agent may use.

Select the aids most in accordance with your objective, the composition and size of the audience where the aids will be used.

Use the aids to reinforce your message. They are there for support, to complement and supplement the spoken word, and should not be expected to communicate their contents without explanation. Refer to them, explain them and ask questions about them.

Make sure that the audience will be able to see and hear clearly. Audio cassettes that cannot be heard or lettering that is too small to be seen can make the audience restless and inattentive.

Practise using the aids beforehand. Where projected aids are used, it is important to be completely accustomed to the equipment. For example, there are seven incorrect ways of loading a slide into a projector but only one correct way.

EDUCATIONAL COUNSELLING

Educational counselling has emerged as a discipline to provide help to students on campuses of schools, colleges and universities, such that they are not tormented by their internal conflicts, do not become cynical and do not resort to self-destructive strategies. Counselling in schools has the ultimate goal of making every individual pupil a responsible individual. The educational counselling is often considered as a philosophy a function, a role and an activity, as a philosophy, counselling, in the educational context, is a process by which educational experiences are related to students' experiences. As a function counselling is a set of responsibilities that the institution should legitimately perform, as a role, counselling should be viewed as the institutions responsibility to provide services to the students. As an activity, counselling comprises a variety of functions that different persons with counselling roles perform for students which are consistent with the philosophy, the function and the role. A student's function is to study and to obtain good results; otherwise, he has failed his role expectation. The school has the responsibility of determining why this has happened, so that the counsellor can help the student reach his expected level of performance.

Need and Significance of Counselling in the Present Scenario

Modern age is noted for the mobility of its population. The sense of security and the atmosphere of love and affection experienced in ideal family, life are lacking in many modern families.

The need of counselling is felt today in different dimensions of man's life. The complexities of modern life and stress and struggles felt by man living amidst the challenges of today call for help from others. Technological changes have made and major impact on people's life and work. Industrialization has resulted in social and vocational mobility. Rapid progress in communication media, fast changing systems, impacts on cultural systems, consumerist value systems etc. have affected many of man's traditional supportive systems and resulted in causing tensions to man's day today life. This demands the help of people who can provide methods and techniques of tension reduction and balancing of life. For, people are in need of help and these helping people can help through meaningful relationships and therapeutic interactions. The help given should be adequate and the people who provide help should be qualified. This help is basically given today by Counselling and Psychotherapy.

- Conflict in social and moral values.
- Modernisation and globalisation.
- Modern age is noted for the mobility of its population.
- The old joint family system to modern nuclear families.

- Isolated parents.
- Broken family.
- Increasing divorce.
- Alcoholic problems.
- Sex abuse.
- Marital problems.
- Increasing suicide tendency.
- Influence of media
- Lack of healthy relationship among (teacher-pupil, family members, friends, peer groups, working place)
- Lack of proper education.

All these problems give us the awareness of the need of counselling in present scenario. As seen above the challenges due to change in the mind process and life style has become uncontrollable and amazing, which is even able to destroy the peace and tranquillity of mankind. Counselling has been defined as an empowerment of a person to face his reality in life. The field of counselling psychology has developed skills and techniques which makes the person capable of tackling the changes.

Summary

- The various approaches to personality are: behavioural approach, cultural approach, type approach, trait approach.
- Freud devide the psyche into three as the id, ego and superego
- Freud saw the libido as general life energy, generated by the id, sexual in origin, but expressed in many different ways.
- Various defense mechanisms are: denial, rationalization, intellectualization, projection, reaction formation, sublimation, regression, fantasy, identification etc
- Jung distinguished between two types of unconscious mind: *the personal unconscious and collective unconscious*
- Jung proposed personality typology.
- Adler believed everybody has feelings of inferiority at times; this is a universal part of human experience.
- Allport believes that traits are essentially unique to each individual.
- Maslow classified and arranged human need called *hierarchy of needs*.
- The various need according to Maslow are: physiological needs, safety and security needs, love and belonging needs, esteem needs and Self-actualization needs.
- The entire personality theory of Rogers is built on a single "force of life" calls *the actualizing tendency*.

- According to Rogers a fully function person have the qualities of openness to experience, existential living, organismic trusting, experiential freedom, and creativity.
- A formal effort aimed at understanding personality of an individual is termed as personality assessment.
- The most commonly used techniques for personality assessment are Psychometric Tests, Self-Report Measures, Projective Techniques, and Behavioural Analysis.
- The World Health Organization defines mental health as ""a state of well-being in which the individual realizes his or her own abilities, can cope with the normal stresses of life, can work productively and fruitfully, and is able to make a contribution to his or her community."
- Anxiety is a psychological and physiological state characterized by cognitive, somatic, emotional, and behavioral components.
- Conflict is actual or perceived opposition of needs, values and interests. A conflict can be internal (within oneself) or external (between two or more individuals).
- Frustration is an emotional response to circumstances where one is obstructed from arriving at a personal goal.
- Hans Selye, the father of modern stress research, defined stress as "the nonspecific response of the body to any demand" that is, regardless of the cause of the threat, the individual will respond with the same physiological pattern of reactions.
- Burnout is a psychological term for the experience of long-term exhaustion and diminished interest.
- Guidance is a personalised assistance made readily available by a sympathetic, mature, experienced and personally qualified person to a needy person.
- Counselling is a process by which a troubled person (the client) is helped to feel and behave in a more personally satisfying manner through interaction with an uninvolved person (the counsellor) who provides information and reactions.
- Different types of counselling are: Directive, Non-directive, eclectic and group counselling.

IMPORTANT TECHNIQUES THAT CAN BE USED FOR IMPARTING GROUP GUIDANCE

Important techniques that can be used for imparting group guidance are as follows: Group guidance is that relationship in which a guidance worker attempts to assist a number of students to attain for themselves satisfactory development or adjustment to their respective individual or collective life situations. It occurs in a setting in which one or more guidance workers encounter students as a group.

Groups are best suited for discussing educational and vocational plans, problems relating to adjustment to college and social situations, problems relating to choice of options and choosing a career, economic and occupational problems, personality adjustment problems, etc. A number of techniques can be used for imparting group guidance:

Techniques

1. Informal discussions: Informal discussions, if done under the table and skilful leaders, can prove very helpful. These discussions should centre on desirable objectives and should be so guided as to result in conclusions that may be helpful to the group as a whole.
2. Group reports: If the students are divided into groups which have certain specific problems to tackle and later these reports are presented in larger groups, they can help all the members of the group in gaining awareness of a number of problems and their solution.
3. Lectures: Lectures delivered by experts on certain problems too can impart group guidance in an effective way.
4. Dramatics: This is another good technique of group guidance. If certain interesting topics are dramatised, the students can be given guidance in an interesting way. How to appear for an interview, how to prepare for an examination, how to prepare notes—all these can be dramatised and guidelines suggested to the students in an interesting way.
5. Question box: "Question-box" says Jones, "If carefully organised and not too frequently used, is also a desirable technique, for it gives the shy and retiring pupil an opportunity to propose a question that is bothering him without revealing that it is his question". Most of the times, we find the shy student remains buried with his problems as he is not vocal. It is also possible that there are quite a few students having the same problem. So if the question could be proposed in a silent way, the same could be discussed in a group and valuable guidance provided to the students.
6. The case conference: Here the problem faced by the majority of the group is stated concretely by way of a case. Each member of the group reviews his own experience in a similar situation.

The group is guided away from the more immediate and temporary advantages to be gained toward more remote and permanent values. Then the effect of the proposed line of action is considered upon others. Possible exceptions may be discussed. Some other conditions that should be considered in deciding a plan of action are also gone through. Some generalisations are also formulated which may prove helpful in other situations. According to Jones, the entire process of the case conference is an experience in social thinking and it has positive and unique values in the group guidance programme.

POSITIVE GUIDANCE TECHNIQUES

Use the Safety Rule

Basic rules and limits are necessary within the early childhood classroom. Children feel more secure if they know what behavior is acceptable and what behavior is unacceptable.

- Reasons for rules and expectations are respectfully explained on a routine basis so children understand their purpose.
- Children and teachers use the Safety Rule to decide on appropriate behavior for themselves and others.

Use Positive Verbal Guidance (Responsive Language)

Children often forget what constitutes appropriate behavior from one day to the next and from one situation to another. They need frequent reminders of the rules; if corrective action is necessary, adults should be clear but non-accusatory. Responsive language utilizes positive verbal guidance that is respectful towards children, labels and validates children's feelings, and clarifies rules and responsibilities. Responsive language gives reasons and explanations to children (Stone, 1993). Adults actively listen to children and respond in a sensitive manner.

State rules in positive terms.

Tell children what to do instead of what not to do. Try to eliminate "stop," "don't" and "no" from your statements to children (except to keep a child safe in an emergency).

"Please walk" rather than "Don't run."

"Eat your food" rather than "Don't play with your food."

"Sit down flat so other children can see" instead of "Don't stand up."

Make requests and give directions in respectful ways.

"When you are finished eating, please throw your napkin and cup in the trash can."

Validate children's feelings.

"I know that it is hard to wait for a turn. But other children want a turn too."

Clarify classroom rules and give reasons for the limits.

"Walk to the bus so that you stay safe and don't fall."

"Use a quiet voice in the hall so you don't disturb the other classes."

Model the Behavior You Want a Child to Follow

All young children benefit from a visual model of what to do, but this is especially important for children with developmental or language delays. Couple the modeling or demonstration of proper procedure, with direct explanation—otherwise children may not imitate the desired behavior themselves at a later time.

- Show the child exactly what you want while giving verbal directives.
- "Put your backpack under your seat like this."
- "After you dry your hands, throw away the paper towel right here."
- Verbal descriptions of desired behaviors are especially needed when the adult wants to model resisting temptation or delaying gratification.
- "It's really hard for me to wait for a turn on the swing. I want to run up there right now, but I will wait until Sarah is done."

Reinforce Appropriate Behavior

The most effective method of managing children's behavior is through the application of positive reinforcement. When teaching a new behavior, it is best to reinforce every time the behavior occurs. New behaviors require immediate and continuous reinforcement to be learned and maintained. For more complicated behavior, it is important to reinforce small steps. For example, to reinforce a child who is cleaning up the block area, which to her appears to have about a million blocks spread all over the floor, ask the child to put five blocks on the shelf, and then praise her. Don't wait until the entire job is completed.

- Behaviors that are followed by positive reinforcement are likely to be strengthened and repeated.
- Use social reinforcers (smiles, praise, pat on the back, wink, OK sign) and activity reinforcers (engaging in a special activity as a reward for desired behavior). Tangible reinforcers (stickers, stars, prizes) should be used only for short periods of time when other types of reinforcement fail to work with a particular child.
- Use effective praise: praise that is selective, specific, and positive.

Use Logical Consequences

Logical consequences make an obvious connection between children's behavior and the disciplinary action that follows. As logical consequences are being carried out, adults remind children of the rule and why the consequence is necessary. They do so matter-of-factly, without humiliating or threatening children. Logical consequences are reasonable, respectful, and related to the behavior.

Logical consequences typically take one of three forms:

1. Rehearsal of a desired behavior: "Ruben, I can see you didn't wash your hands before you sat down for lunch. You need to keep yourself safe and wash away germs before you eat. Please go wash your hands now and then come back to the table."
2. Restitution—making amends for misbehavior: "Jeffrey, I cannot let you draw in the book. We need to take care of books and keep them safe. You need to get an eraser and erase the pencil marks. Would you like some help?"
3. Temporary loss of privilege: "Alex, I reminded you that it wasn't safe to splash your friends at the water table. You will have to find another place to play today. Tomorrow you can play again at the water table if you remember the Safety Rule."

When a new consequence is being applied or a situation is new for a given child, give one clear reminder or warning before applying the consequence. "Remember, the ball must stay in the play yard. If you throw the ball over the fence again, you will have to play with something else."

Once a rule and its consequence are well-known to the children, the consequence should be stated and applied in a matter-of-fact way immediately following an infraction, without blame, criticism, or extended discussion. Primary grade children can be involved in determining the consequences for behavior. One first-grade group developed the following consequences (Letts, 1997).

PROCESS AND PRACTICE GUIDANCE FOR REFERRING PROFESSIONALS

A Family Group Conference (FGC) is a decision-making meeting. It is arranged and run by an Independent Coordinator. 'Family' is defined broadly, to include the child, parents, extended family and significant others. At the FGC, the family will be given 'private planning time' to produce their plan for the care and protection of the child.

FGC's are based on the principles of partnership as defined in the Children Act 1989. They are a means of enabling families to find solutions to their own difficulties within a professionally supportive framework. The process aims to make use of the family's strengths and resources, and seeks to respect each family's own values and culture. Working Together to Safeguard Children (2010) (now archived) supports FGC's as "a positive option for planning services for children and their families". While it is recognised that families are currently offered packages of support and care, experience has concluded that it is the process of the FGC that makes a difference to the outcome, i.e. families feeling empowered if in control of the decisions. When a referrer discusses this model with a family you will need to be clear that the Independent Coordinator will contact all key family members and invite them to the Family Group Conference. Parents or care givers cannot select which family members are invited or informed. This is to challenge any collusion there may be within the family system. If the parent/parents cannot agree to this, the Family Group Conference cannot proceed.

The parent/s and/or those with Parental Responsibility will need to consent to share information openly at the FGC; this is done with the use of a report, which will include the reasons for the meeting, what the referring agency is concerned about, what the child's needs are, what resources could be available to the family and the non-negotiable position (the 'bottom line' should the family not be able to plan). Without the family's consent to share this report and the information within it, the FGC cannot proceed.

The Independent Coordinator's Role

The Independent Coordinator's role is to meet with child and family and map out who is 'significant to them', ('family' used in the wider context of the word). The Coordinator will help facilitate a family meeting, which will involve the Coordinator, referrer, and possibly other professionals who hold relevant information. They will organise the venue and agree dates with the family and the professionals. They will ensure the family understands the cause for concern via the report, and the purpose of the meeting. They will ask the referrer to explain to the family what the main issues of concern are and, in social worker referred cases, what constitutes unacceptable care of the child in child protection cases and the actions that will be taken if the child continues to be placed at risk of Significant Harm. The Independence of the Coordinator allows successful participation, as throughout the process they remain independent of any case management issues and work within their clearly defined role.

Circumstances where a Family Group Conference should be Considered

Children's Social Workers:

- Where children are being considered as in need of accommodation or are at risk of becoming Accommodated - referral by Team Manager and social Worker;

- Where children are being considered for Initial or Review Child Protection Case Conferences, or at any time when a child's name is subject to a Child Protection Plan - referral by Team Manager and social Worker;
- At a Planning Meeting which is considering children already looked after (including children in out of County placements) – referral by Service Manager and Team Manager;
- At a Looked After Review - referral by Team Manager and social Worker;
- At Legal Panel meetings – referral by Service Manager, Team Manager and Legal Services - for further information see Care Proceedings and the Role of the Legal Panel;
- Other situations affecting the care of children to be considered on a case-to-case basis, e.g. contact arrangements – referrals by Service Manager in consultation with Legal Services;
- Children subject to Interim Care Orders – referral by Team Manager and social worker Where ongoing family support has been assessed as being needed - referral by Team Manager and social worker;
- Where the Care Plan indicates that neither parent would be a suitable carer, and alternative carers are being sought - referral by Service Manager, Team Manager and Legal Services. An FGC should be considered alongside adoption and, in appropriate cases, long term fostering as alternatives.

Other Circumstances:

- When a child is at risk of exclusion from school - School/ Behaviour Support Managers through Integrated Support Services;
- Unauthorised absences – referral by the school;
- Any long term absences that give rise to concern – referral by the school;
- When a child is at risk of further offending – referral by YOT Officer.

8

Research in Counselling and Psychotherapy

Theory plays an important role in guiding the Counsellor or therapist in helping clients. However, every theory must be subjected to research to determine its truth or validity, as well as the efficacy and effectiveness of its applications in actual practice. Research is therefore another crucial dimension in the field of Counselling and psychotherapy. Scientific and systematic research on the processes and outcomes of Counselling and psychotherapy only began in the 1940s when Carl Rogers started recording his therapy sessions, which could subsequently be studied and evaluated. Since then, research in this field has mushroomed, although some controversies and issues still remain.

OVERVIEW OF COUNSELLING AND PSYCHOTHERAPY: PRACTICE

As suggested, briefly cover the following topics: primary theoretical orientations of Counsellors and psychotherapists in practice in the United States; major types of therapists or mental health practitioners and the settings in which they practice; several contemporary developments in the practice of Counselling and psychotherapy; and examples of major professional organisations and their Web sites for Counsellors and psychotherapists.

Primary Theoretical Orientations of Counsellors and Psychotherapists

Prochaska and Norcross have summarised the major findings from several surveys or studies of the self-identified primary theoretical orientations of clinical psychologists, Counselling psychologists, social workers, and Counsellors in the United States. The most popular theoretical orientation self-reported by most of these mental health professionals has been *eclectic/integrative therapy* (using theories and techniques from various approaches): 29 percent of clinical psychologists, 34 percent of Counselling psychologists, and 26 percent of social workers. However, *cognitive therapy* is self-reported as the primary theoretical orientation by 28 percent of clinical psychologists and 29 percent of Counsellors (the highest percentage for Counsellors). Only 23 percent of Counsellors selected eclectic/integrative therapy as their primary theoretical orientation. Judith Todd and Arthur Bohart note that while eclecticism is the most popular approach among practicing psychotherapists, cognitive therapies and theories are now the dominant therapeutic orientation in many professional contexts including university clinical psychology programmes.

Prochaska and Norcross have also summarised the main findings of a Delphi Poll they conducted with sixty-two expert panelists; its composite ratings indicate what will happen in the field of psychotherapy over the next ten years. In terms of primary theoretical orientations of the future, *cognitive behaviour therapy* was ranked first for the greatest increase over the next decade, followed closely by culture-sensitive/multicultural therapy, cognitive therapy (Beck), interpersonal therapy (IPT), technical eclecticism, theoretical integration, behaviour therapy, and systems/family systems therapy.

There was also consensus that psychotherapy will become more directive, psychoeducational, technological, problem focused, and brief in the next ten years. One of the major predictions concerns the length of therapy: long-term therapy will significantly decrease, while short-term therapy will become predominant.

Major Types of Mental Health Practitioners and Practice Settings

There are over a dozen major types of mental health practitioners in the United States who may provide Counselling and psychotherapy. Les Parrott lists the following:

- *Psychiatrists* are medical doctors who have specialised training in the diagnosis and treatment of mental disorders. They are qualified to prescribe psychotropic medications and can practice Counselling and psychotherapy. Some psychiatrists have also been trained in psychoanalysis.
- *Psychoanalysts* have received advanced training of at least three years in Freudian psychoanalysis or some other more contemporary version of psychoanalysis at institutes of psychoanalytic training. Such training institutes often require their psychoanalytic trainees to be licensed psychologists or psychiatrists.
- *Clinical psychologists* are educated at the doctoral level (PhD, PsyD, or EdD), including internship training in psychological assessment and psychotherapy. They must be licensed in the state in which they practice.

- *Counselling psychologists* are usually educated at the doctoral level with internship training in helping people deal more effectively with their problems in living. Counselling psychologists also must be licensed to be in independent practice. They function very much like clinical psychologists do, except that Counselling psychologists tend to see clients with less severe psychopathology, although this is less often the case today than in the past.
- *School psychologists* are usually educated at the doctoral level to closely work with educators and others to facilitate the holistic development of children in school. They often assess and counsel children with different types of problems, as well as consult with teachers, parents, and other school staff.
- *Industrial/organisational psychologists* are educated at the doctoral level. They are involved in enhancing the effectiveness of organisations and helping to improve productivity and the well-being of employees as well as management staff.
- *Marriage and family therapists* are trained at the master's or doctoral level in marital and family therapy. In most states they must be licensed to practice as marriage, family, and child Counsellors (MFCC) or marital and family therapists (MFT).
- *Social workers* usually have a master's degree in social work. They also must be licensed in many states as clinical social workers in order to do individual as well as family Counselling and therapy.
- *Psychiatric nurses* have an associate's or baccalaureate degree, specialising in psychiatric services. A psychiatric nurse with a master's degree in nursing (MSN) and psychiatric/mental health certification can also do private practice.
- *Pastoral Counsellors* are ministers, usually with master's degrees in theology or divinity, who also have had special training and experience in Counselling from a spiritual perspective. Many of them have received training from a clinical pastoral education center in the United States, which has over 350 such centers.
- *Vocational Counsellors* have a master's degree that prepares them to counsel people in order to help them in their vocational choices and professional development.
- *Occupational Counsellors* have a bachelor's or master's degree and internship experience that prepares them to help people with physical challenges to make the best use of their resources.
- *School Counsellors* have an advanced degree in Counselling psychology and are involved in helping people with career and educational issues.

- *Substance-abuse Counsellors* have bachelor's or master's degrees and counsel people with alcohol and/or drug addictions or substance-abuse problems.
- *Paraprofessional or lay Counsellors* have limited training in Counselling but do not have advanced degrees in Counselling and are not licensed mental health professionals. They usually do their Counselling work under the supervision of a licensed mental health professional.

Another group of mental health practitioners not mentioned by Parrott (2003) is the category of *professional Counsellors* or *licensed professional Counsellors* (LPCs) with master's degrees in Counselling who have also been licensed in the state in which they practice. There are several major practice settings in which mental health professionals do Counselling and related work including: private practice, community mental health centers, hospitals, human service agencies, and schools and workplaces.

Some Contemporary Developments in Counselling and Psychotherapy

Several significant contemporary developments in Counselling and psychotherapy have occurred in recent years. Not surprisingly, given the computer and Internet revolution in this information age, one such development has been in the area of *technological applications and innovations*.

Examples include the use of computer technology in *virtual therapy*, in which virtual reality is used as a therapy intervention for the treatment of anxiety disorders. Psychotherapy can also be provided by telephone, videoconferencing, and videotelephone, in what has been called *telepsychotherapy*. Such therapies, of course, raise serious ethical and logistical issues, but such technological innovations in psychotherapy are here to stay.

Another contemporary development in clinical practice is the *integration of religion or spirituality and psychotherapy*. Since Allen E. Bergin published his seminal article on psychotherapy and religious values over three decades ago, religiously or spiritually oriented psychotherapy has become an important part of the current practice of Counselling and psychotherapy. More specifically, Christian approaches to therapy have further developed in recent years, and research findings so far have provided some support for the efficacy and effectiveness in actual clinical settings of Christian therapy.

Contemporary clinical practice has also been significantly impacted by multicultural perspectives, feminist therapy, and postmodern approaches such as narrative therapy, solution-focused brief therapy, and social constructionism. As a final example of another significant contemporary development in therapeutic practice, let us turn to a major movement in psychology today called *positive psychology*.

Martin Seligman and Mihaly Czikszentmihalyi introduced the emerging science of positive psychology over a decade ago, referring to the study of positive emotion, positive character, and positive institutions and how to nurture them. This movement has really taken off with a mushrooming body of literature as well as recent empirical attempts to validate or support positive psychology interventions. Martin Seligman, Tayyab Rashid, and A. C. Parks reported findings from two research studies that provided empirical support for the effectiveness of *positive psychotherapy* employing exercises or interventions explicitly aimed at increasing positive emotion, engagement, and meaning in treating depression. A more recent meta-analysis of 51 positive psychology interventions with a total of 6, 018 participants showed significant enhancement of well-being (effect size =. 29) and significant alleviation of depressive symptoms (effect size =. 32). Positive psychology (including positive psychotherapy) focuses more on identifying the character strengths and virtues of clients and less on their psychopathologies or psychological deficits.

DEFINITIONS OF COUNSELLING AND PSYCHOTHERAPY

There are many different definitions of psychotherapy, none of which is precise. James Prochaska and John Norcross have chosen to use the following working definition of psychotherapy: "Psychotherapy is the informed and intentional application of clinical methods and interpersonal stances derived from established psychological principles for the purpose of assisting people to modify their behaviours, cognitions, emotions, and/or other personal characteristics in directions that the participants deem desirable".

Similarly, there are also several possible definitions of Counselling. Christian psychologist Gary Collins has defined Counselling as "a relationship between two or more persons in which one person seeks to advise, encourage and/or assist another person or persons to deal more effectively with the problems of life". He further states: "Unlike psychotherapy, Counselling rarely aims to radically alter or remold personality". Some authors therefore try to differentiate Counselling and psychotherapy on a continuum, with psychotherapy dealing with deeper problems and seeking to significantly change personality. However, most authors in the mental health field today do not differentiate between Counselling and psychotherapy, agreeing with Charles Truax and Robert Carkhuff, who, years ago, already used the two terms interchangeably. In fact, C. H. Patterson emphatically asserts that no essential differences exist between Counselling and psychotherapy. This is the view I take in this textbook on Counselling and psychotherapy from a Christian perspective.

John Sommers-Flanagan and Rita Sommers-Flanagan also use Counselling and psychotherapy interchangeably and define it as a process that involves *"a trained person who practices the artful application of scientifically derived principles of establishing professional helping relationships with persons who seek assistance in resolving large or small psychological or relational problems. This is accomplished through ethically defined means and involves, in the broadest sense, some form of learning or human development".*

Psychotherapy and Psychological Treatments

More recently, David Barlow has attempted to differentiate psychotherapy from psychological treatments, which may add more confusion rather than clarity to the already diverse definitions available for Counselling and psychotherapy. He suggests that "psychological treatments" should refer to those dealing primarily with pathology, while "psychotherapy" should refer to treatments that address adjustment or growth. Psychological treatments are therefore those that are clearly compatible with the objectives of health-care systems that address pathology. He further stresses that the two activities of psychological treatment and psychotherapy would not be distinguished based on theory, technique, or evidence, but only on the problems they deal with. He is aware that these are controversial recommendations. However, I believe Barlow's recommendation is not only controversial, but it is also potentially confusing and may not really help to clarify the definition of terms. Examples of psychological treatments provided by Barlow include *"assertive community treatment, cognitive-behavioural therapy, community reinforcement approaches, dialectical behaviour therapy, family focused therapy, motivational interviewing, multisystemic interpersonal therapy, parent training* (for externalising disorders in children), *personal therapy for schizophrenia,* and *stress and pain management procedures"*. We can see that many of these examples of psychological treatments are already part and parcel of Counselling and psychotherapy.

THEORY OF COUNSELLING AND PSYCHOTHERAPY

Although over four hundred varieties of Counselling and psychotherapy presently exist, most of them can be subsumed under the major schools of Counselling and psychotherapy that are usually covered in textbooks in this field of people-helping. There are ten to twelve major ones, depending on the author and the text. In this book the following ten major theoretical approaches to Counselling and psychotherapy will be covered in some detail, based on the theories and techniques developed by their founders and practitioners: psychoanalytic therapy, Adlerian therapy, Jungian therapy, existential therapy, person-centered therapy, Gestalt therapy, reality therapy, behaviour therapy, cognitive behaviour therapy and rational emotive behaviour therapy, and marital and family therapy.

Psychoanalytic Therapy

The key figure of psychoanalysis and psychoanalytic therapy is Sigmund Freud. He originated a theory of personality development focused on experiences in the first six years of life that determine the subsequent development of personality. Freudian or psychoanalytic theory emphasises unconscious factors, especially sexual and aggressive drives in motivating human behaviour. Psychoanalytic therapy employs techniques such as *free association* (allowing the client to say whatever comes to his or her mind without censorship); *dream analysis* (interpreting the latent or hidden meaning of the dream mainly through the use of symbols that have consistent significance for almost every person); and *analysis of transference* (when the client responds to the analyst or therapist as a significant person of authority from his or her life, thereby revealing childhood conflicts he or she has experienced). The goal of psychoanalytic therapy is to help make the unconscious conscious and strengthen the ego. Contemporary versions of psychoanalytic therapy such as object-relations theory focus more on attachment and human relationship needs rather than on sexual and aggressive drives.

Adlerian Therapy

Alfred Adler founded Adlerian therapy, which was originally called individual psychology. Another major figure in this approach is Rudolph Dreikurs, who was responsible for making it better known in the United States. Adlerian therapy is based on a growth model of the human person. It emphasises the need for the client to take responsibility in making choices that help determine one's own destiny, and that provide meaning and direction for one's life. Adlerian therapy uses techniques such as *investigating the client's lifestyle* or *basic orientation towards life* by exploring birth order, early recollections from childhood years, and dreams; *asking "The Question"* ("What would be different if you were well?"); and *paradoxical intention* (encouraging clients to do or exaggerate the very behaviours they are attempting to avoid).

Jungian Therapy

The key figure of Jungian therapy, or analytical psychology, is Carl Jung. Jung's interest in mystical traditions led him to conclude that human beings have a significant and mysterious potential within their unconscious. He described both a personal unconscious as well as a collective unconscious. Jungian therapy encourages clients to connect the conscious and unconscious aspects of their mind in constant dialogue, with the goal of individuation or becoming one's own person. Jungian therapy techniques include the extensive use of *dream analysis* and the *interpretation of symbols* in order to help clients recognise their *archetypes* (ordering or organising patterns in the unconscious).

Examples of archetypal images include major ones such as the persona, the shadow, the anima and animus, and the Self, as well as others such as the earth mother, the hero, and the wise old man.

Existential Therapy

The key figures of existential therapy include Vicktor Frankl, the founder of logotherapy; Rollo May; Ludwig Binswanger; Medard Boss; James Bugental; and Irvin Yalom. It focuses on helping clients experience their existence in an authentic, meaningful, and responsible way, encouraging them to freely choose or decide, so that they can create meaning in their lives. Existential therapy therefore emphasises more the relationship and encounter between therapist and client rather than therapeutic techniques. Core life issues often dealt with in existential therapy include death, freedom, meaninglessness, isolation, and the need to be authentic and real in responsibly choosing one's values and approach to life. Existential therapists can be optimistic or pessimistic to the point of being nihilistic, and they include those who are religious as well as those who are antireligious.

Although techniques are not stressed in existential therapy, Frankl has developed several techniques in logotherapy, a particular approach to existential therapy. Some examples are *dereflection* (encouraging the client to ignore the problem and focus attention or awareness on something more pleasant or positive); *paradoxical intention* (asking the client to do or exaggerate the very behaviour he or she fears doing); and *modifying the client's attitudes or thinking* (especially about the past, which cannot be changed, so that more meaningful or hopeful ways of looking at things become the focus).

Person-Centered Therapy

Carl Rogers founded person-centered therapy, which was previously called non-directive Counselling or client-centered therapy. Person-centered therapy assumes that each person has a deep capacity for significant and positive growth when provided with the right environment and relationships. The client is trusted to lead in therapy and is free to discuss whatever he or she wishes. Person-centered therapy is therefore not focused on problem solving but aims instead to help clients know who they are authentically and to become what Rogers calls "fully functioning" persons. Three therapeutic conditions are essential for facilitating client change and growth; these are the major person-centered therapy "relationship techniques": *congruence or genuineness; unconditional positive regard* (valuing the client with respect); and *accurate empathy* (empathic understanding of the client's perspective or internal frame of reference).

Gestalt Therapy

Frederick (Fritz) Perls and Laura Perls founded Gestalt therapy, an experiential therapy that emphasises increasing the client's awareness, especially of the here and now, and integration of body and mind. The Gestalt therapist assumes a very active role in helping clients become more aware so that they can solve their problems in their own way and time. Examples of Gestalt therapy techniques that focus on doing include *dream work* that is experiential; *converting questions to statements*; *using personal nouns*; *assuming responsibility*; *the empty chair*; *exaggeration*; and *confrontation*.

Reality Therapy

William Glasser founded reality therapy, which focuses on the present and emphasises the client's strengths. It is based on choice theory as developed by Glasser, which asserts that people are responsible for choosing their own thinking and actions, which then directly influence their emotional and physiological functioning. Choice theory also posits five basic needs of all human beings: survival, love and belonging, power, freedom, and fun. Reality therapy helps clients to become more responsible and realistic and therefore more successful in achieving their goals. Examples of reality therapy techniques include *structuring*; *confrontation*; *contracts*; *instruction*; *role playing*; *support*; *skillful questioning* (e. g., "Does your present behaviour enable you to get what you want now, and will it take you in the direction you want to go?"); and *emphasising choice* (e. g., by changing nouns and adjectives into verbs).

Behaviour Therapy

The key figures of behaviour therapy include Joseph Wolpe, Hans Eysenck, Arnold Lazarus, Albert Bandura, B. F. Skinner, and Donald Meichenbaum. Behaviour therapy applies not only the principles of learning but also experimental findings from scientific psychology to the treatment of particular behavioural disorders. It is therefore an empirically based approach to therapy that is broadly social learning oriented in theory.

Behaviour therapists view human beings as products of their environments and learning histories. The behaviour therapist plays an active and directive role in therapy. Behaviour therapy has developed many techniques that continue to be refined through systematic empirical research.

Examples of therapeutic techniques used in behaviour therapy include *positive reinforcement* (reward for desirable behaviour); *assertiveness training* (role-playing with clients to help them learn to express their thoughts and feelings more freely); *systematic desensitisation* (pairing of a neutral or pleasant stimulus with one that has been conditioned to elicit fear or anxiety); and *flooding* (exposing the client to stimuli that elicit maximal anxiety for the purpose of eventually extinguishing the anxiety).

Cognitive Behaviour Therapy and Rational Emotive Behaviour Therapy

The key figures of cognitive behaviour therapy (CBT) and rational emotive behaviour therapy (REBT) are Aaron Beck, the founder of cognitive therapy (CT), and Albert Ellis, the founder of REBT. Donald Meichenbaum is also often noted as an important figure in CBT because he developed cognitive behaviour modification (CBM) and stress-inoculation training (SIT), which are incorporated into CBT.

Beck's CT approach focuses on how maladaptive and dysfunctional thinking affects feelings and behaviour. It attempts to help clients overcome emotional problems such as depression, anxiety, and anger by teaching them to identify, challenge, and modify errors in thinking or cognitive distortions.

Similarly, Ellis developed REBT as an active and directive approach to therapy that focuses on changing clients' irrational beliefs that are viewed as the root of emotional problems. CBT and REBT assume that clients have the capacity to change their maladaptive thinking and hence to change problem feelings and behaviours.

CBT and REBT employ a wide range of therapeutic techniques, many of which have been empirically supported by documented results or systematic research. Examples of CBT techniques include *coping skills training* (helping clients use cognitive and behavioural skills to cope more effectively with stressful situations); *cognitive restructuring* (helping clients to change or modify maladaptive, dysfunctional thoughts); and *problem solving* (helping clients to explore options and implement particular solutions to specific problems and challenges).

Examples of REBT techniques include *use of the A-B-C theory of REBT* (A refers to Activating Events, B to Irrational Beliefs, and C to Consequences—emotional and/or behavioural—of such beliefs) and more specifically *keeping an A-B-C diary* of daily experiences; *disputation* (of irrational beliefs); and *action homework*.

Marital and Family Therapy

Marital and family therapy is an umbrella term referring to over twenty systemic therapies. The important figures in this approach include Salvador Minuchin, the founder of the *structural* approach; Jay Haley and the Milan Group, who developed the *strategic* approach; Murray Bowen, who developed family systems theory and transgenerational (multigenerational) family therapy; and Virginia Satir, who developed conjoint family therapy. More recently, Susan Johnson and Leslie Greenberg have become well known for their development of emotionally focused therapy for couples. Other key figures include Nathan Ackerman, Carl Whittaker, Ivan Boszormenyi-Nagy, Steve de Shazer, Michael White, Neil Jacobsen, John Gottman, and Alan Gurman. Marital and family therapy approaches assume that the crucial factor in helping individuals to change is to understand and work with the interpersonal systems within which they live and function. In other words, the couple and the family must be considered in effective or efficacious therapy for individual problems as well as marital and family issues.

Examples of marital and family therapy techniques that seek to modify dysfunctional patterns of interaction in couples and families and effect therapeutic change include *reframing* (seeing problems in a more constructive or positive way); *boundary setting* (either to establish firmer limits or lines of separation or to build more flexible boundaries for deeper connection); *communication skills training; family sculpting* (asking a couple or family members to physically put themselves in particular positions to reflect their family relationships); and constructing a *genogram* (a threegenerational family tree or history).

Counselling theory is important. It provides a framework of understanding and practice that guides the Counsellor and psychotherapist in their attempts to help clients.

Every one of us has his or her own implicit, if not explicit, theory of Counselling. We may, or may not, be aware of our basic assumptions and views of how to best help people with their problems in living.

Kevin Fall, Janice Holden, and Andre Marquis have provided the following questions for clarifying and articulating one's theory of Counselling, which you may find useful in formulating your own theory, no matter how basic it may be:

- *Human nature*: Are people essentially good, evil, or neutral? How much of personality is inborn or determined by biological and/or other innate factors? Are there inborn drives, motives, tendencies, or other psychological or behavioural characteristics that all human beings have in common? How much of a person's individuality is determined by heredity or other innate factors?
- *Role of the environment in personality development*: How influential is one's physical and/or social environment in one's personality development, and how does the environment affect personality development?
- *Model of functionality*: What constitutes functionality/mental health or dysfunctionality/mental unhealth in an individual? How do innate and environmental factors interact in influencing a person's functioning, be it relatively healthy or unhealthy?

- *Personality change*: How does personality change after it is to some extent developed? What conditions are necessary but not alone sufficient for personality change to occur, and what conditions are both necessary and sufficient?

These are the kinds of questions we need to ask ourselves in reflecting on our own theory of Counselling. Combs has noted that many Counselling theorists value a theory of Counselling that is complete, clear, consistent, concrete, current, creative, and conscious, that is, that has the seven Cs.

Bibliography

Allcock, R.S.: *Development Training: A Personal View*, Birmingham, Endeavour Training, 1988.

Anderson, L.W.: *International Encyclopedia of Teaching and Teacher Education,* Oxford, Pergammon Press, 1995.

Anthony, K.: *Technology in counseling and psychotherapy: A practitioner's guide,* Houndmills:Palgrave Macmillan, 2003.

Bandura, A.: *Social Learning and Career Development,* New York, Holt, Rinehart, and Winston, 1963.

Barnes, D.: *From Communication to Curriculum,* London, Pelican, 1990.

Beane, J. A.: *Toward a Coherent Curriculum*, Alexandria, VA: Association for Supervision and Curriculum Development, 1995.

Buehl, D.: *Classroom Strategies for Interactive Learning*, Newark, International Reading Association, 2001.

Carl R. Rogers: *Client-Centered Therapy: Its Current Practice, Implications and Theory,* Boston, Houghton Mifflin, 1965.

Clifton, C., & Grant Haworth, J.: *Curriculum in Transition: Perspectives on the Undergraduate Experience,* Needham Heights, MT: Ginn Press, 1990.

Colbert Judy : *Career and Guidance Opportunities in the Travel Industry*, Facts on File, 2004.

Damon, William: *Social and Career Development: Infancy through Adolescence,* New York, Norton, 1983.

Donaldson, Gordon A. : *Cultivating Leadership in Schools*, New York, College Press, 2001.

Elliott, J. : *Action Research for Educational Counselling*, Milton Keynes, Open University, 1991.

Evers, C. & Lakomski, G. : *Knowing Educational Guidance*, Oxford, Pergamon, 1991.

Fogarty, Robin: *How to Integrate the Curricula,* Palatine, IRI/Skylight, 1991.

Galbraith, M.W. : *Education Through Community Organizations,* San Francisco, Jossey-Bass, 1990.

George, J.: *Taking issue: Debates in guidance and counselling in learning*, London: Routledge/ Open University, 1998.

Giroux, H. : *Critical Theory and Educational Practice,* Geelong, Australia, Deakin University, 1983.

Glover, J.: *The Philosophy and Psychology of Personal Identity*, London, Penguin, 1988.

Greenaway, R.: *The Training and Development of Development Trainers,* Ambleside, Brathay Hall Trust, 1986.

Grittner, F.: *A Guide to Curriculum Planning in Foreign Languages*, Madison, Wisconsin Department of Public Instruction, 1985.

Halverson, Charles: *The Developing Structure of Temperament and Personality from Infancy to Adulthood*, Hillsdale, Lawrence Erlbaum, 1994.

Johnson, C.: *Meeting the Ethical Challenges of Leadership*, Thousand Oaks, Sage, 2005.

Kelly, G.A.: *Theory of Personality : The Psychology of Personal Constructs.* New York, W.W. Norton, 1955.

Kolb, D.A.: *Experiential Learning: Experience as the Source of Learning and Development*, New Jersey, Prentice-Hall Inc., 1984.

Markee, N.: *Managing Curricular Innovation*, New York, Cambridge, 1997.

Morrell, J. : *Employment in Teaching*, London: British Tourist Authority, 1985.

Nancy, N.: *Choosing a Career in Teaching*, New York, Rosen Pub. Group, 1997.

Okech, J.G.; Asiachi, A.J. : *Curriculum Development for Schools*, Nairobi, Educational Research Publications, 1992.

Potter D. : *Information Technology and Higher Education: A Twenty Year View*, Unpublished Paper, 1996.

Rosenfield, M.: *Counselling by telephone*, London, Sage, 1997.

Schuster, C.: *The Process of Guidance*, Boston, Little, Brown & Co., 1980.

Wiggins, Jerry: *The Five Factor Model of Personality: Theoretical Perspectives*, New York, Guilford Press, 1996.

Index

M

N

P

R

S

T

U

V

❑❑❑